UNIX® Networks

An Overview
for System Administrators

Bruce H. Hunter
Karen Bradford Hunter

P T R Prentice Hall
Englewood Cliffs, New Jersey 07632

Editorial/production supervision: **Ann Sullivan**
Buyer: **Alexis Heydt**
Cover designer: **Design Source**

The publisher offers discounts on this book when ordered in bulk quantities.
For more information, contact:
Corporate Sales Department
PTR Prentice Hall
113 Sylvan Avenue
Englewood Cliffs, NJ 07632
Phone: 201-592-2863,
FAX: 201-592-2249

Printed in the United States of America
10 9 8 7 6 5 4 3 2 1

ISBN 0-13-089087-1

Prentice-Hall International (UK) Limited, *London*
Prentice-Hall of Australia Pty. Limited, *Sydney*
Prentice-Hall Canada Inc., *Toronto*
Prentice-Hall Hispanoamericana, S.A., *Mexico*
Prentice-Hall of India Private Limited, *New Delhi*
Prentice-Hall of Japan, Inc., *Tokyo*
Simon & Schuster Asia Pte. Ltd., *Singapore*
Editora Prentice-Hall do Brasil, Ltda., *Rio de Janeiro*

This book is dedicated to our children

Eric, Joanna, and Chad

With love

Table of Contents

285   Chapter 17 — DNS

PREFACE

Computers used to be free-standing. Users all logged on to the same machine, and if they communicated at all, they communicated only with each other. Also, all file transfers were done by "sneakernet" (hand carried magnetic media).

Today the computer has reached out beyond itself. Not only can it communicate with other computers, but most computers are part of a larger system of distributed resources. To understand these systems, called clients and servers, system administrators and power users must know how networking is done. There are no shortcuts. There is no networking without protocols, and protocols do no good without the physical media and the devices on which they run. UNIX networking is constructed in this manner, so this is how a reader's understanding of networking must be built.

To give our readers a sufficient understanding of networks and networking, this book builds on the readers' knowledge of the network, starting from basics like network topology, and building up to topics about the physical part of the network, like the media. Then some theory is discussed, starting with the protocols, and building some more until the reader will be able to handle clients and servers. Then the book goes on to advanced topics like `sendmail` and DNS (domain-name service).

The material in this book was created from a series of seminars originally written by Bruce H. Hunter for system and network administrators. This material was developed on a large-scale computer system at a major electronics manufacturer. The authors have revised this material and developed it into a book.

Network advances take place daily, and keeping current is a full-time job. If this work accomplishes what the authors intend, its readers will be well on their way to understanding the complex topic of networking well enough to administer their own UNIX networks.

CHAPTER

1

An Introduction to UNIX Networking

Networking has changed computing forever. In the old days, we had proprietary operating systems that didn't talk to one another, but eventually some machines with the same operating system were tied together, and the idea of *connectivity* began to take hold. Naturally, users and administrators started pushing for full connectivity among all the machines on their sites, and although OEMs (Original Equipment Manufacturers) initially resisted that as contrary to their own self interests, software finally became available that would connect machines with different operating systems in one network, and they could slowly talk to one another and exchange files.

This was such a good thing that computer people began to want connectivity with *interoperability* — that is, once connected, someone on one machine in the network would be able to log on to a different machine and transfer files from one machine to another, regardless of the operating system. In fact, some degree of interoperability is available today. The `telnet` command is heterogeneous in that it allows remote logins, and `ftp` allows file transfers. Thus, if you have the appropriate software, you can `telnet` to an IBM PC running MS DOS, an IBM running CMS, a

1

DEC VAX running VMS, or any UNIX machine, and you will be logged on to that machine; however, once on that other machine, you need to know that machine's operating system to function there. On the other hand, the file transfer program ftp allows file transfers across the network from one operating system to another without having to know the sending machine's operating system. For example, UNIX users on Sun workstations can grab files from DEC VMS systems on the same network, and they don't need to know VMS.

As desirable as pure interoperability might be, it will probably never become a reality. If computer vendors wanted to pursue interoperability among all computer systems, all operating system commands would have to be identical, an unlikely prospect. However, at this writing the POSIX[1] standards are still being written for UNIX, and one day we may see a relative degree of command uniformity in all major UNIX versions. For now, non-UNIX operating system vendors claim that they will make their operating systems POSIX-compliant, and that could be as close to interoperability as the computer industry will get.

Efforts towards greater connectivity and interoperability have been made by several major players in the computer field over the years, but this book is about UNIX networking, and UNIX contributions to this field have been very significant indeed. One reason that UNIX is different from most other operating systems is that it doesn't rely on outside software for networking; networking was built into the UNIX operating system practically from its inception. Early UNIX versions allowed file transfers and remote logins, albeit at extremely low speeds. However, the magic of today's UNIX networking began when the people at the University of California at Berkeley joined the existing nonproprietary network protocol suites: the Ethernet protocol for data transmission across the wire, the Internet protocol for internetwork connectivity, and the TCP protocol for port-to-port computer communication. They brought them together into their versions of BSD UNIX, and they left the technology open to anyone

---

1. POSIX is an acronym for portable operating system interface for computer environments. This standard was started in 1984 by /usr/group, the international UNIX users' organization now known as UniForum, and it was taken over by the Institute for Electrical and Electronics Engineers (IEEE). The federal government is now specifying POSIX compliance as a basic requirement of most UNIX contracts.

with an AT&T UNIX source license and enough gumption to do something with it.

Other UNIX networking developments soon followed. AT&T added some refinements at the kernel level to speed transmission and to simplify layered protocol handling. Then some clever people at Sun introduced the idea of Networked File Systems (NFS) and Yellow Pages (YP or NIS).[2] NFS allows remote mounting of another machine's files, and YP allows the machine's administrators to share critical system files and allows common system files to be shared among systems within the same domain. YP is currently considered irreplaceable at networked UNIX sites because of its time savings, convenience, and accuracy.

Two of the most important recent networking developments are: 1) network mail delivery via SMPT and `sendmail`, and 2) domain-name-to-address-resolution via DNS and BIND. In this book one chapter is devoted to each, because they have become vital to UNIX networking.

There have been many other interesting developments in UNIX networking as well. They may not be as flashy as YP, NFS, `sendmail`, and DNS, but they are just as important. For example, time synchronization daemons run continually to make sure all machine clocks run at the same speed. They not only check the time but also check the small differences in time since the last check. These tasks may not seem important, but appearances can be deceiving. They are, in fact, critical to today's UNIX networks, because the security algorithm of Secure NFS requires that the clocks on server and client are at exactly the same time.

In short, UNIX networking has evolved over time into a highly complex and sophisticated scheme for data transmission, and UNIX administrators need to understand most of it inside out to be able to install and maintain it. Today over half of a UNIX administrator's work is network-related.

---

2. The name Yellow Pages was changed to NIS for Network Information Systems because of a legal action by an English telephone company, but in spite of the change, most people in the trade still call it YP.

The Evolution of the UNIX Network Administrator

The revolution in UNIX networking has changed everything about UNIX computing and everyone who comes in contact with it, including administrators. Time and distance are no longer a barrier with the Internet. Files and mail can be exchanged with ease, and users can log in anywhere they have privilege. Unfortunately, this bountiful gift is not without a price, for it requires time and skill to maintain it. Countless UNIX system administrators are finding themselves having to add network administration tasks to their repertoire.

A historical perspective to UNIX networking reveals why it has become such a time-consuming task. UNIX networking is a still-emerging subset of a much larger data communications set known as *datacomm*. Whereas today we have networked workstations and servers that require both hardware and software knowledge to maintain, years ago hardware and software computer people lived in two different worlds.

Let's go back to the late 1970s for a moment and remember what computer sites were like. Datacomm people were hardware-oriented, and they maintained voice networks such as the telephone lines and PBX systems in companies, although gradually their domain was extended to include digital networking, particularly the hardware side. Computer systems groups, on the other hand, were software-oriented and in charge of system software and applications. To complete this picture, recall that back in the 1970s, some computers were available for purchase, but most computer sites leased relatively expensive hardware, such as IBM mainframes, and the computer software also had to be leased. Included in this leasing cost was a bevy of support people called field engineers, ready to help whenever you needed hardware or software support.

So if you were a technical system manager in the 1970s and you needed to "network" some machines at your site, you would call in some datacomm people to put in the lines for you and some support people to install the specialized network software, and all you had to do was learn how to use that network software. If you had any problems whatsoever, you would call in the vendor's field engineers, and it would be up to them to fix your problems.

Computer sites have changed a lot since then. First of all, companies buy more machines than they lease today because of the proliferation of small, powerful systems that can be networked together. Leases are expensive and a thing of the past, a holdover from mainframes. Outright purchase and ownership of the much less expensive workstations and servers is far cheaper and is part of a pervasive "downsizing" trend in the industry. Also, companies buy almost all of their own software outright nowadays. All this is more cost effective for companies, but it also means that system administrators need to do more hardware and software maintenance than they used to.

The hardware side of UNIX networking is a departure from traditional system administration duties. In large companies administrators can ask existing datacomm people to lay down the backbone and some of the network lines, or they may be allowed to use an existing physical network, but that's probably all the help they are going to get with the hardware side of the network. They have to take it from there, including things like physically attaching their own computers, servers, and workstations, as well as doing most of their own local wiring.

However, the hardware side is only one side of administering a UNIX network. A significant part of UNIX networking is the network service software, such as NFS and YP. In other words, UNIX network administration requires a mix of hardware and software knowledge.

Obviously, there is a lot to learn about UNIX networking, and you should start at the beginning. The best place to start learning about UNIX networks is by studying network models and protocols.

Networking Models and Protocols

You need to learn about network models and protocol suites to understand UNIX networking, and that requires a protocol layering diagram. Take a look at the International Standards Organization Open Systems Interconnection (ISO/OSI) model:

```
-------------------
7
Application              User applications
-------------------
6
Presentation             Applications preparation
-------------------
5
Session                  Applications preparation
-------------------
4
Transport                Port-to-port transportation
-------------------
3
Network                  Internetwork routing
-------------------
2
Data Link                Data preparation and network linkage
-------------------
1
Physical                 Wire or cable transmission hardware
-------------------
```

Figure 1.1: ISO/OSI network layer functions

Each layer has its own special purpose. The *physical* layer is the *medium* on which data travel. The *link* layer establishes the connection among host machines, and it can reach any machine on a local network segment, but it can't easily get out to another network segment. That's where the network layer comes in, for it goes beyond the local network segment and handles internetwork addressing. Then the transport layer gets the data from one computer's port to another's.

However, traditional UNIX networking is firmly founded in the three protocol layers that form what is commonly called TCP/IP-Ethernet. In fact, by its very definition, TCP/IP encompasses the third and fourth network layers: TCP resides in the transport layer, and IP controls the network layer:

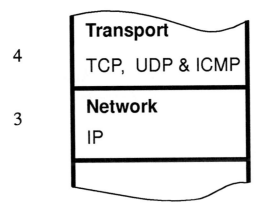

Figure 1.2: Third and fourth protocol layers

Ethernet and 802.3 comprise the lowest two layers of the network. Ethernet is straightforward:

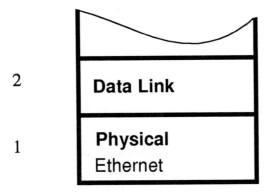

Figure 1.3: First and second protocol layers

IEEE 802.3 is more complicated because it splits the link layer into two parts, a link portion and a *media access control* (MAC) layer:

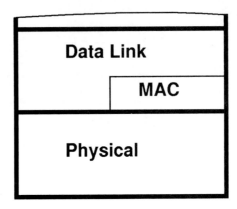

Figure 1.4: 802 Protocols

The link layer is free to maintain a link connection to other nodes, while the MAC layer confines its duties to getting outgoing data ready for the physical layer and preparing incoming data streams for the link layer.

You will find that a shorter, informal UNIX model for TCP/IP-Ethernet is all you will need for most UNIX networking tasks:

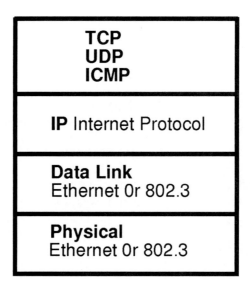

Figure 1.5: Protocols of the first four layers

The TCP family of transport protocols (TCP, UDP, and ICMP) running on top of the Internet Protocol (IP) have been around for a long time, and TCP/IP has been successfully running on top of Ethernet for so long, it is firmly entrenched in most UNIX sites today.

The UNIX TCP/IP-Ethernet combination as we know it today started at the University of California at Berkeley with Release 4.1C, where the first successfully networked version of UNIX was created and run. By Release 4.2, the basics were established, including the BSD R protocols. This Berkeley-UNIX heritage is significant because most non-AT&T UNIX versions are direct descendants of BSD UNIX. For example, SunOS is a BSD 4.3 derivative, and DEC's ULTRIX is a 4.2 derivative. Even the first AT&T UNIX commercially networked systems were running glue-on packages that were Berkeley-based and offered by companies like Wollongong. And all contemporary UNIX systems, such as Solaris and AIX, use Berkeley-based network software.

Thus, Berkeley's networked UNIX owed much of its success to Ethernet's ability to get data on the wire and over to other systems, the Internet protocol layer to get data from one network segment to another, and the TCP family of transport protocols to get data to and from individual computer ports (thus the name *trans port*). At the time Berkeley UNIX networking was developed, other network schemes were proprietary, but this technology was available in the public domain. Berkeley added its own software in the applications layers above, and the rest is history. TCP/IP-Ethernet continues to run successfully on UNIX.

You need to understand how each of the network layers work to manage a UNIX network. For those of you completely unfamiliar with UNIX networking, sending data via Ethernet TCP/IP will seem a bit bewildering at first. The mechanism that gets data through the protocol suites is *data encapsulation*, and the following allegory will give the uninitiated a general idea of what's involved.

Data Encapsulation — A Nontechnical Approach

Imagine that you live in a country made up of three separate republics with entirely different languages, customs, and laws —

Ethernet, TCP, and IP. These three independent and distinct republics form one country, but each republic is independent of the other two; so the Postal Service has three agencies, one representing each republic, each with its own bureaucratic powers to make regulations as it sees fit. In addition, each post office in this country has three sections, one representing each republic of the country.

The post office regulations are elaborate and involved. Each republic has its own limit on a letter's size. If the letters are too long, they are carefully cut up into pieces and put into special envelopes by the post office staff. In fact, all envelopes are controlled so strictly by the regulations of the separate republics that each section has its own envelopes made precisely to suit its own specifications, and each envelope has a different name. TCP's section of the post office has envelopes called *packets*; IP's section's envelopes are called *datagrams*; and the Ethernet section's envelopes are called *frames*.

Also, letters going out of the post office can only go through in a certain preordained order: through TCP's section, then through IP's, and finally through Ethernet's. Likewise, letters coming into the post office have to go through each section in reverse order: first through Ethernet's section, then through IP's, and finally through TCP's.

To mail something in this country, you can write your letter and bring it into the nearest post office where one of TCP's clerks measures it, cuts it into pieces of precisely even sizes, and then carefully inserts each separate piece into separate packet envelopes, which are then taken over to IP's section of the post office.

The TCP packets fit TCP's specifications, but IP's section has dominion over all the envelopes coming from TCP's section, and packets don't fit IP requirements. IP uses datagrams. So the TCP packets are cut into pieces and put into datagram envelopes according to IP regulations. Then all these envelopes are addressed and carried over to the Ethernet section of the post office.

However, the Ethernet section has little use for packets or datagrams. The purpose of this section is to send all mail in frames for delivery to the next post office en route, and the datagrams that come from IP's section of the post office frequently are not the right size, so they are cut up into the size specified by Ethernet regulations and inserted into frames. Frames are the only way envelopes could be delivered from post office to post office.

How is mail delivered in this country? That's the most amazing part. The frames travel from post office to post office throughout the country. Ethernet clerks at each post office sort through all mail received, strip off the frames, and carry the datagrams to the IP section. There the IP clerks look at the addresses on the datagrams. If they are going to destinations outside of their own postal district, they address them to the next post office along the route, put them back into other frame envelopes, and carry them back to the Ethernet clerks who send them onward. But when they spot some envelopes addressed to people within their own postal district, they strip off the datagram envelopes and reassemble the packets. The IP clerks look carefully at the packet headers so they can not only mark to what address to send the mail but also into which boxes the mail should be placed. These boxes are known as *ports*. All these reassembled packets are finally taken to TCP's section of the post office, where they are carefully reassembled into the original letter form and delivered to the proper ports.

Despite its curious regulations, mail delivery is reliable in this country, even though the letters are read by the post office staff.

Data Encapsulation — A Technical Approach

Now that you have a basic idea of this kind of data encapsulation, let's take a technical approach which will reveal just how ingenious, intricate, and interesting UNIX data transmission really is.

TCP

TCP uses its transport protocols to form *packets*, one form of data encapsulation, from the data stream, and it associates the data with both machines' sending and receiving ports. The protocol starts each packet with information needed by the transport layer on the receiving machine, and it uses that information to find out to which port (program) to send it. This part of the packet information contains the source and destination ports, for the transport layer's primary job is to establish port-to-port communication. Next the sequence number of the packet is added, because the packet may very well arrive out of sequence and have to be reassembled. There are a lot of variables involved, but as an example, depending on whether UDP or TCP is used, reordering and resending packets is sometimes necessary.

IP Routing

Since the transport layer only uses port addresses, how does the routing to real (Internet) addresses occur? IP takes the packets and forms Internet *datagrams*. It treats the entire TCP packet as if it were data and adds its own header containing the Ethernet version number, Internet header length, type of service, total length, several flags, a fragment offset, and *time to live* (the number of allowable hops left). The header information also specifies which upper protocol has been used (TCP, UDP, or similar protocols), and it contains a checksum and the source and destination Internet addresses, the two most critical fields, comprising the 32-bit (4-byte) Internet address. Finally comes options and padding. It seems like a lot of stuff to cram into one protocol layer, but it is all necessary for routing, and that is the name of the game at this level. Meanwhile, the system still has no concept of an Ethernet address, and it won't until it reaches down one more level.

Encapsulation at the Link Layer

You can write a letter, but you can't send it until you put it in an envelope. We have done data-to-packet encapsulation with TCP and packet-to-datagram encapsulation with IP, but we still can't send data down the wire to its intended destination because the wire needs Ethernet addresses. The package type used on the wire is a *frame*, another level of encapsulation at the data link layer, which has the job of setting up the link from one node to the other. The data link layer does almost everything but send the data. Unlike IP's header, the frame header is simple: It consists of the destination and source Ethernet 6-byte addresses, the Ethernet type, and the preceding data. The data, which include all previous datagram and packet information, are followed by a simple cyclic redundancy check (CRC).

While we're at this level, it's a good time to mention that Ethernet is similar to IEEE 802.3, a protocol and hardware specification, but not the same. The *type* field in Ethernet is a *length* field in 802.3; they are not interchangeable. You must be aware of this if you have Ethernet or IEEE 802.3, because they cannot easily coexist on the same wire. For example, if you have ULTRIX machines that require DECnet running on 802.3, and then you try to bring in some Sun machines running on Ethernet, you will have some technical glitches in your network. (Fortunately, you can work around them.)

Physical Layer

The physical layer of the Ethernet system converts bits to analog electrical impulses and does the actual transmission to the wire. It also looks for *carrier*, the presence of signal on the wire, and handles *collisions*, which happen when two sets of frames go on the wire simultaneously. If the data are coming in, the physical layer takes the impulses off the wire, converts the Manchester encoded signal into bits, and readies them for the network layer.

All Together Now

All of these layers act in concert. They pass the data stream from transport to IP, IP to link, and link to physical for outgoing data. The transport layer packetizes the data and adds its protocol header information. The packets are passed down to the IP layer, where they are made into datagrams and the routing information is added. The datagrams are passed down to the link layer, where they are made into frames and the Ethernet address is added so they can be delivered on the physical network. The frames are finally flushed down to the physical layer, made into a transmittable Manchester encoded analog stream, and sent out onto the wire.

From one host to another, the data stream has to pass through transceivers and may have to pass through repeaters (where it will be retimed), bridges (where it will have its link layer modified and rebuilt), routers (which will read its third-level IP information and rewrite both the IP and link information), or even to a gateway (where everything short of the original data will be rewritten).

At the receiving host, the stream arrives at the physical layer of the receiving node, where the frames are reconverted to bits. They are then passed up to the link layer where the frame headers are stripped. The datagrams are passed up to the link layer, stripped to packet form, and handed up to the transport layer, where they have their transport headers stripped. What's left is the original data.

In a virtual sense, all layers act as if they were handing data from their own layers directly over to the corresponding layers on the receiving system; that is, the data seem to go from transport layer to transport layer, IP layer to IP layer, and link layer to link layer. Of course, data actually do go from physical layer to physical layer. Thus, these protocol layers are called *peer-to-peer protocols* because the data seem to go directly across parallel layers. Protocols and protocol layering are the heart of UNIX networking.

Streams in AT&T UNIX System V Releases 3 and 4 are ideal for peer-to-peer protocols. In fact, BSD sockets have been functionally replaced by streams in AT&T UNIX 5.4, but sockets are maintained for backward compatibility. A BSD socket is a combination of the node address and the port address, and those of you who run BSD UNIX 4.2 (ULTRIX) or 4.3 (SunOS) need to understand sockets in order to deal with network diagnostics.

In the computer industry, the only constant is change, even AT&T's seemingly unbreakable association with UNIX. UNIX ownership is now in the hands of the network giant, Novell. What this company does with UNIX remains to be seen, but we can assume that DOS or Windows connectivity to UNIX will be one result.

Ethernet-TCP/IP versus ATM, ISO, and Other Rivals

At this writing, in the United States, Ethernet-TCP/IP has a dominant position in UNIX networking. Right now, its position is comparable to that of a heavyweight champion in boxing. However, just as every heavyweight champion eventually loses the title, so will Ethernet-TCP/IP give way one day to another networking scheme. And there are a lot of other contenders out there.

ISO's suite of network protocols goes back as far as Ethernet-TCP/IP's does. The major difference between the two is that OSI started out as a model created with painstaking care by a committee, whereas TCP/IP-Ethernet was a joining of working technologies. Governments and large industries will commit to standards long before the creation of an actual working model — recall that the Department of Defense picked Ada as its programming language of choice before there were any working Ada compilers. The federal government committed to the OSI suite of networking protocols and incorporated it into the Government Open Systems Interconnection Profiles (GOSIP); therefore, the adoption of OSI by the general computer industry seemed inevitable. However, in reality, private industry has been about as enthusiastic about meeting this standard as it was about changing over to the metric system, and today the government is reconsidering its singular commitment to GOSIP.

Similarly, there is strong interest in ATM as a base protocol. It makes a great deal of sense for multimedia networking: Its small packet size has many advantages for applications like the transmission of video images, for example. As of this writing, however, most of industry is still consumed with the best way to transmit data.

Thus, although Ethernet-TCP/IP has been firmly established on UNIX sites for a long time, one day Ethernet or TCP/IP may take a back seat to OSI, ATM, or some other rival. In fact, year after year new approaches to networking come out that show great promise. However, although UNIX networking may eventually incorporate ATM or OSI protocols, this will take time, and there will be resistance to change by users and administrators.

Let's compare the classic-protocol ISO/OSI model, TCP/IP-Ethernet and IEEE 802.3 protocols, one OEM UNIX version that has already incorporated some of the ISO protocols, and DEC Phase V.

OSI	802.3	Ethernet	DECnet Phase V
application			
presentation			presentation
session			session
transport	TCP	TCP	TP0 /TP2/TPY
network	IP	IP	ISO / CLNS
link	802.3 MAC	link	802.3 / MAC
	802.3 Link		802.3 Link
physical	802.3	physical	802.3

Figure 1.6: A comparison of protocols

Looking at the diagram, you can see that TCP/IP depends on IP, the Internet protocol, but the 4-byte Internet address was an unfortunate oversight. Class B[3] Internet addresses have almost reached their limit, and it is only a matter of time before there are no addresses left in any class. That is one of the reasons why Ethernet-TCP/IP is being challenged. UNIX will some day have to give up Internet addresses, and OSI is not tied to IP's 32-bit addressing.

To fully understand the Open System Interconnection, it helps to think of it as a network platform. Each of the seven layers supports multiple protocols, not dissimilar to TCP/IP's transport layer supporting TCP, UDP, and ICMP. To achieve success in the UNIX community, initial UNIX OSI releases will rely on traditional physical and link layer protocols, particularly IEEE 802.3 and Ethernet, to ease the transition over to OSI.

---

3. Classes will be discussed in further chapters.

Major manufacturers of Berkeley-based UNIX workstations and servers, such as Hewlett-Packard, DEC, and Sun Microsystems, were farsighted enough to see that the OSI would take hold in Europe, and therefore each of these companies made its own commitment to OSI in case it swept the United States market. It seemed like a good strategy, but industry changes are difficult to predict, and so far, OSI's acceptance in the U.S. has been more tepid than many players anticipated.

DEC, for example, committed early to OSI, even pushing their OSI development ahead of Ethernet-TCP/IP development. In fact, DEC's networking products, joined under their Phase IV umbrella, are based on the OSI standard, DEC putting its upper-layer ISO protocols on top of existing physical and network layer technologies. Note how DEC's Phase V generation network product is OSI through all seven layers, paralleled by DEC's own NSP session layer and DNA session control at layers 4 and 5. Whereas DEC's phase IV product line relies on IEEE 802.3 to negotiate with the wire, DEC's Phase V products also support TCP/IP, leaving backward compatibility to their Phase IV products. Unfortunately, hindsight reveals that spending more money on Ethernet development would have been a better strategy for DEC. Perhaps DEC's commitment to OSI would have been more credible if DEC hadn't lost a large part of its workstation market share.

Berkeley has traditionally been the bellwether of networked UNIX, and even it had an OSI entry — Berkeley 4.3 Reno. Berkeley Reno ingeniously implements the lower three OSI layers at the kernel level. The kernel is the heart of UNIX, negotiating with the hardware "below" and interacting with user interfaces and applications "above." The OSI session and presentation layers are handled above the kernel, like all UNIX applications. OSI physical and link network layers rely on a plethora of protocols, including the ones basically designed around coaxial cable — Ethernet 1, Ethernet 2, and IEEE 802.3 — as well as other protocols, such as Fiber Distributed Data Interface (FDDI) fiber-optic networking. By putting ISO layers 3 though 7 on top of an existing standard protocol, 802.3, Berkeley Reno uses a known, accepted, working technology at the base that will be easier for UNIX people to accept. However, although this is historically interesting, it may be academic, because Berkeley is no longer a major force in UNIX development. The information is included here to give you an idea of how tenuous a hold Ethernet-TCP/IP has on UNIX networking. Everyone in the industry keeps their eyes and ears open for the latest trends and developments, knowing that a change will eventually be forthcoming.

For a long time OSI was just a model, but now you can buy operating systems with OSI networking software. While many UNIX administrators may worry that a transition over to OSI will be painful, if it ever occurs, on the positive side OSI networking software has many interesting new features. Newer technologies are incorporated into the link and physical layers, such as the 100,000,000 bps FDDI fiber optic standards and ISO DIS 9314-1 and -2. The increased speed and signal quality that FDDI cable offers their networks is promising. However, other technologies are promising, too. CDDI has been trying to upstage FDDI, ATM is the latest rival to Ethernet-TCP/IP, and using Fast Ethernet has been suggested as a way to buy some time before any commitment is made to changing industry-wide networking protocols.

The IP (network) layer isn't the only reason Ethernet-TCP/IP is being challenged. The Ethernet (physical layer) is also being challenged because it's not fast enough. In the early days of UNIX internetworking, the Ethernet and the Internet addressing scheme seemed to be an unlimited resource. There weren't that many machines, they were slow, they only ran the R protocols, and network file serving was still an idea. But now the bandwidth is maxed out. Our machines are larger, more powerful, and more sophisticated. System clocks are set and skewed on the net, name-to-address resolution outside of the current name space is provided, endless streams of mail are routed, all of our files are provided, diskless workstations and X terminals are booted, and the network interfaces with PC networks such as Novell, Banyon, and Windows NT. All this adds up to less room on the bandwidth.

It's not an all-UNIX problem either. UNIX networks now have to face the problem of interfacing with PC networks, PCs running Windows and networked to each other via NT, Novell, and Banyon servers. In other words, we must bring PC networks together with UNIX networks, and not by using a quickie gateway solution. UNIX will have to have all the required hooks built in so it can run

NT, and NT, Netware, and Vines will have to have all the necessary UNIX hooks built in. The magnitude of this problem is so overwhelming at UNIX sites today, it makes alternatives to Ethernet seem like a minor issue.

Be that as it may, Ethernet-TCP/IP is what you will study in this book. It will be around for a long time to come, even when a gradual changeover to another networking scheme occurs. Just be aware that a change will be coming eventually.

What You Will Learn in the Rest of This Book

There is much to learn about UNIX networking, and there are many ways you could go from here, but the introductory approach we are taking is an overhead view of how networks are laid out, in Chapter 2. Once you have a handle on that, you'll go down to the hardware level in Chapters 3 and 4 to examine network media and hardware devices. But before you can fully understand a UNIX network, you need to learn something about network design in Chapter 5. Because UNIX networks require a thorough understanding of network software, you'll also need to study network addressing in Chapter 6 and closely examine network protocol details in Chapter 7. Then you will be ready to learn in detail about the computers and computer-like devices that live on the network: routers (Chapter 8), NFS servers (Chapter 9), YP servers (Chapter 10), print servers (Chapter 11), and clients and workstations in Chapters 12 and 13. That will take you through the basics.

In the intermediate section of the book, you'll learn about some of the things you need to do once the network is up and running. You will soon discover that running the network presents problems of its own, and in Chapter 14 you'll study access control and security. The study of monitoring and diagnostics in Chapter 15 will give you an idea of how to keep tabs on your net.

Networks become complicated quickly, and the last part of the book deals with more advanced topics. You must learn about `sendmail` because it's the innermost layer of the mail systems and allows mail to be sent to other machines. You also need to study DNS, because it's the mechanism used both on the Internet and within company internetworking to resolve names so that things like mail can be delivered. Because you'll be installing and administering networked software, you will learn how to install and administer the X Windows system. It is the most pervasive because it is what the users see. And finally, in Chapter 19, you will look at how a UNIX network administrator does problem determination by studying actual network scenarios. By the time you're through reading this book, you will discover that networks have become as important as the computers they serve.

CHAPTER

2

Network Topology:
The Basics

Network Topology refers to the way a network is laid out. Some networks are simple and straightforward, but many UNIX networks are so complex that you need a map to understand them. Understanding the basics of network topology is a good place to start, because it will lay the groundwork for learning about network addressing and network design.

A Simple Network

TCP/IP-Ethernet networks used to be simple and straightforward years ago, but very few networks are like that anymore. On a simple network, the heart is a thick coaxial cable called a *thickwire* (10BASE5) that acts as a bus:

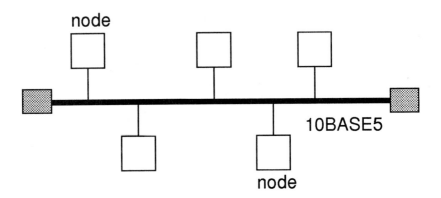

Figure 2.1: A coaxial cable network with termination

The *nodes* are any computer-like devices that attach to the network, including general-purpose computers, workstations, and servers. This network may go from office to office or to the computer room, but wherever it goes, the network wire is terminated at both ends with 50-ohm resistors, and that's all there is to a simple network.

All these nodes are attached to thickwire in a special way. Every time you attach a node to the network, you prepare the cable so you can attach a device called a *transceiver*. (This preparation is called *tapping* the cable.) A transceiver is a powered device that interfaces between the network bus and a node, electrically preparing the signal for the attachment wire that connects to the node. Transceivers also check for *carrier*, the presence of a signal on the wire, and for *collisions*, which happen when frames hit the wire simultaneously. Attached to each transceiver is an AUI (application unit interface) or *drop cable*, which attaches to the network controller interface card within the computer.

Ethernet networks used to run only on thickwire, but after a while *thinwire* (10BASE2) came along. It was so much cheaper than thickwire that it was dubbed *cheapernet*. Thinwire is similar to the kind of coaxial cable used for cable TV, and it can be used successfully to connect small networks over short distances. If you network three small computers in one room or if you have only small PC-type units with transceivers built into the interface cards, all you need is cheapernet.

What Happens When Simple Networks Grow Larger?

Networks start to get complicated when they become larger. What happens when a network in one building needs to be extended to another building? You can't have one continuous coaxial cable running from building to building — various length restrictions prevent that. For one thing, extra cable length increases the impedance, and the signal peters out. The limit of a single thickwire cable is 500 meters, approximately 1650 feet, and the thinwire cable limit is only 200 meters.

The effective length of a network coaxial cable can be extended by using *repeaters*. A repeater allows 500 meters to be added to each end of the network:

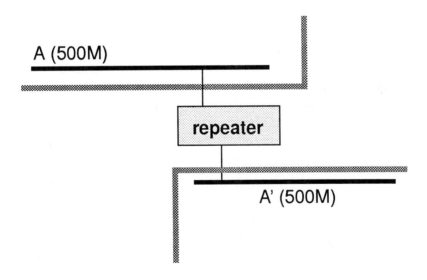

Figure 2.2: Using a repeater to cross buildings

Thus, networks can go from building to building with repeaters. The use of fiber optic cables has reduced the number of repeaters necessary.

What Happens When Networks Become Overloaded?

When TCP/IP-Ethernet was in its infancy, most UNIX computing was done on large minicomputers. Although these systems were the physical size of small mainframes, they only had the power of today's PC ATs. They were always loaded, and you spent a lot of time waiting for the prompt to come back to your screen. Computers were a lot more expensive in those days, and so there were fewer computers per site to network, and they weren't powerful enough to overload the wire.

We've come a long way since then, but the technology we've used to make computers more powerful has created new sets of problems. Computer systems today are not only more powerful, but there are a lot more of them. Network wires are now taxed to the limit by a proliferation of small but powerful systems like 486- and Pentium-based PCs, and large powerful workstations and their servers. More often than not there are too many systems on a site for a single wire network to handle.

There is a lot more network *traffic* to handle today as well. A network used to be used for remote logins and occasional file transfers, because only freestanding, standalone machines were networked together. Today, freestanding machines are the exception rather than the rule. Workstations depend on servers for files, printing, mail, and many other necessities. As a result, workstations contact their servers constantly, and workstations and servers never stop talking to each other. For example, when a workstation needs to execute a program, it must take the binary image from the server. The data it needs for that program are also on the server, so it takes that too, and the results of the workstation's program execution need to go back to the server to be stored. This represents only a small portion of the total amount of network traffic standard on most of today's networks.[1]

---

1. The maximum design rate for Ethernet and 802.3 network traffic is an incredible theoretical 10,000,000 bits per second, but on a network with heavy traffic the actual data transfer is substantially less — about 1 to 3 megabits per second. FDDI fiber optic technology increases the bandwidth, but workstations and servers are becoming more powerful at a proportional rate.

The ultimate in server dependence is the diskless workstation. Because it has no disk, it has no operating system, swap area, or files of any description. Diskless workstations represent early workstation technology. The idea was to have a cheap, per-chair (per-user) solution. However, today the new paradigm is the use of X Window servers as the cheapest per-chair solution. Both start to boot from their boot proms and complete the boot process from the network and their servers. Even their Internet numbers and names must be retrieved from a file server, and when they come up, they must use the server's disks for their swap areas.

Clearly, with this amount of machine interdependence, it's not surprising that many Ethernet networks become overloaded, and when that happens, the network must be broken into smaller network *segments*. Remember that a bus is like an antenna; it broadcasts to everything that attaches to it. Moreover, each network segment is a separate bus. These segments are connected so they can talk to each other, but they must be protected, even isolated, from other segments in order to be able to keep their local traffic to themselves and to send to the next network segment only data that need to be sent. The repeaters mentioned earlier cannot do this. Specialized devices must be used: *bridges, routers,* or *gateways*:

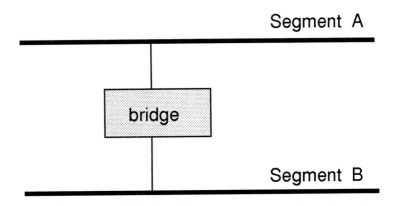

Figure 2.3: Bridging network segments

In Figure 2.3, we see a bridge connecting the two network segments, A and B.

Network segments can be isolated by bridges to keep the local traffic from getting out to other segments, but the long-range solution requires *subnetting*. Routers and gateways are the devices used to isolate the network segments. Whereas bridges can only deal with the Ethernet addresses of network protocol levels 1 and 2, routers and gateways can handle the level 3 IP addresses. When you subnet, each network segment is given a separate Internet address under the umbrella of a common Internet address: thus, on network 62.0.0.0 you will have subnetworks 62.1.0.0, 62.2.0.0., and so on. We will go further into network addressing and the differences between bridges, routers, and gateways in later chapters.

Some Problems with Thicknet and Thinnet

Thickwire and thinwire coaxial cables used to be the essential building materials of networks, but they aren't anymore, for many reasons. They require some skill as well as specialized tools to tap them, terminate them, put them in cable trays, do the routing, and do other installation and testing tasks. Coaxial cable is also expensive, and it doesn't work well with very closely spaced machines because it doesn't bend easily and requires large bend radii. If you have a large, square room, the cable has to be snaked laboriously back and forth in order to make the connections to each machine. Coaxial cable can never be exposed because it is extremely vulnerable — one accidental trip over a thinwire cable can take out the entire network. Therefore, the cable is run in the ceiling or under raised floors in the computer room. Because thick coaxial cable is heavy, when it is run through ceilings cable trays have to be used or the ceilings will collapse. When it is run up walls, wire ladders have to be used for the same reason. But perhaps the most irritating and time-consuming problem with coax is that faults and opens are difficult to detect and isolate.

You might ask, why did people use coaxial cable if it was all this trouble? Indeed, the frustration level of the people who installed and ran the network increased as the number of networks increased, and better solutions were eventually found. Today inexpensive wire, like the telephone company's unshielded twisted-wire pair, is used for parts of the Ethernet.[2] It was a logical solution, because the telephone system is the ultimate network. Thousands of twisted-wire pairs come together in a company's telephone closets, and from there they branch out to every office on the site. Somebody finally figured out that if part of the Ethernet branches away from a central point like that rather than having to come off of a linear bus, it would be easier to cable a lot of machines to the network. And if Ethernet networks tapped into and ran on some of the twisted-wire pair wiring already expertly installed by the telephone company, a lot of networking costs and logistics problems would go away.

It is therefore not surprising that today, twisted-wire pair Ethernet star networks have nearly taken over the UNIX-network world, and telephone closets have become data communications closets. Today's media of choice are fiber optic cable for long runs at high speed and twisted-wire pair for short runs.

Network Star Topology

Network star topology is not a new concept. Recall that only computers such as workstations and servers and computer-like devices such as routers and gateways can be network nodes; terminals cannot. However, because terminals need to be attached to minis and mainframes, star topology is used. The terminals are hooked up to communications controllers, devices external to the mini or mainframe:

---

2. Twisted-wire pair wiring consists of from one pair of conductors on up to hundreds of pairs within a large cable. Its name comes from the fact the each pair of wires is twisted around one another and color coded so that they can be readily distinguished from the other pairs.

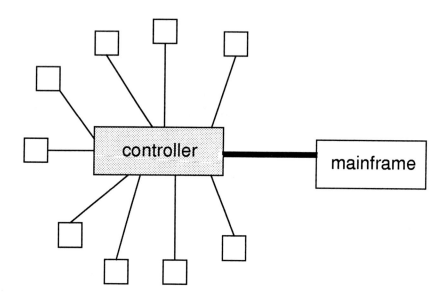

Figure 2.4: A star off a mainframe controller

UNIX network designers used this kind of network star topology to create small Ethernet stars using multiport Ethernet devices. More sophisticated devices called *concentrators* gradually evolved, and they are so important to UNIX networking that there is an entire chapter devoted to them in this book. In the most common network configurations, the concentrator is connected to the network backbone from thickwire or fiber optic cable. It fans out to the nodes through *host* modules:

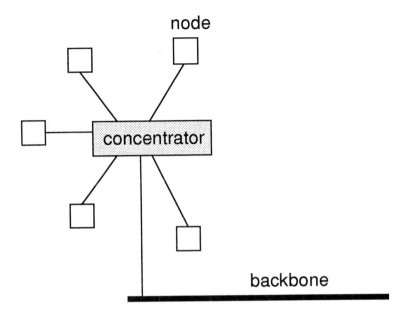

Figure 2.5: A star off a concentrator

The most popular media from the concentrator to the nodes is good old telephone wire, the unshielded twisted-wire pair available in every office.

Typical concentrators are fitted with as many as eight host modules, each having six to eight ports, thus allowing a a single concentrator to service over sixty nodes. Multiple concentrators can be used in parallel or they can cascade from concentrator to concentrator so that you have stars feeding stars feeding stars — a network using concentrators can grow exponentially. However, this design has its limitations. This kind of network proliferation works well enough for PCs, but not so well for workstations running NFS because the bandwidth of the Ethernet is quickly met.

From Small Networks to Large-Scale Network Systems

Separate Ethernet networks can become network segments and subnetworks. The following diagram shows a simple example of a network divided into two subnetworks:

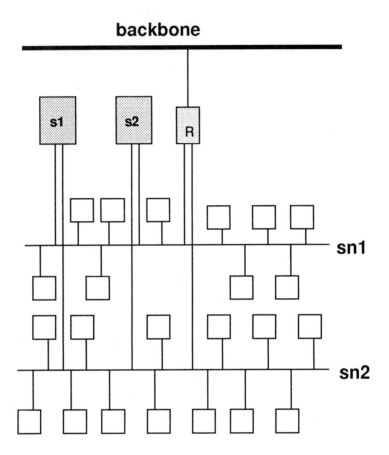

Figure 2.6: A two-segment using multihomed servers

The twisted-wire pair network stars that are joined to concentrators become "subnet satellites" because the star handles all the node traffic on one concentrator, and it sends traffic from one star's node to another. There is no reason to go into great detail now, because subnetworking will be covered in later chapters, but this will give you an indication of how quickly networks can grow to connect together hundreds, even thousands, of machines, including standalone PCs, workstations, servers, minis and mainframes. And the simple bus network that started it all can become buried in the massive, large-scale network system.

Thus, network topology is dictated by the media used. The inadequate, clothesline-like design of coaxial cable has given way to twisted-wire pair starring away from concentrators. (Concentrators are so common, they are even used in the computer room.) The geography actually develops as segments grow around the concentrators. And as organizations grow, concentrators cluster about routers which in turn connect to the backbone, while fiber optic cable connects the concentrators to the computer rooms that provide the servers. Concentrators can be cascaded with one concentrator reaching out to the other concentrators, but UNIX networks and subnets become loaded far too easily for the large numbers of hosts that can be cascaded from multiple concentrators.

How many concentrators are used is a function of the number of systems served, and how they are subnetworked. Systems with high throughput and clustered to the file servers will have very few systems on one subnetwork and still manage to load the wire to capacity. As these networks become laden with traffic, their complexity can become overwhelming. Multihomed servers[3] have become a necessity, and frequently devices like Etherswitches are used to gain a high degree of parallelism of data flow to eliminate or reduce bottlenecks between file servers and concentrators.

In short, network topology always tends to move in the direction of increasing complexity. In fact, it can get so complex, no one on the site knows exactly what's out there; you need maps and network analyzers to figure it out. Actually, the topology would be totally unmanageable if it weren't for network analyzers because the network keeps changing as you add machines, upgrade workstations, fix bottlenecks, and so on. Some analyzers require that you construct a graphic map of the net, while others draw it for you. They then track changes and watch the flow of traffic, recording a summation of the header information so they can be relied upon later to track problems or graph or report data flow and errors on all protocol levels and for most protocols. It would be wise to plan on using more than one network analyzer, because

---

3. Servers with multiple Ethernet interfaces.

each concentrator takes its own type, and another will be needed to analyze the network as a whole.

A well designed net may have a useful life of two to three years, if you're lucky, before it has to be expanded and redesigned. The primary reason is that technologies constantly change. A few years ago, a six-port router was the biggest you could get, but now they have more ports. Also, file servers used to have only one good Ethernet port; other server ports didn't have the same access to the bus as the primary card. But now, the presence of multihomed servers are taken for granted.

The high turnover of expensive machinery is enough to make a bean counter lose sleep nights. Perfectly good units that are still being depreciated often have to be replaced. In today's competitive world, gaining throughput is often more important than having a machine reach the end of its bookkeeping life before it is retired.

In order to make the best use of your money, it's a good idea to make two plans of your proposed network, one as large and grandiose as you can imagine, and the other large enough to meet your perceived needs for the next three years. You go with the smaller version, but you make sure you are always thinking ahead. For example, if you are installing fiber optic cable, it will probably be cheaper to put in *all* the lines you think you will eventually need in one installation session. Why pay for installation costs twice?

Another part of your network topology plan must include the "PC" network. For years, many UNIX sites have separated the PC network from the UNIX network, because that was the best solution at the time. But it seems clear now that these two networks will have to be joined well enough so that users on PCs on Novell NetWare, NT, or Banyon Vines can access UNIX files and do work with the X Window System. At the same time, UNIX users will need to access files on the Novell or Banyon servers and do their work, while on their UNIX workstations, in Windows. The technology is available from Novell and Banyon. It is also provided by SCO on the Open Desktop Systems and their network server products.

The joining of PC and UNIX networks will affect network topology planning, because PCs have network servers and UNIX systems don't. Plan your layout accordingly, because you will need a place to interface. You may end up with network servers in your closet or in your computer rooms.

An Overall Picture

Network topology is an excellent introduction to UNIX networks because it gives you a rough idea of the way networks are laid out. This will make it easier to learn network addressing, for you cannot create accurate addresses if you are unable to identify your network, network segments, and subnetworks. In the next chapter we go down to the network level and examine some of its actual components more closely, starting with network media.

CHAPTER

3

Network Media

It could be said that the first wide-area UNIX network medium was the telephone wire, because UUCP relies on telephone lines for anything other than hardwire connections. "The Net" became a worldwide source of news, mail, and software exchange, and people still use UUCP to this day. Ironically, the UUCP network has also become the way for small installations to reach the Internet. Of course, UNIX networking has evolved since the heyday of UUCP, and now most UNIX-based companies use the Internet to communicate. They lease special T1 lines from the telephone company for the purpose of networking, and these massive, high-speed digital communication lines are switchless; that is, their circuits do not rely on switches to route the information the way telephone lines do.

Data sent on switched circuits like PBX systems rely on mechanical or computer switches to be set in order to route the data from one point to another. Switchless networks, more often referred to as packet-switched networks, rely on the computers that handle the routing to look up the destination address on the packet headers to route the information. Any computer that is able to see information on a packet-switched wire simply ignores packets that don't have its own Ethernet addresses. However, all machines on the network respond to a broadcast address.

Packet-switched networks and the layered network protocols that made them possible were brilliant innovations, and UNIX networking has blossomed with the use of Ethernet TCP/IP protocols and the Internet. The Internet is often referred to as *the wire*, but you are not limited to a wire or fiber optic cable for networking, for many kinds of exotic media can be used to connect networks worldwide, including satellite, microwave, and AM and FM broadcast. However, because in this book our main concern is the setup and maintenance of local UNIX Ethernet TCP/IP networks, let us leave the wider world and concentrate on the media used to set up a local UNIX network within a local-area network.

We've already mentioned the three types of media used for local-area UNIX networks: coaxial cable, twisted-wire pair, and fiber optic cable. Now let's take a closer look.

Coaxial Cable

For years the media of choice for UNIX networks has been coaxial cable. With an Ethernet transmission speed of 10,000,000 bits per second, it opened the way for remote logins, file transfer, NFS, and distributed computing, markedly changing the nature of computing and the entire computer industry:

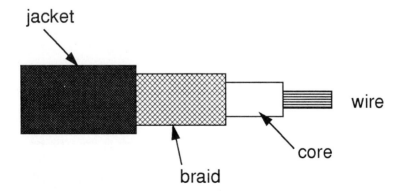

Figure 3.1: Coaxial cable

Coaxial cable, most often called *coax*, consists of a single wire through which data are transmitted, surrounded by an insulating layer, which in turn is surrounded by a grounding braid.

When you think of ordinary, household electric signal media, you think of something with two ends, one hooked up to the source and the other hooked up to the destination. For example, you plug in one end of your TV cable to the television and the other end to the cable outlet. However, as far as UNIX networks are concerned, coaxial cable is considered a *bus* media, terminated at either end by resistors attached from core to grounded outer braid. Although it exists as a single wire with two termination points and no branches, tees, or crosses, the cable can be repeatedly cut and spliced with special BNC connectors to make it longer or shorter. Beyond a simple splice, the cable cannot be attached or extended without the aid of an active electrical device, such as a transceiver to connect it to a computer, or other devices such as repeaters, concentrators, routers, and bridges.

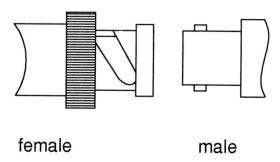

female   male

Figure 3.2: BNC connectors

The coaxial cables used on UNIX sites have specific names that indicate their networking capabilities. The first part of the name is the line speed in megabits, which is followed by the word BASE or BROAD for baseband or broadband, and this is followed by the maximum length in hundreds of meters. Thus, a 10-megabit-per-second, baseband, 500-meter cable specification is 10BASE5.

Whenever you transmit intelligence, you have to deal not only with the actual signal you want to transmit but also with *noise*, similar to the "snow" on a TV set or static on a radio, which is noise that interferes with the transmission. However, noise on a digital line is more than an irritant because it corrupts data, and some media are noisier than others. The quietest long-distance coaxial cable is 10BASE5, called *thicknet*, a thick cable (about 1 centimeter in diameter) with a thick center wire surrounded by Teflon[1] insulation. The insulating layer is covered by a layer of metallic braid which, in turn, is covered by another insulating layer. Thicknet can create a single network segment 500 meters (half a kilometer) in length.

Thicknet's bargain-basement relative is *thinnet*, known as 10BASE2, much thinner than thicknet with an insulating layer that is potentially toxic under fire. Thinnet cables are limited to anywhere from 160 to 200 meters, depending upon which authority you are quoting. They are more noise-susceptible and more fragile than their fat-cable cousins, and a lot cheaper.

The impedance of both thinnet and thicknet is about 50 ohms. In order to avoid having a signal reflect back and forth along the wire and garble the data, 50-ohm resistors are placed at either end of the cable so a signal can travel the length of the wire and be absorbed. These resistors are called terminators and match the impedance of the line. The signal must travel from any tap to either end of the cable and then disappear.

When adding devices to thinnet, the cable must be cut, but nodes[2] (computers, repeaters, bridges, concentrators, and routers) can be attached to thicknet by *tapping* the cable. This is done by cutting a small hole through the outer (ground) braid and clearing away all wire fragments. Then the hole is continued by carefully drilling down to the center conductor, taking great pains not to cut it. A *tap* is then clamped to the wire, and its center probe touches

---

1. Teflon is a registered trademark of Dupont Corporation.
2. A node is 1) a computer router or gateway; 2) any device with an address.

the center wire. Two shallow probes, one to each side of center, tap into the outer ground braid.

With the tap in place, a transceiver is attached — a powered device that transmits and receives data, and also monitors for carrier (traffic), detects collisions, and passes such data back to the Ethernet controller card, where they can be acted upon intelligently. A transceiver must be used between the media and any network device, such as a repeater, computer, bridge, router, or concentrator. Taps can be placed no closer than 2.5 meters apart on thick wire and 1 meter apart on thin, and it is best to use even multiples of these numbers. In fact, thickwire is marked every 2.5 meters for this purpose.

Thinnet is not tapped. Instead, you cut the cable and attach common *BNC connectors* to either side of the cut. These connectors can then be directly attached to the computer's Ethernet card, called an NIC[3] by datacomm people. Most PC cards intended for use with thinnet have the transceiver built into the card. Since this method is cheap and simple, this is the way to go if you want to install a small network for very little money.

Thinnet has problems: Its length limitation is restricting, and its connections are fragile. If users want to move their computers a few inches forward from where they are, and a move pulls apart the connector by mistake, the entire network will come down. Like a cheap set of old-fashioned Christmas tree lights, if you lose one connector on a thinnet bus, you lose them all. 10BASE5 doesn't have that problem because it is tapped to make a device connection rather than spliced, and the connection from the transceiver to the node is done with an application unit interface (AUI), also known as a *drop cable*.

An interesting feature of coaxial cables is their electrical propagation speed. 10BASE5 sends the signal down the wire at 77 percent the speed of light. On the other hand, 10BASE2 only

---

3. NIC is a network interface card. All computers interfacing with the network must have a network interface, which is usually a separate card.

sends at 66 percent. Nevertheless, that's still a lot faster than "sneakernet."[4]

Twisted-Wire Pair

Today, most installed UNIX systems use twisted-wire pair in some part of the Ethernet network, because, like Everest, it's there. Industrial architects always specify plenty of twisted-wire pair from each and every office and cubicle to the floor's phone closets, so twisted-wire pair, known as 10BASEt, is an ideal network medium from phone closets to the various offices on a site.

A device called a concentrator allows a single network cable to be run from the servers and shared computers to a multitude of workstations. Concentrators fan out to the twisted-pair wiring, and thus into each office and cubicle needing a connection for a PC or workstation. Consequently, concentrators and similar devices known as multiport transceivers have picked up the nickname *fanout units*.

Twisted-wire pair comes in different varieties, but the common kind found in voice communications and telephone closets is unshielded t1. Longer distances can be run with shielded twisted-wire pair (t2 and t3). Although the capabilities of the humble twisted-wire pair medium seem paltry compared to the flashy, close-to-light-speed capability of fiber optics, its impact is significant. Twisted-wire pair is cheap, omnipresent, and allows network star topologies, something coaxial cable cannot do.

Fiber Optic Cable

Fiber optic cable has been around for a long time, but as an affordable media for digital communications its day was slow to come. Initially, it was expensive and difficult to terminate properly.

---

4. Sneakernet occurs when someone puts a tape under his or her arm and runs it from one building to another.

Fortunately, these problems have been overcome, because fiber optic cable has distinct advantages as a network medium. It is free from electrical noise, it has a high bandwidth, and it has an extremely high rate of transmission. Fiber optic cable is rapidly replacing coaxial cable for network backbones and long, uninterrupted spans. The final seal of approval came with the FDDI fiber optic standard transmission rate of 100,000,000 bits per second.

Fiber optic cable used to be exotic and expensive, but today the *installed* cost of fiber optic cable is closer to thickwire because labor is the largest part of installation cost. When you hold the cable in your hand, you marvel at how slender it is compared to thicknet and thinnet. It consists of a thin glass core or a slightly thicker plastic core surrounded by cladding, which prevents the light being transmitted down the core from scattering, and the core and its cladding are protected by an outer braid or jacket.

Making end connections for fiber optic cable used to be a specialized task for technicians, but now end connections can be made easily with a few inexpensive tools and a little training. Like any other network medium, fiber optic cable runs from transceiver to transceiver, and from there is attached to any network device, whether node, repeater, bridge, concentrator, router or gateway.

Whereas fiber optic cable was once used only for high-speed network backbones and to interconnect segments, it now has its own physical-media layer specification: FDDI. The demands placed on the network by our heavy reliance on workstations and servers has pushed 10,000,000-bit-per-second Ethernet and 802.3 transmission beyond capacity, and FDDI is a possible alternative. For this reason, most new installations are planning ahead and going to fiber optic cable wherever practical.

An Administrator's Approach to Contemporary Media

We've looked at several kinds of network media in this chapter and earlier chapters. We have seen that although the Ethernet was born on coaxial cable, it found a second life on twisted-wire pair, fiber optic cable, and semi-exotic hybrids, such as CDDI (FDDI technology on twisted-wire pair). We have learned that for some time, the established standard has been fiber optic cable from computer room to distribution centers, like wire closets, and from building to building. The thin, spaghetti-like orange cable is so common now that most people take it for granted. We have also learned that the established standard from closet to node is twisted-wire pair.

But learning facts about network media isn't enough. Where do they fit into your planning? Administrators have to participate in planning the network, because they are the ones who take care of it. Let's review the media we've covered from an administrator's point of view.

Coaxial cable used to be favored because it could be installed by the local staff. Tools and fittings were available, and it only took a little skill to terminate the cable or tap it. You may still have some coaxial cable on your site.

Twisted-wire pair is favored today for the same reason. It is easy to install, it is even easier to run, and it is far easier to troubleshoot. The toughest part of TWP is punching it down to the punch-down blocks, but that requires only one tool, and the skill is easily learned. And TWP is so cheap that if you doubt the quality of a run of wire in the wire closet, you don't feel a bit guilty about pulling it out and punching down a new run of wire.

Fiber optic cable, on the other hand, is far more difficult to terminate, and although it can be terminated by anyone with a little training, many sites still call in specialists. However, don't be intimidated by fiber optic cable. To be sure, if a connection is brushed at a concentrator it is easily broken, but you can learn to cut the cable, strip it, pot it to the connector, and optically polish it. If you fix it yourself, you can be back on line in an hour. On the other hand, waiting for a tech to come out can take an entire day.

You can leave open the possibility of future technologies, but it's still a good idea to plan your topology around known technologies. Fiber optic cable doesn't go bad, it is free of problems with electrical noise, and it is fast. Twisted-wire pair is cheap, it works well with concentrators, and it is everywhere. Even if the base (Ethernet) technology changes, you are safe with either.

All Media Are Not Created Equal

Most network electrical wiring schemes have the same DC resistance, but that is of no significance unless you are checking the wire for continuity. The wire's AC impedance is the characteristic that much be matched, and naturally none of the three major wire types do match, so you cannot simply splice one to another.[5] Going from one type of medium to another requires devices like repeaters, bridges, or gateways, and in the next chapter we will unravel some of their secrets.

---

5. Twisted-wire pair can be joined with a device called a BALUN which will match its impedance, but it is only used in limited applications and only at terminal end points.

C H A P T E R

4

Devices and CSMA/CD Protocols

Ethernet and 802.3 are protocol suites that use CSMA/CD for access control management, CSMA for *collision sense, multiple access* and CD for *carrier detect*. In this chapter, we will look at how transceivers and the network interfaces to which they attach handle CSMA/CD protocols, and we will also introduce repeaters, concentrators, bridges, routers, and gateways.

When you look at the network from a totally electrical point of view, it is useful to divide it into two parts, passive devices and active devices. Passive devices are unpowered, such as terminators and the wire, but active devices are powered. The transceiver is the smallest active device on the network, and it draws power from the network interface card to which it is attached. Other active devices are repeaters, bridges, routers, and gateways. A few specialized devices are multiport transceivers, repeaters, and concentrators, designed to allow a network leg to *star* out to multiple wires or cables.

Transceivers

In terms of numbers, the transceiver is the most common device on a network. With rare exceptions, a transceiver is required to connect from the wire to any network device, such as a computer. If you don't see an external transceiver, it's probably built into the device's Ethernet controller card. As a powered unit with minimal circuitry, a transceiver takes the signal from the network cable and puts it on the drop cable, the line that connects to a node's Ethernet controller card. Be aware that there are often more than one name for network media and network devices. For example, a drop cable is also known as an AUI, for *application unit interface*, and a transceiver is sometimes called an MAU, for *medium attachment unit.*

Ethernet is based on CSMA/CD for access management, which works hand in hand with transceivers. Because the wire is intended for multiple access, the hosts must test for the presence of traffic on the wire. The wire will be a zero-voltage reference when idle, but when data are on an Ethernet or 802.3 wire with a Manchester-encoded binary signal, the wire voltage will fluctuate approximately two volts from the zero reference at an effective rate of 10,000,000 bits per second by running at 15 to 20 Mbaud (depending on the bit stream).

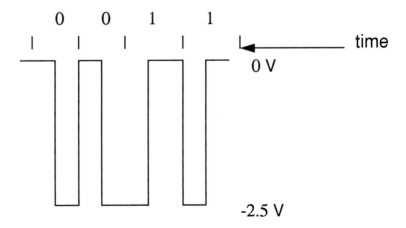

Figure 4.1: Manchester encoding

There are two important points to note about Manchester encoding: First, as a timing consideration, the voltage must fluctuate once for each bit sent; second, the bit value (0 or 1) is determined by the voltage at the end of the time cycle. Inside the machine it's a digital signal, a beautifully sharp-edged square wave. If you monitor the network with an oscilloscope, the wave is rough, irregular, and semisinusoidal because it's an analog signal. The transition from one wave to another takes place in the transceiver and the Ethernet card. (Recall that the Ethernet card is also referred to as the NIC, for *network interface card.*)

In a perfect world no data would ever be sent if a signal were already on the wire, but in the real world collisions start to occur as soon as network traffic increases much beyond 30 percent of wire capacity. Initially, several systems sense no data on the wire, and so they start to send. A collision occurs when two or more systems send data simultaneously. The transceiver *monitors* the line, and while the transceiver is receiving, or when it senses carrier or collision, it stops the NIC from transmitting. When the transceiver and NIC sense a collision, the NIC sends a bit sequence called a *jam,* and all sending units back off and immediately stop sending. They will reattempt transmission after an interval selected by random number generation. Should a second collision occur, the unit immediately backs off for a time interval exponentially larger than the first.

Not only do the transceivers monitor the line for carrier and collisions, some also test the collision-detect circuit continuously after each transmitted frame. This is called a heartbeat, or SQE for *(continuous) signal quality test.* Because Ethernet transceivers do this and 802.3 transceivers do not, the SQE should be enabled for Ethernet and disabled for IEEE 802.3.

Transceivers must also exert *jabber* control, the control and termination of excessively long data streams. All forms of data encapsulation have a maximum length, and the length of a network frame is exceeded only if a transmission malfunctions. When jabber control sees a transmission that is too long, it interrupts the transmission, which is good because jabbers should never get from the MAU to the Ethernet card.

Transceivers come in flavors. Although similar in function, the network requires different transceivers for thickwire, thinwire, fiber optic cable, and twisted-wire pair. PC thinwire controllers (NICs) have the transceiver built into the card.

Streetwise network administrators soon learn that all transceivers are not created equal. Most specifiers think of them as commodity items, but it goes well beyond getting a transceiver from your favorite vendor or from the lowest bidder. Sugar is essentially the same, no matter what the brand, but you have no idea how a transceiver will behave on your net. Is the transceiver you selected able to switch SQE on and off? If it can, how reachable is the switch? If you have to take each transceiver apart to set or disable SQE, it is going to be costly in the long run; you might prefer ones you can set with a switch. Be sure to request samples before making any major purchase of new transceivers, because all of them won't work well on your type of network. Give one a trial period before committing.

Stock Cable

The switch to twisted wire to the individual nodes has made the use of J connectors popular, replacing the older and costlier IBM hermaphrodite connectors. Not a lot can go wrong with a cable that has J connectors, but you will run into occasional problems from time to time. If a workstation fails and leaves the network, simply replace a suspect cable and see if the network returns for that particular node. If it doesn't, replace the transceiver.

AUI cables for DB connectors present problems constantly. The sliding locks look like a good idea when you first see them, but they are not reliable. Luckily, there is a little, plastic after-market device to lock the lock, well worth the few cents it costs to keep the connector connected.

On critical AUI connections, like your file servers, the ones to the routers or concentrators, and so on, protect yourself and form a loop of cable just before the connection. Use a nylon tiewrap to secure it to the chassis of the shelf so if the cable is stepped on or brushed against it won't pull out.

The Ethernet NIC Card

To appreciate the way the NIC and the MAU work in concert, let's look at an illustration of an outgoing frame traveling through the interface card, through the transceiver, and out to the cable:

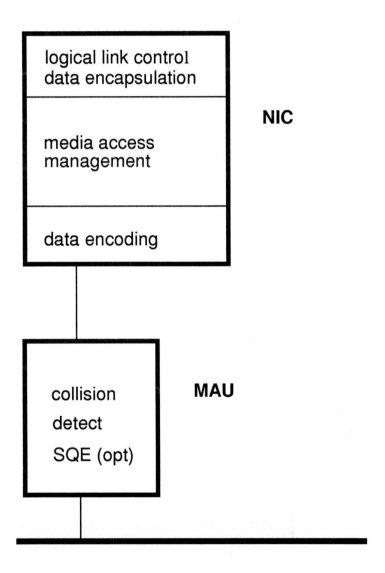

Figure 4.2: MAU and NIC functions

Once the information enters the MAC layer, it is encapsulated into a frame. The media access management section of the MAC layer waits until the transceiver tells it there are no other data on the cable, and then it will encode the data into the final datagram and make an analog signal of it to be sent to the transceiver.

A signal coming the other way is picked up by the transceiver as an analog transmission. The transceiver sends it up to the network interface card unless it is part of a jabber or a collision. There the Ethernet address is examined, and if the datagram is a broadcast, a *multicast*[1], or it has the system's address as its *to* address, the NIC will accept it and it will be unencapsulated. Note how the media access management is shared between the NIC and the MAU, for although only the MAU can sense carrier or collision, the NIC has the intelligence to act on it.

Multiport Transceivers and Concentrators

Many multiport, fanout transceiver units exist today, but the golden oldie was the DEC DELNI. A single tap from a coaxial cable led to eight or more hosts with a DELNI, and it became the hub of its own little star subnetwork.

Since the introduction of the DELNI, fanout units have evolved into sophisticated machines. SynOptics, Racal InterLan, and Cabletron all make specialized fanout units called concentrators, which have separate modules that can be mixed and matched to create just about any kind of network star you can imagine, such as a fiber optic input from the network segment, twisted-wire pair outputs for several dozen computers, and a fiber optic output to allow the concentrator to be connected to one or more similar units to extend the net. These port connections can be monitored by software to show the traffic and condition of any part of the LAN.

---

1. Whereas a broadcast goes out beyond the boundary of the local-area network to all possible destinations, a multicast is confined to the LAN or at least to a subpart of the area reached by a broadcast. With a broadcast, all possible destinations (within a defined subgroup) are referenced. With a multicast, a subset of all possible destinations is referenced.

The monitor can also actively turn ports on or off, allowing the network administrator to kill a jabbering device or some other similar nuisance as close to the source as the nearest monitored concentrator port. Concentrators and their applications are so important to UNIX networking today that they are covered in their own chapter in this book.

Repeaters

A 10BASE5 cable can't be over 500 meters long, and 10BASE2 is limited in length to only 200 meters. Most of the time neither length is long enough, so repeaters are used to extend the effective length of the cable. Imagine running the same LAN between two buildings. There are only a few dozen systems, and they not only need to be at the same network and subnet address, but they also have to be on the same segment (cable) as well. Let's say Building A uses a few hundred meters of thickwire to service their nodes, and then they go to a fiber optic repeater to use fiber optic cable between buildings, a typical use for fiber optic media. The repeater-connected fiber optic cable crosses the tunnel to Building B, where it connects via transceiver to another piece of thickwire, also several hundred meters in length.

Ethernet specifications allow only two repeaters between nodes, but this does not mean that only two repeaters can be used in any one LAN. On the contrary, you can use as many as you need, and you can use a multiport repeater to branch to several separate network segments, as long as they are parallel and not serial. With this sort of a fanout, you can have over 1000 nodes on the network and only one repeater between any one of them:

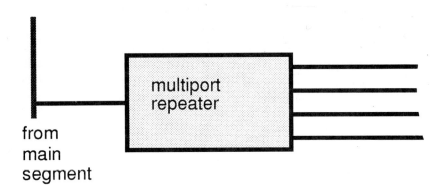

from
main
segment

Figure 4.3: Multiport repeaters

Repeaters operate at the physical level of the network. They don't alter the data or frames in any way, although some of them retime the preamble. Older repeaters used to pass on electrical noise, but fortunately, newer ones are more sophisticated and clean up the signal.

Multiport Repeaters

Multiport repeaters allow the single network cable to branch off to several cables, forming a network star. A typical multiport repeater will have a single (AUI) port to pick up the main part of the network as well as about eight thick or thinwire connectors to branch out to the extended part of the network. Contemporary repeaters will retime the signal (preamble) and extend collision fragments, and there are even multiport repeaters for fiber optic cable.

Routing and Protocol Layers

Remember that a network segment is like an antenna in that it broadcasts everything to every node attached to it; therefore, delivering a datagram to any node on that segment is easy. The trouble starts when you try getting datagrams over to another network segment.

Let's review the bottom three network protocol layers again:

3 Network
2 Link
1 Physical

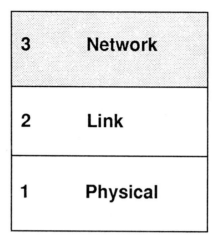

Figure 4.4: The bottom three protocols

The link layer (MAC layer in 802.3) exists to get datagrams from node to node on the local segment, but it has no mechanism to get over to another network or subnetwork. However, the third layer of the OSI model is designed to take care of routing across networks, and fortunately it can route across subnetworks as well. You can see why if you look at a datagram header:

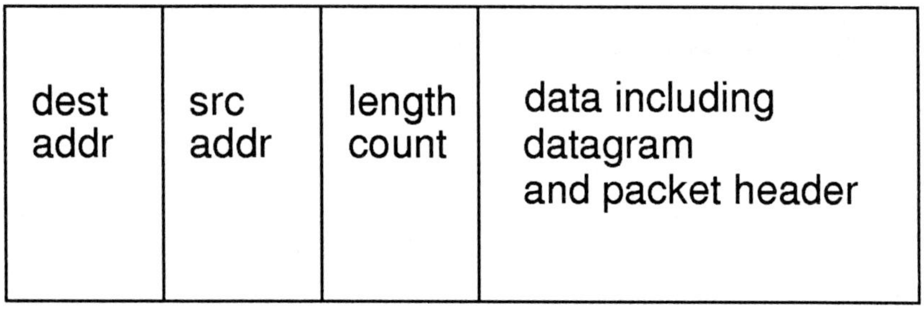

dest addr
src addr
length count
data including datagram and packet header

Figure 4.5: Network (internet) layer encapsulation

At the link layer only the source and destination addresses can be seen, but any routing information is hidden in the data part of the datagram and cannot be examined, which is why routing gets complicated so quickly. Bridges and routers solve this problem in different ways, bridges working at the link layer and routers working at the network layer.

Adaptive bridges operate at the link layer, seeing and working with source and destination addresses, but they also have a short-term memory which enables them to learn about the network by remembering all the source and destination addresses that they see. In other words, an *adaptive* bridge stores the source addresses and ports of each datagram and builds a routing table of destination addresses and bridge port numbers. To adapt to changes in the network topology or the loss or gain of a node, it will "forget" the address and port after a specified period of time and reinitialize it the next time it sees the address.

Routers work at the network (IP) layer. Older routers work from tables created manually by the people who set up the router at their site, but newer dedicated routers have the intelligence to create their own tables of Internet addresses and their corresponding Ethernet addresses. In either case, when data come into the router with an IP destination address, if the router finds that address in its table, it looks up the corresponding Ethernet number and port number, rebuilds the datagram header, and sends the data to that port.

The key is that bridges work at the link layer, and routers work at the network layer. Let's take a closer look at bridges and routers and examine their similarities and differences.

Bridges

A bridge connects two segments on the same medium. Networks with workstations that rely on network-intensive devices like file servers, YP-domain servers, mail servers, and print servers will get saturated quickly. PC networks can have hundreds of nodes on a network leg and not saturate, but a server/workstation environment will pass the capacity of the wire very quickly after 50 nodes.

To ease the network overload, the nodes must be *isolated*. One method is subnetting. Each segment becomes a subnet by virtue of its network address. Take the case of a network with the internet class B address of 128.213.0.0 using a router to achieve isolation:

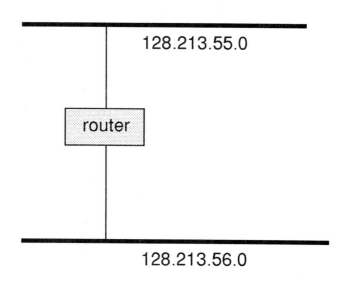

Figure 4.6: A router connecting two segments at different addresses

One leg of the LAN has the subnet address 128.213.55.0, and the next segment has the address 128.213.56.0. When a router is used to separate the two segments, only data intended for 128.213.56.0 pass from the 128.123.55.0 segment, and vice versa.

Routers join subnets and networks, and they require maintenance, but bridges can also be used for isolation. When smaller network segments need only partial isolation rather than absolute isolation, adaptive bridges are used.

Let's re-examine that network with the Internet class B address of 128.213.0.0, this time using an adaptive bridge to separate the two legs:

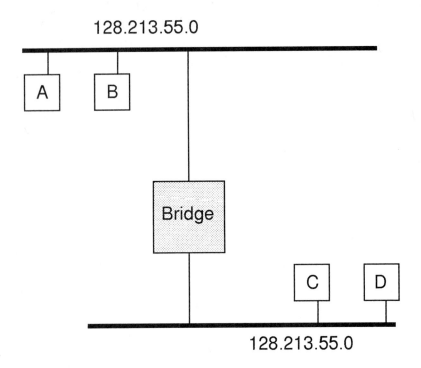

Figure 4.7: Bridging segments at the same address

Operating at a single network address and spanning two segments, the bridge forwards data from A or B to C or D, and vice versa. Because the bridge learns of their locations by remembering the source address of the datagrams it forwards, it also blocks data that should not be sent. When the bridge receives a packet (datagram), it looks at the destination address and does a scan of a hash table to see where to forward the datagram or where to discard it. Then it looks at the source address if it is not in the hash table and adds it to the hash table. Thus, if A sends to B, the bridge will keep the data from going over to the side where C and D live; this is called *bridge isolation*.

To reiterate, whereas the third network protocol layer takes care of IP routing and the first layer gets the data on the wire, the second link layer on which bridges operate exists to get data from one node to another, and with a few exceptions its primitive routing is limited to "on-this" or "on-the-next segment."[2] Anything beyond that needs to be handled at the IP layer with routers, but a bridge's ability to partially isolate network traffic should never be overlooked. As you develop your fledgling network, often the first steps you will take toward network isolation will involve bridges, for they are cheaper than routers and require much less maintenance.

Routers

The next logical step from bridge routing is to get past the adjacent segment to send to another destination node, whether it be several segments away or on another network. Recall that a repeater won't help you, because it only knows about its own segment. We have just seen that a bridge knows about its own segment and those to which it is directly attached, and it can figure out the next node and the paths belonging to other networks, but it has a built-in short-term memory so it remembers them only for a limited time. More sophistication is needed to go any further, and so we must start thinking about routers.

Routers are also used to connect networks over different media, sometimes at a great distance. Routing requires that a datagram be sent to the next segment that is on the way to its ultimate destination. If a datagram must route from network A to B just to get to C, the *fixed router algorithm*[3] requires that the datagram be routed to B before it gets to C:

---

1. Bridges operate at the media access control (MAC) section of the link layer.
3. First-generation routers depended on fixed routing based upon routing tables set manually by the people setting up the router. Second-generation routers build their own routing tables.

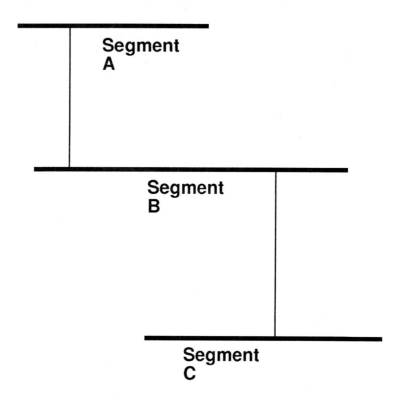

Figure 4.8: Spanning three segments

A is the source, and C is the destination, but B is the *next* segment. Routing to C requires a device that can operate at the IP layer, which can route by way of routing tables. Routers keep internal routing tables which allow them to resolve routing by host name and through routing complexities far beyond the capabilities of bridges. Combined with the name-to-address resolution of DNS, data can be accessed from anywhere in the domain to anywhere in the world.

Physically, all it takes to make a router out of an ordinary computer is to add a second Ethernet card. These improvised routers are much slower than bridges because they have more work to do. Dedicated multiprocessor routers solve the speed problem, for they are quite sophisticated and rely heavily on their multiprocessors to bring their throughput at normal loading to line speed. Because routers are high-maintenance devices that must be well understood to be maintained, and because routing algorithms are numerous and complex, they will be covered in greater detail in Chapter 8.

Gateways

Gateways used to be general-purpose computers that were fitted with additional Ethernet cards and programmed to do protocol conversion. Typically, they would be used to get from a VT100 terminal to an IBM mainframe by converting terminal protocols. Today, gateways are highly capable routers that route network to network over similar or different media and protocols. The differences between routers and gateways is that a router can act on and alter header information through the IP layer, while gateways can change header information and protocols, leaving only the original data unchanged. To get beyond the LAN requires a router or gateway, and the Internet relies on gateways. In one of the Star Trek adventures, "City on the Edge of Forever," a gateway was used to get from one time frame to another, and that is where the network gateway got its name.

Bridges or Routers — That Is the Question

Although a bridge works at the link network protocol layer and the router works through the IP network protocol layer, networking is developing at such an explosive rate, who can say what additional characteristics they will acquire in the future? At this writing we will compare the two by pitting the adaptive bridge against the dedicated multiprocessor router.

Since the bridge can't distinguish one network or subnet from another, it can be used to join segments with any internetwork address. Unlike routers, bridges do not discriminate — to them each system is an Ethernet number. They are called *adaptive* because they dynamically map out where the nodes are relative to their own ports. If 128.213.56.37 *sends* a datagram and it arrives on the bridge's Port A[4], the router marks 128.213.56.37 as Port A. When a datagram *arrives* for 128.213.56.37 on Port B, the router knows to send it to Port A. Whether the node is one *hop*[5] away or 14, the bridge neither knows nor cares.

The contemporary router also learns, but in a much more sophisticated fashion. Its most important source of information is other routers, and it exchanges routing information freely with adjacent routers to get its picture of the current network topology. A second-generation router deals with fixed routing information as well as getting its own picture of all nodes, regardless of the types of devices in the immediate vicinity (that is, one to a few hops away). In actuality, an intelligent bridge running with a spanning-tree algorithm can map destinations to almost anywhere within the network since it shares information with other bridges.

Both devices can get a fair picture of a small network, and a good adaptive bridge can even be programmed to some extent. By attaching it to a PC, you can program the bridge to do a reasonable amount of filtering. Picture a bridge that spans a small, 70-system, departmental UNIX network to a campus network backbone heavy with all kinds of traffic, including extraneous PC network traffic:

---

4. Bridges and routers have more than one port.
5. Any time a node has to forward a datagram, it's called a hop.

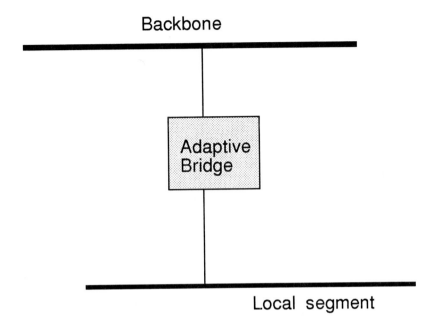

Figure 4.9: Using an adaptive bridge

If this adaptive bridge is programmed to filter IP traffic only, it will not forward anything other than datagrams with Internet protocol encapsulations.

Let's extend the local part of our department network for computing that includes DECnet:

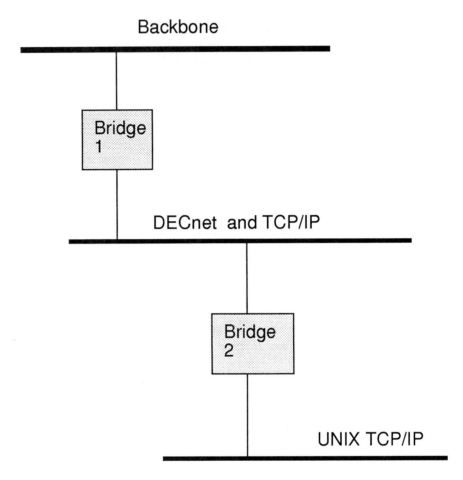

Figure 4.10: Bridging dissimilar protocols

To live with this new topology, Bridge 1 is programmed to accept both DECnet and IP traffic, while Bridge 2 permits only IP traffic to come through. In this way the entire departmental network is isolated from any extraneous PC data that flows through the main network backbone, and the UNIX-*sans*-DECnet segment sees nothing but local traffic and incoming IP datagrams.

Bridges are low-maintenance, and those who administer them don't need extensive schooling in their care and maintenance. They adapt quickly to changes in the network. Let's say that in the following network a node is moved from Segment C to Segment B:

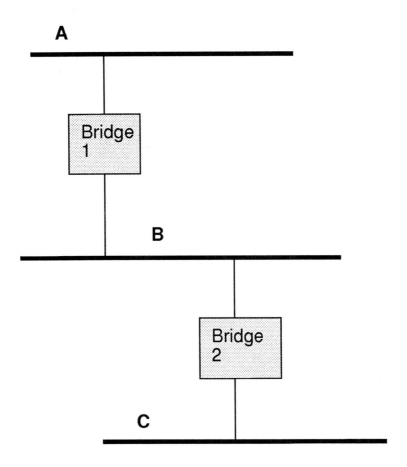

Figure 4.11: Two bridges spanning three segments

Bridge 1's picture of the node's location would not change, but Bridge 2 would flounder for a bit or eventually forget about the node's old location until the new node sends a datagram through Bridge 2, and then it would reorient its picture of that node's location.

If adaptive bridges work effectively to partially isolate a network, then why use routers? It's surprising how quickly network traffic increases to more than the Ethernet's theoretical capacity, and this departmental network will degrade quickly if we stubbornly stick to bridges. Timeouts will soon become a regular occurrence, and major jobs requiring NFS will start to fail. Everything on the network will still work, but it will no longer be able to provide reliable communications and file sharing. That's when routers can come to the rescue.

We all grow and change, and networks do the same. One way to save departmental network 128.213.0.0 from the horrors of timeouts is to divide it into four segments, each segment on its own subnet. Each segment carries the work of separate groups, each with their own file servers. Now the segments are separated by routers which will block all traffic except any intended for a particular subnet:

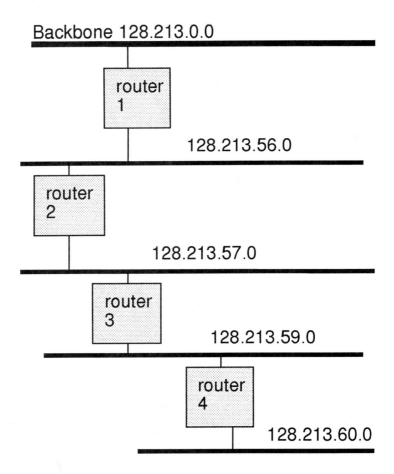

Figure 4.12: Routing multiple subnets

If the number of segments is doubled, the network traffic diminishes by half. If this new network setup will remain static and nothing changes, adaptive bridges could do the job pretty well, but networks never stay the same — they always change. This new network topology is starting to reach a level of complexity that will soon exceed the capabilities of bridges, and to plan best for the future, routers should be used.

Routers are more flexible, easier to program, and they permit subnetworking, but they also require special skill and training to program and maintain. They are more work-intensive to set up and more costly than bridges, but a $5000 two-port router would rescue this overloaded department network, and full service would be restored.

We'll go into routers and bridges in further detail later in the book, but now is a good time to put routers and bridges in perspective. A short time ago, no one except the central network authority bought a router or a gateway. A few brave souls may have bought a bridge or two for isolation, but local network groups didn't buy routers because subnetworking was a dirty word. Now subnetworks and routers are commonplace.

The reason bridges used to be favored is because they were cheaper, faster, and easier to maintain. But a good dedicated router requires little attention once it is set up, and it can double as a bridge or a gateway. They are highly specialized, multiprocessor devices, and in the long run they are cheaper than buying a bridge and having to replace it with a router. Old network equipment has no resale value.

The point is to take your time before committing to anything. If you are administering a small network, you may opt for simple bridge isolation. However, if the network grows, and they all do, then you may need routers because bridges won't work. On the other hand, you can also consider something called bridging routers, because they do both tasks. Never put a router between a workstation and its server, because it is easier and cheaper to put a half dozen subnets onto a server through a half dozen internet interfaces than attempting to do it by the routing of Etherswitches (a switching device that allows a lot of lines to come through a central hub).

There is an alternative to using routers to solve network traffic problems. UNIX provides for multiple Ethernet interfaces, and although normally only routers take advantage of it, a high-capacity file server with multiple ports can become a router of sorts. You add additional Ethernet ports by adding additional Ethernet cards. Thus, a file server with two active ports can serve two subnetworks. If you have 200 machines all coming off the same file server, a dedicated functional multiprocessor file server like an Auspex can easily handle a half dozen subnets without the aid of routers.

Multihomed servers are another, even better alternative. They are designed to have a high number of Ethernet ports but also to favor Ethernet traffic internally. Make maximum use of multihomed servers, and be rigid about subnetworking before you exceed the capacity of the wire.

We are currently in a time of rapidly changing technology. The best way to protect yourself is through education. If you understand basic networking concepts, you will more intelligently select the best technology for the present and have a better idea of how to plan for the future. You need to walk a thin line, ignoring fads and wild promises made by the vendors and the trade press, but you also need to keep an eye open for possible future changes that will affect your site. For example, an important question to consider if you are on an Ethernet is whether you should buy your next router to be ready for FDDI or ATM. If you see multimedia in your future, ATM may be promising, but talk to your router sales engineer to see if the product can be *upgraded* to ATM when the time comes.

Challenges to CSMA/CD Protocols

The use of CSMA/CD protocols does not go unchallenged. Some say token ring is more sensible because it allows only one transmission at a time. Ethernet not only has collisions, they happen quite often. However, when you go from theory to fact, token ring is much slower. While token ring politely waits for its turn to access the wire, Ethernet shoves transmissions on the wire as fast as it can. Two out of five transmission may be clobbered as a result of collisions, but they will be retransmitted. In fact, the existence of collisions is not a major problem if 1) they stay below a reasonable level, and 2) the software handles them gracefully.

FDDI uses token ring, and while its transmission speed is 10 times faster then Ethernet, it runs only 2.5 times faster than conventional Ethernet. Any increase in speed in line transmission is welcome, but anything less than a full order of magnitude fails to get much attention and certainly is not enough to get a site to junk its investment in copper cable and Ethernet equipment and start from scratch in FDDI. However, a site creating a new installation might look at it differently.

You have to look at how software handles failed transmissions. The specifications for the lower protocol layers all state that they are unreliable. Ethernet and IP do a great job, but they don't guarantee that any single datagram or packet will arrive. However, TCP is considered "reliable" transmission, and it *does* guarantee that a packet will arrive. How can it claim to be reliable if the lower layers can't guarantee delivery? Simple. If it doesn't receive all the packets, even if only one is missing, it requests that the entire transmission be resent.

And what about TCP's partner, UDP? It is known as "unreliable," but NFS uses UDP, and NFS is quite reliable. The reason? The end-to-end packet delivery needed by NFS is put there by NFS itself.

A Foundation for Network Design

Now you have a background in network topology, network media, and network devices, but that isn't enough to set up a UNIX network. You still need to learn a little bit about network design, and that is the subject of the next chapter.

CHAPTER

5

Network Design, Creation, and Implementation

You need not only network knowledge to design a local area network, but also common sense, because you will have to administer your creation for a long time. The best way to design a network is one piece at a time. You should also consider some basic network design goals before you purchase anything:

- Accessibility — You must be able to reach every node on the network from every other node. The only exceptions are during emergencies or special maintenance tasks.

- Reliability — You expect your phone to work every time you pick it up, making rare allowances during severe, unusual circumstances such as storms. Similarly, you want to achieve less than one percent unscheduled downtime on any part of the network.

- Cost — Cost is a major consideration, for network design is always restricted to some extent by economic limitations.

- Extensibility — Networks must be designed ahead of time for growth, or you will spend extra money replacing some of the devices that you put in when building the original network. You never want to pay for the same function twice.

- Interoperability — Every vendor's hardware and software should work with other vendors' equipment and software. If your network components aren't compatible, you will have to spend extra money and extra time trying to hold everything together. For example, you could find yourself having to purchase a gateway or special software solely for the purpose of getting certain network protocols to work with the other vendors' software and hardware on your net. You could design your network around one vendor, but why limit your capabilities and paint yourself into a corner? Design interoperability into your net before you make any purchases.

- Security — If you have a need for higher security than UNIX normally offers, make sure that you build it into the network during the design phase. Some operating systems like SunOS, SCO, and AIX have optional security packages.

- Isolation — Your network will quickly grow to the point where you will need to isolate network segments with routers or bridges in order to maintain the bandwidth of the segments. Whether you choose routers or bridges will depend on the ultimate size of the segments joined.

- Ease of Maintenance — Purchase network devices with your specific maintenance capabilities in mind. On smaller, less complex networks, bridges are cheaper and require little maintenance, but if something goes wrong with the net, they are much harder to troubleshooot than routers. If you create a large, heavily segmented local area network, you will need the more expensive routers in order to be able to troubleshoot the network, and you will also need a larger staff to maintain them. A bridging router does both bridging and routing.

- Ability to Monitor the Network — Eventually you will need to monitor your network to identify network problems. Plan for this in advance when you design your network.

Design goals sometimes appear to be at odds with one another other. For example, it's difficult to achieve easy accessibility without compromising security, and ultimate security can only be achieved by sacrificing accessibility. However, some goals work hand in hand. Your network will be easier to maintain if you have carefully planned for adequate monitoring hardware and software.

Networks always grow faster than planned, so look at the broadest possible picture: imagine the way it will be when network segments hook up workstations or terminals in every office on the entire floor. Start small, but if you know you are going to grow, select equipment and vendors that are capable of expansion, such as expandable concentrators.

We could continue to talk about network design in general terms, but instead let's get right down to the nitty gritty and study some basic network designs.

The World's Smallest Network

Let's design a tiny computer network, one that you might use in your own home or in a very small business. The simplest, smallest computer network would consist of two PC-type machines in the same room hooked up by a single piece of thinnet cable.

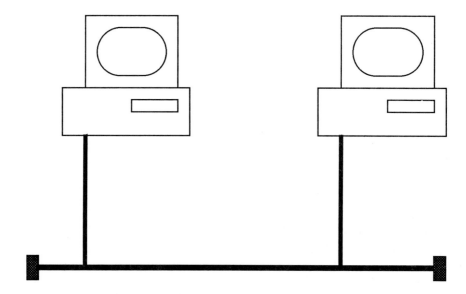

Figure 5.1: The smallest network

Thin coax is hooked up directly to the Ethernet card in PC-type systems, and so external transceivers are not needed. The cable is fitted at either end with a BNC-type female connector crimped to the wire end. These ends are then fitted with a tee and a 50-ohm terminator. The tee connector is connected to the Ethernet card on the system, and one (and only one) terminator is grounded. For this tiny network, the only cable-length restriction to consider is that the cable from one system to another be no shorter than one meter.

You will have to fit the system with an Ethernet card, plugged directly into the system's bus or motherboard, and the jumpering for the board will be peculiar to your system. The card itself will have to be set for interupts. PC-type machines require an IRQ setting that has not already been used by another COM port or slot, done by jumpering the motherboard of the PC. Also, a memory address or DMA channel addition may be necessary. Be sure to consult the manufacturer's manual. You must also select an I/O base address (base addresses 300 and 310 are usually available), one of the configuration parameters. Once the card is jumpered, record the jumper settings, and button up the system.

Be sure to run the cable where it is not likely to be kicked loose. Thinnet systems are notorious for failing when someone accidentally kicks the cable under the desk or moves a machine and disconnects it.

That's all there is to the world's smallest network — little design is involved.

An Expandable Thickwire Coax Network

Let's design a small thickwire Ethernet LAN for a large, one-room engineering office and a raised-floor computer room on the same floor. In the larger there are many people working, but for now you are limiting the network to one mechanical engineering group consisting of two PC-class systems and five workstations doing computer-aided design. One UNIX file server and two old minis are in the computer room now, but within two years the company plans to buy several more servers and network devices, so rapid network growth is an integral part of your design plan.

The size of the facility limits the size of the network, and small machine rooms limit the number of servers and therefore limit the site to small networks. However, computer rooms can be very large indeed. I've seen them bigger than 100,000 square feet, with huge mainframes, modem banks, DASD farms, water chillers, controllers, and other major devices. The computer room for this engineering office is more modest in size, about 500 square feet, large enough to hold several file servers, a departmental workstation (larger and more powerful than a personal workstation), communications equipment such as bridges and routers, and the older, general-purpose minis that were around before the network project began.

Start by planning your cable layout in the computer room. If the room is long and narrow, you may be able to run the cable the full length of the room down the center under the floor tile. If the room is wide enough, you might want to consider extending the length of the cable by running the cable in a full U around the room or snaking it to maximize the number of systems that can be attached to it in the future by branching off a small concentrator. Don't forget the cable trays to keep the cable off the floor.

Coming out of the computer room, the cable will run up into the ceiling space as it enters the office area. There it will be fitted with taps and transceivers, and drop cables will be brought down the partitions to the individual systems. The rule is 2½ meters between taps, minimum, so plan to lay your cable where it can access every possible system location. Although you are setting up the network for one engineering group for now, remember that you are planning as if the network will eventually expand to include every engineer and secretary at every desk on that floor. Before you know it, you may have to go to concentrators and twisted-wire pair in this room.

Before installing the cable, start at one end and mark it at periodic intervals, say every 10 meters. The cable will already have a mark every 2.5 meters to remind you where to put your taps, but you can add your other measurements alongside. These distance marks will be helpful later when you troubleshoot the network and find out how many feet or meters away the problem is from wherever the diagnostic point is.

Now lay the cable, install all taps and transceivers, and have a TDR[1] picture taken of the new network. A timed pulse will be sent down the cable from its beginning in the computer room to the far terminator at the other end in the office, and an oscilloscope will record the reflected wave form coming back on the wire, showing any faults in the network such as shorts (where the inner core comes into electrical contact with the outer braid), opens (any place where the inner core is broken), and severe bends (where the cable has been bent too tightly). A reading should be photographed and stored safely away. Eventually you will experience a network failure, another TDR snapshot must be used to troubleshoot the net, and the original reading will be useful for comparison. The TDR output should also indicate barrel connectors, T connectors for thinwire installation, and tranceiver locations. These normal cable distortions marked in the output will help identify and document where those devices are.

Recall that PC-type machines have their transceivers built into their interface cards; however, PC-type machines on a thickwire net must have transceivers directly on the wire which, in turn, must bypass the internal transceivers.

If you are putting Sun systems on this network, they will also need transceivers, but don't try to find a network interface card. Sun workstations have the Ethernet function built into the motherboard, obviously designed with networking in mind.

When designing a thickwire network, using common sense is as important as sophisticated network knowledge:

- Be sure that there is enough cable in the floors and overheads for future connectivity needs.

- Don't run your cable near sources of electrical interference or radiation, like transformers or fluorescent light ballasts.

- Ground one end of the cable shielding only. (The outside shielding is the ground reference, and the inner core is the

---

1. TDR stands for time-delay reflectometer.

signal conductor.) If both ends are grounded and there is a potential at one end, a current will continually flow over the ground braid until it heats up the cable and destroys it.

• Be careful not to bend the cable severely or kink it. Use cable ladders to and from cable closets because they allow large bend radii.

• Use cable trays in floors and ceiling plenums to lay cables rather than laying them loose on the ceiling tiles, because the ceiling will eventually collapse from the weight.

Fanning Out with Twisted-Wire Pair

Now let's imagine that you already have a thickwire Ethernet network on your site, but your network has been expanding at such a rapid rate that you must now consider using concentrators and twisted-wire pair. Concentrators are used when there is a high concentration of nodes in a small area, like an office floor. It's hard to beat twisted-wire pair for branching out to office nodes, because miles of twisted-wire pair are already installed in walls and ceilings of commercial buildings. The typical layout includes data communications closets[2] that distribute both voice and data connections, and essentially you will run into three conditions in the offices: 1) you have extra twisted-wire pair originally meant for telephone lines that terminate with RJ-type[3] connectors, in which case you will have to use RJ-type connected drop cords to hook up the workstations; 2) you have several RJ-type connectors on a wall panel specifically meant for computers and voice, and you will need drop cords with RJ-type connectors for those; or 3) you may have an older combination of unshielded and shielded twisted-wire pair, unshielded for voice and shielded for data (innovated

---

2. These rooms used to be called telephone closets, but now that networking has become so important, the wires carry both voice and digital data.

3. "Telephone" type connectors, RJ-45 jacks (8-conductor), RJ-12 jacks (6-conductor), and others have come into common usage for connecting twisted-wire pair, concentrator connections, telephones, keyboards, and similar applications.

originally by IBM), and you will know you have that if you see boxes in each office with a RJ-11 phone connector *and* an IBM hermaphrodite drop cable connector.

Whatever condition you find, twisted-wire pair Ethernet installations are relatively easy to set up and maintain. The wires are already in — each office is usually designed with at least two sets of twisted-wire pair per office — so getting from the offices to the data communications closets is almost a done deal. Your main network design task is determining how to get the network from the closet to the computer room. If it is a short distance from the closet to the computer room, use thicknet. If FDDI is even vaguely perceived by your company as part of its network's future, or if there is a reasonably long distance to travel, go with fiber optic cable and lay at least two lines.

The key to successful Ethernet twisted-wire pair networks are the concentrators, requiring a transceiver and attaching to the segment by coax or fiber optic cable. The concentrator fans out through RJ or DB connectors to the twisted-wire pairs running to the individual offices. In the future, this site will have several concentrators which will need to be monitored carefully, so when you enlarge this part of the network pay special attention to the monitors that will be watching the concentrators.

A Modular Approach to Creating a Network Segment

No matter how large or small a network you design, take a modular approach. If it is a site network, start with the *backbone*, the main segment to which all other segments will be attached. When you have to cover any distance, think fiber optic cable. Design each subnetwork separately, give them letter designations, such as subnet A, B, and C, and then worry about how to tie them together. If you are adding only one network segment, take care of the servers in the computer room first before worrying about how you will add the workstations. Taking the whole and breaking it down into manageable pieces makes the job of designing and maintaining the net manageable.

Imagine another engineering group that wants to go over to a network of 20 to 30 graphical workstations with 3 servers, and they must be on the company's larger network. Start your design with the network segment for the workstations. First you must determine if all the engineers are in the same physical area and if sets of twisted-wire pair for workstations are available in the engineers' offices. Let's say that the answer to both questions is yes — all the offices have twisted-wire pair, and all the engineers are on the same floor. However, this office area is too large to be serviced by one datacomm closet (twisted-wire pair has severe length limitations), and so you have two datacomm closets to deal with. The servers are in a computer room on another floor, about 400 meters away from the first closet.

Let's add an additional wrinkle: this group is sharing the machine room with several other groups. For flexibility, your servers are attached by a small fanout unit like an old DEC DELNI or a small concentrator such as a Synoptics 3030. The reason we're using these old units is to add a realistic flavor of what it's like to work at real sites. All sites have to deal with monetary limitations, and if you have an old machine sitting around that you can make use of, you do so. Most sites buy as many new machines as they can, but you'll always see an accumulation of older machines that are slowly being phased out.

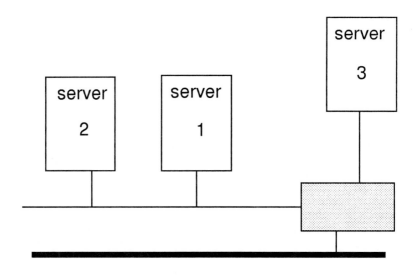

Figure 5.2: Multiport server connections

The next step is to get from the servers to the first datacomm closet, and the distance between floors requires the use of fiber optic cable. Now the plot thickens, because in this first closet you need a *departmental concentrator*. Aside from its regular ports, this type of concentrator also has a special ports module that allows it to attach to the concentrator in the other datacomm closet that services the rest of the workstations on the floor.[4]

Attaching the workstations completes the creation of this network segment, and now you can give it a unique subnet address and attach it by way of a router to the nearest leg of the company's larger network backbone. For a company of this size, router isolation is an absolute necessity. When the need arises, you can isolate this segment from the rest of the company's network by bringing down the router, a handy technique when systems start dropping like flies and you don't know why. All the workers on the segment can still get their work done until the network storm passes.

Extending the Net by Designing Subnetworks

Let's imagine that your engineering section has been on the network for quite a while, and now your segment is reaching its limits, bursting its seams by exceeding the bandwidth of its medium. The telltale signs are the slowness of the network and the high incidence of collisions and runts. Your network is sick, and you must fix it as soon as possible.

Communication between PCs, mainframes, and multi-user systems doesn't result in a significant amount of network traffic, because it usually involves remote logins, occasional file transfers, and mail transactions. However, you will see your network

---

4. Concentrators can be cascaded to accommodate new nodes as your installation grows, and departmental concentrators allow branching from one concentrator to another until reaching slave concentrators, which represent the end of the line, with no further branching possible. Branching from main concentrators to slave concentrators can be done either on the same locality or at great distances via fiber optic cable.

become overloaded quickly when you add servers. A network segment with 30 to 40 workstations and 3 to 4 servers is about as much of a load as any 10 megabit-per-second LAN can handle. After that, you need to subnet.

Assume that this hypothetical engineering section is divided into three groups: engineering, design, and checking; and although they share very little data, they do need to communicate with each other occasionally. Each group works out of separate disk partitions in the file server, so dividing the network segment into three subnets is a perfect solution to this section's network problems.

In order to subnet, you must understand addressing. A site is given a class B Internet address, say 123.156.000.000. The simplest, but by no means only, way to look at this address is

```
123.156.sss.nnn
```

where **sss** is the subnet part of the number and **nnn** is the part of the node number. Look at the two network segments, A and B:

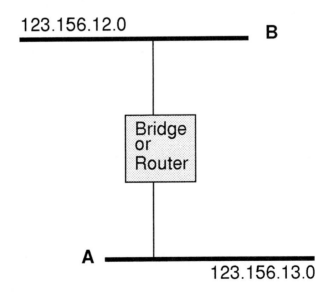

Figure 5.3: Spanning segments

If a router is used, A will forward 123.156.13.0 addresses only to B. If a bridge is used, it will forward on a node-by-node bases as it learns each node's location.

True subnetting can only be achieved by using a router. Routers used to be a lot slower than bridges, not surprising when you consider how much extra work they do, but today dedicated multiprocessor routers are extremely fast, and they are less expensive than they used to be. When designing a network that you know will eventually have to be subnetted, do not discount using routers to perform as virtual bridges until you actually need them as routers.

On the other hand, don't overlook the possibility of using a server as a router in a pinch. Just because a computer has multiple Ethernet cards does not mean that it has to function as a router. Most servers have either two ports on each Ethernet card or two cards, so you could add another Ethernet card to one of the engeineering section's servers and use it as both router and server. Then when you enable the routing daemon on the server, your subnets are ready to go. Or you could use multihomed servers, specially designed for this. They take the worry out of subnetworking.

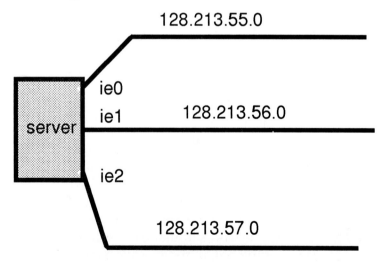

Figure 5.4: Multihomed server connections

The `ie` numbers are the servers' Ethernet interface device numbers with an Intel device.

Now let's take a look with new insights at the illustration first presented on page 30.

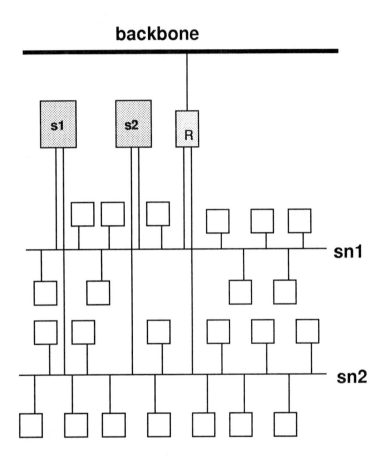

Figure 5.5: A two-segment network using multihomed servers

This is a practical network design for multiple subnetworks using multihomed servers (s1 and s2) to eliminate the use of multiple routers. The way it works is that each subnet is directly connected to one pair of Ethernet ports on each server. Only one router is needed to handle the occasional offsubnet traffic.

The next illustration shows the actual implementation using concentrators at the workstation end by twisted-wire pair.

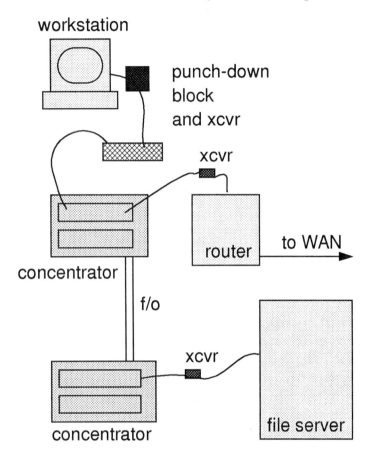

Figure 5.6: Workstation to file server implementation

The concentrator connects to a concentrator in the computer room by way of fiber optic cable. The smaller concentrator in the computer room connects to individual file servers. Additionally, the concentrators in the datcomm closet also connect to the one router used for the entire domain.

Network Monitors and Managers

There are several things to consider when designing a network, and this chapter has given you some insights into a few. However, network monitors and network managers are so important to the maintenance and health of today's networks that they merit further discussion.

Network monitors keep an eye on the network and give you relevant data on its general health. A network manager is a software platform on which a monitoring system can be built that is capable of managing the entire network. Network diagnostic tools and monitors allow you to watch traffic at any point along the network that is instrumented, that is, having some kind of device that will pass intelligence about what is happening on the wire. From your desk you see the condition of various network devices, such as concentrators, and shut down ports or bring them up, individually or collectively.

In spite of these appealing qualities, it is tempting not to include network monitors and network managers in your initial network design, because they cost extra money. Your desk flooded with brochures, your head buzzing with trying to understand all the new network technology, it's all too easy to buy workstations and servers from Company A, concentrators from Company B, routers from Company C, and put off purchasing monitors until later.

Unfortunately, if you don't have any network monitoring capability, you will become a victim later when your network becomes overloaded, because you won't be able to diagnose the problem without them. Up to your hips in alligators, you may have to pay outside experts who will tell you that you need to purchase network monitors. That's when the real fun begins. You will find out that the manufacturer of some of your network equipment has monitors only for its own concentrators, and the manufacturer of some of your other network equipment has other monitors only for its own concentrators and bridges. Although your computer manufacturer may have network manager software that watches the entire network, you will still end up purchasing extra monitors for all the different network equipment that you bought.

If you had carefully researched network monitors when you researched the network hardware you purchased, you would have picked monitors that covered most of the hardware you bought and enabled the monitoring capability of your network the minute it started growing. Then you would have been be able to tackle your network problems without hiring outside help. In short, a complete network design plans ahead for the most interoperable network monitors and network managers possible, even if you don't install them right away.

Network monitors are used for more than keeping tabs on the condition of your network; they are also handy network administration tools. Picture a scenario in which, during a power loss, all your workstations stay up but all of your servers go down. When you try to bring up the servers, the workstations flood them with so many mount requests that they drown trying to come up. It's no problem, though, because you can use the network monitor to shut off the concentrator ports between the workstations and the servers. The workstations are still frantically looking around for servers, but they are no worse off than they were before, and meanwhile the servers can take their time coming up, blissfully undisturbed. As soon as your servers are alive and well, use the network monitor to turn on the concentrators' ports. The servers can now respond to the workstations' anxious mount requests, and your network is up and running again.

Monitoring software keeps a careful eye on the increasing network traffic, timeouts, collisions, and whether the ports are active or inactive, so choose the monitoring software as carefully as you choose your concentrators, bridges, and routers. Some monitoring capabilities are built into the devices themselves, and others are added later by a pluggable module.

The Battle for the Telcomm Closet and Other Issues

Do you design your own local domain, or do you let a central organization do it for you? Supposedly, a well-run centralized systems management team can provide services for its users better than local support groups, but is that always the case?

Some centralized systems support groups work well when they provide true expertise, have beneficial, consistent policies, and give timely service. But in large companies some of them fail to provide adequate service because bureacratic delays bog down response time. The good intentions of central groups are great, but only when they work, and they don't always work.

Whether technical service is provided locally or centrally, it must be high quality, and the response time must be as rapid as possible so that user downtime is minimized. Service is the key here. Whichever user service policy works best should be used. But the entire issue pivots on whether users are being adequately supported.

Some central support is mandatory, such as central maintenance of mail gateways and Internet gateways. But who is going to have the keys to the telephone closet? If you give control of the network closets to a central organization, will they let you in when you need access? What if a network connection fails and you prove, to your own satisfaction, that the system, cables, and transceiver are all right? You need the closet-side of the connection checked immediately, but can you get that kind of service? If administrators can't get into their own closets to fix the problem without waiting for service from a central authority, hours could be wasted, or even days. But if you maintain control of the closet, you will have someone you can depend on — you!

Here's another example. Imagine that your organization has been successfully running DNS for two years. You have successfully solved your main problems, keeping host tables down to a manageable size and maintaining a rapid resolution of names outside of your own name space. Now imagine that a corporate MIS-type comes to you with a proposal — he wants to provide centralized DNS service, and he wants you to buy in.

This is a good idea, to be sure, but just because a centralized support group talks the talk, it doesn't necessarily mean they can walk the walk. In other words, promising technical support doesn't ensure that it will be delivered. And since your budget is limited, you need to make sure that your dollars are well spent.

If this offer had been made before you set up DNS, it would have been a bargain. But offering it after the fact won't save you any money. So before you buy in, you need to find out how much this group knows about DNS before you commit; don't surrender to any central "authority" until you ascertain that they truly have the competence to do the job. Downtime delays are too costly to take a chance on a good idea. Leave yourself a way to back out if the service doesn't live up to your expectations.

A combination of local and central support is probably the best way to go. For some services, central support is the best solution, but for other services local support will be the fastest way to get the job done.

Here are some other important issues to consider. Consult with company-wide gurus to see what their plans for the backbone are, what kind of routers they are using, and if they plan to join with NetWare, Vines, DECnet, SNA, or what have you. How do they plan to get mail to you? If you are a full Ethernet domain, it's hard to get excited about SoftSwitch or any other mail system, because you'll go crazy making `sendmail` work with whatever system they elect unless they can deliver mail to you on Ethernet using SMTP.

You should be knowledgeable enough to design your own segment, even if you let someone else do it for you. Who is going to check their plans for accuracy if you don't? Today, you get away with 20 workstations on a subnet. At 20 MIPS each, it works. But next year they may all be multiprocessor with over 100 MIPS each, so how many on a subnet then? This kind of foresight needs to go into network design.

Don't rely on one salesman, either. The vendor that sold you your high-end file servers has an even faster system now, but do you need high computational power or the best and fastest network access possible? If you need a fast network, the computational power of a Cray supercomputer won't buy anything. High-speed multiple network interfaces, each with its own processor are what you need. We will continue to discuss these kinds of issues throughout the book.

The Importance of Addressing

When a network grows to the point at which it exceeds its bandwidth, you need to subnet with routers, and this requires a thorough knowledge of addressing, router setup, and router maintenance. The next chapter introduces some important addressing concepts.

CHAPTER

6

Addressing

For dependable mail delivery, you must have the correct address. If you specify the wrong address or forget to write it down, your mail will be delivered to the wrong place or spend its last days languishing in the dead letter pile at some post office somewhere. Network addresses are as important to the network as mail addresses are to the post office.

Computers see everything as numbers. Network programs have port addresses, every node has its own unique Ethernet number, each network, subnet, and host has its own Internet number, and so on. You need to know Internet addressing when you set up the network, you need knowledge of both Ethernet and Internet addressing when you diagnose network problems, and you must understand port addressing to fix sick network software. In short, you must understand how these addresses work at each protocol layer in order to set up the network and maintain it.

Ethernet-TCP/IP, OSI, and 802.3 network protocols achieve virtual delivery at the transport, network, and link layers, and each layer has its own address type and data form:

Layer Name	Address Type	Data Form
Transport	Port	Packets or Segments
Network	Internet	Datagrams
Data Link	Ethernet or 802.3	Frames

Figure 6.1: Data forms

Let's look at the addressing involved in each of these layers, starting with the transport layer.

Port Addressing

We've already discussed to some extent how data come off the wire at the physical layer and are processed at the Ethernet and Internet layers, but we haven't talked much about what happens at the transport layer. The machine deals with the ports for network programs at this level, such as `telnet` and `rlogin` for doing remote logins, `ftp`, `tftp`, and `rcp` for doing remote copies, `rsh` for executing a remote shell, and `smtp`, which gets mail across the network. TCP isn't the only protocol used; others include UDP and ICMP. In order for the transport-layer protocols to get to and from these network applications, they operate through a "well-known port."

The idea of a well-known port is that its address (port number) is known to all systems, and each network program has its own unique number. These programs are also called *services*, and the system uses the `/etc/services` ASCII file to keep track of services, aliases, and protocol types. Let's take a look:

```
% cat /etc/services
#
# services
#
echo            7/udp           ping
echo            7/tcp           ping
discard         9/udp           sink null
discard         9/tcp           sink null
.
.
```

The form is *service_name port/protocol aliases*. The first field has the names of the network programs or services. The socket and protocol used are in the second field, and the third field is the list of alternate names by which the service might be requested.

Use `rpcinfo` to see which services are currently running:

```
% rpcinfo -p stalker
program     vers    proto   port
   100000   2       tcp     111     portmapper
   100000   2       udp     111     portmapper
   100004   2       udp     642     ypserv
   .
```

`rpcinfo` is particularly useful for getting port information when used with utilities like `etherfind`, which tears apart datagrams. The following command line will give you information about every packet that goes to and comes from `stalker`:

```
% etherfind -src stalker -o -dst svr4
                                                     icmp type
lnth    proto      source      destination      src port    dst port
 146     udp         ws27           svr4           1017        2049
 154     udp         ws27           svr4           1017        2049
 146     udp         ws27           svr4           1017        2049
 146     udp         ws27           svr4           1017        2049
 154     udp         ws27           svr4           1017        2049
 158     udp         ws27           svr4           1017        2049
 150     udp       galadriel        svr4           1022        2049
 150     udp       galadriel        svr4           1022        2049
 150     udp       galadriel        svr4           1022        2049
 162     udp       galadriel        svr4           1022        2049
 162     udp       galadriel        svr4           1022        2049
 166     udp       galadriel        svr4           1022        2049
 162     udp       galadriel        svr4           1022        2049
 166     udp       galadriel        svr4           1022        2049
 150     udp       galadriel        svr4           1022        2049
 162     udp       galadriel        svr4           1022        2049
 174     udp       galadriel        svr4           1022        2049
 146     udp         svr2           svr4           1023        2049
 146     udp         svr2           svr4           1023        2049
 .
 .
```

This output went on for pages, but in this short excerpt, the various source nodes you see originate the packets, and svr4 is the node that is receiving them. Let's find out why port 2049 is dominating the dst port field by delving a little further for information with rpcinfo and grep:

```
% rpcinfo -p svr4 |grep 2049
 100003   2     udp     2049      nfs
```

The mystery is solved. Naturally, the NFS port is bound to get a lot of traffic!

Port addresses control traffic at the transport layer. Without port addresses, you couldn't get anything from the network to the application or from the application to the network, and network administrators must understand these port addresses in order to maintain the tables in which they are stored and to use transport-layer diagnostics.

Internet Addressing

The 4-byte (32-bit) Internet addresses get data from network to network; they are assigned by a central authority and are guaranteed to be unique. Written as four bytes, called *octets*, each number is separated by periods and is a decimal representation of one byte:

```
128.216.155.54
```

An Internet address has two to three different parts: network, host, and (optional) subnet. Think of how you find a normal street address, like 1234 Alder Lane. The number, 1234, identifies a particular house, but if you don't have the street name, you aren't going to find that house. Having only the street name is a help, but without the address number you're still up a creek. You definitely need the number and the street name to get to the right house, the street name corresponding to the network part of the address and the house number corresponding to the host part. The subnet part of the address is similar to an apartment number.

There are three classes of Internet addresses in use, A through C. The ranges of each class vary, depending on the relationship between the host part of the address and the network part. As the host part of the address gets larger, the network part gets smaller, and vice versa:

Class	Networks	Hosts	Net Size	Host Size
A	few	many	8 bits	24 bits
B	mid	mid	16 bits	16 bits
C	many	few	24 bits	8 bits

Figure 6.2: Network class size comparison

The bit patterns and the length of the address limits the ranges of each class, and the first one to three bits of the high-order byte reveal its class. Let's look at each class separately to see why.

Class A Internet Addresses

Class A was intended for networks that have a multitude of hosts and only a few networks. Its original form looks like this:

```
net.host.host´.host´´
```

Notice that it takes three bytes to form the host part of the number in a Class A network. Thus, a Class A network number 120.5.40.215 has a network part of 120 and a host part of 5.40.215. Look at all this from a binary point of view:

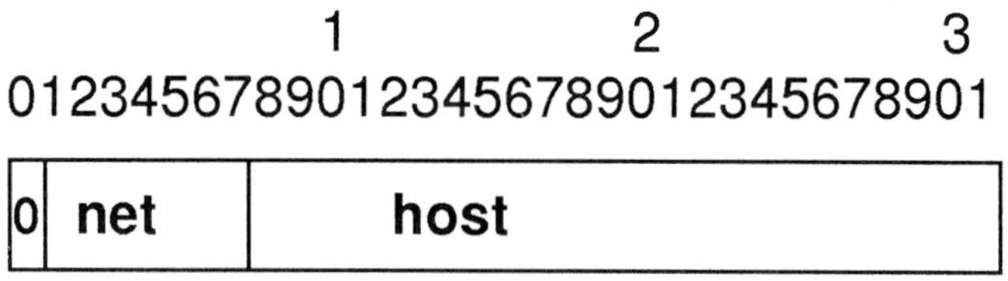

```
                1               2               3
      01234567890123456789012345678901
```

Figure 6.3: Class A Ethernet numbers

The high-order bits (1 through 7) comprise the net field, and the first bit is always a 0.

Class A addresses range from 1.0.0.0 to 126.0.0.0, with 127.0.0.0 reserved as a loopback address:

```
$ grep ´127\.´ /etc/hosts
127.0.0.1  localhost  lcl  me  loopback
```

Class A addresses not only have the highest potential for a large number of hosts but also subnets, as these alternate forms show:

```
net.subnet.host.host´
net.subnet.subnet´.host
```

Class B Internet Addresses

Class B addresses were intended for use with a medium number of networks and a medium number of hosts, and most new installations prefer this scheme, which divides the network and host address parts evenly:

```
net.net´.host.host´
```

It looks like this, broken down by bits:

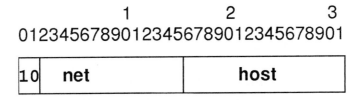

Figure 6.4: Class B Ethernet numbers

It takes two bytes for the host part of the number and two bytes for the net part. The range of possible Class B addresses is 128.1.0.0 to 191.254.0.0. From a binary perspective, the first two bits of the first byte of a Class B 32-bit Internet address are 10.

Class B addresses are also ideal for subnetworking in this alternate form:

```
net.net´.subnet.host
```

Class C Internet Addresses

A Class C network address, the default, was intended for a multitude of networks supporting a few hosts each. In other words, it handles the minimum number of subnets and hosts:

```
net.net´.net´´.host
```

Only one byte is allowed for the host number, so it doesn't lend itself to subnetting.

Here's how it looks when we break it down by bits:

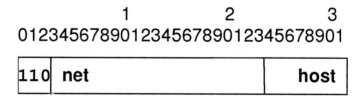

Figure 6.5: Class C Ethernet numbers

The Class C address range is 192.0.1.0 to 223.255.255.0. The binary characteristics are easy to remember, because the first three bits of the first byte must be 110, and the bits remaining to 23 comprise the large net part of the address.

Broadcasts, Multicasts, and Other Address Conventions

In a sense, all packets on a network are broadcast, because they are received by every host on the wire. The network is not a filter, it is an antenna, sending to everyone, and the filtering takes place because each host knows its own Ethernet address and accepts only those packets addressed specifically to it. Some exceptions are network *broadcasts* and *multicasts*, which are machine-generated, such as ICMP packets.

If the bits in the host portion of an Internet address are all binary ones (255 decimal), the address is intended for all hosts on that network segment. Thus, the network address 128.213.0.0 would have a multicast address of 128.213.255.255 to reach all hosts on its Class B LAN.

The Internet address 255.255.255.255, all binary ones, is the broadcast address, picked up by every host on the entire network, including subnets.

If the bits in the host portions of an Internet address are all zeros, the address is for a specific network. Thus, 128.217.0.0 is solely a network address and does not refer to any hosts.

If the net portion of the address is all zeros, the address is for a specific host on that local network. Thus 0.0.55.58 is for host 55.58 on the local Class B network.

Subnets have their own conventions, and it is customary to reserve the lowest host numbers for the subnetwork's routers. Subnet 128.123.55.0 would have address 128.213.55.1 for its router, for example. You may want to reserve the range 10-15 for servers. Some people also reserve the highest number in the range, 254, for a temporary address for demo systems and other extraneous machines that come and go.

Network Masks

The creation of network masks is a necessary part of network setup, because they determine which part of a network address will be interpreted as the network part of the host number. A mask is a template held over a piece of data that causes some of it to be read and some to be ignored. The software uses a mask to isolate the network or host part of the network number. When you subnet, you're the only one who knows which part of the address is net and which subnet. In order to do routing, all the router wants to see are the net and subnet part of the address, not the host, and you accomplish that by giving the software a mask. The network's Internet number and network mask are stored in `/etc/netmasks`. A typical entry:

```
128.213.0.0 255.255.0.0
```

This Class B network address is masked with the value of `0xffff0000` or 255.255.0.0 decimal, clearly defining the last two bytes as the host part of the number. It also shows no subnetting, for the third byte would have been used as a subnetwork number. Simple network masks are:

Class	Mask
A	255.0.0.0
	0xff000000
B	255.255.0.0
	0xffff0000
C	255.255.255.0
	0xffffff00

Figure 6.6: Network class byte comparison

You supply the masks when you set up the machine and store them in places like `/etc/masks`. At boot time the masks are used by commands, such as `ifconfig`, which needs the Internet masks to set up the machine's Ethernet interface.

Subnet addressing is an address within an address. If a Class B site has the network portion of its Internet address of 128.213, and the site wishes to subnet and reserves the third byte for subnetting, the address 128.213.50.1 is a different node on a different subnet than 128.215.51.1.

There is a myth going around that subnetting slows down the network because the net must use routers to move data from one subnetwork segment to another, but in actual practice, subnetting picks up the overall speed of the network when used with dedicated routers, because the subnetwork is no longer flooded with extraneous traffic. A well designed subnetwork has 85 to 95 percent of its traffic internal to the subnet (and therefore 5 to 15 percent is "off net"). Subnetting is particularly beneficial because it obtains the isolation needed where workstations and servers dominate the network and would quickly overload any network of over 50 workstations.

Subnet Masks

Subnet masks are similar to network masks in that they mask out the nonhost portions of Internet addresses. If subnet numbers were divided on even byte boundaries, subnet masks would be easy. If a Class B network actually used the third byte for the subnet number, the /etc/netmasks listing would be:

```
128.213.55.0 255.255.255.0
```

In practice, subnet portions of the "host" field can be on a bit boundary, and you must refer to a table of byte-subnet masks:

Subnet Bit	Mask (Base 10)
0	0
1	128
2	192
3	224
4	240
5	248
6	252
7	254
8	255

Figure 6.7: Bitwise subnet masks

To set up the interface, you must supply the mask. We'll go into subnet masks further in a later chapter.

Limitations of Internet Addressing

It would have been better if Internet addressing had been designed with a larger address size, such as 48 or 64 bits, because the current scheme is close to being out of numbers; however, at the time the addressing scheme was conceived, no one imagined that the Internet would grow to its current gigantic proportions.

Ethernet Addressing

Ethernet addresses get data from host to host and are used at the physical and link layers for the actual delivery of data on the local area network. At six bytes (48 bits) in length, they are larger than Internet addresses.

The outermost encapsulation of networked data is the *frame*, and the only addresses used in frame transmission are Ethernet addresses.[1] Every host reading a frame can only read the Ethernet number in order to make its accept or reject decision on that frame, for the Internet number is encapsulated.

Ethernet addresses are expressed as six hexadecimal numbers:

```
08 20 0 02 1C D3
```

There are no classes or special meanings to the numbers, but they are handed out to OEMs in blocks, and the well informed can trace a number back to the OEM.

The most special feature about any one Ethernet address is that it is unique. A system with a built-in Ethernet address is the only

---

1. Ethernet addresses are not limited to Ethernet protocols; they are also used in 802.3 protocols and current OSI schemes as well.

system in the world with that particular number, for it is literally built in, burned into an EPROM on the system's Ethernet card or even on the motherboard of some dedicated workstations and networked SBCs (single board computers).

Recall that frames are the link layer's encapsulation form. Let's compare the frame header for 802.3 and Ethernet. First 802.3's:

```
            1             2             3             4
01234567890123456789012345678901234567890123456789012345 67
```

destination address		
source address		
length count	data	
data		CRC

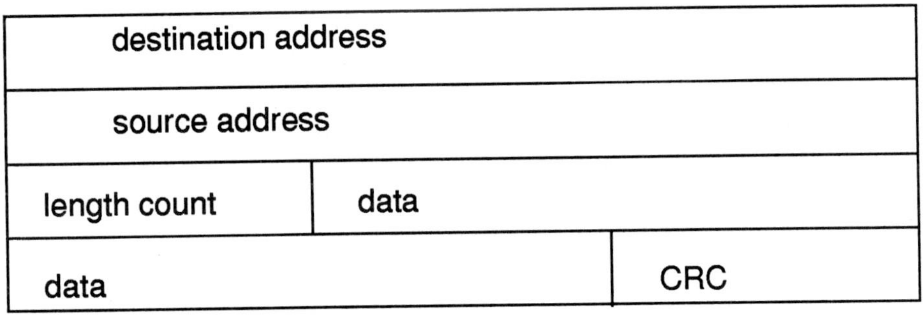

Figure 6.8: 802.3 encapsulation

Now Ethernet's:

```
            1             2             3             4
01234567890123456789012345678901234567890123456789012345 67
```

destination address		
source address		
type	data	
data		CRC

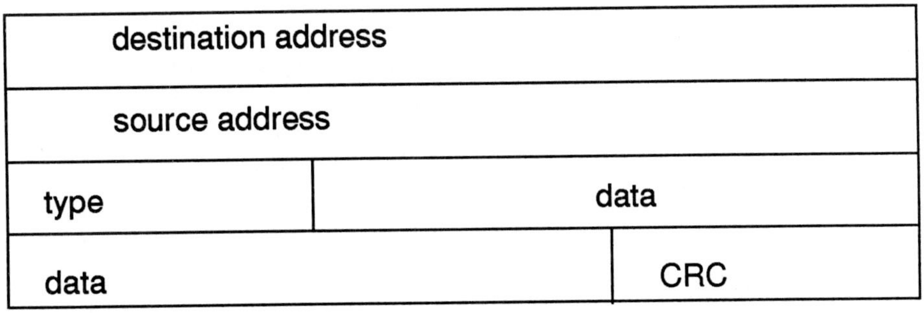

Figure 6.9: Ethernet encapsulation

Notice that they are the same except that Ethernet's `type` field is replaced by 802.3's `length` field. The first 48 bits comprise the destination in both, and the next 48 make up the source address.

The very first thing a host reads from an incoming frame is the destination address, and based on this it can accept or reject the frame. Most are rejected because they are not the host's Ethernet number. The point to remember is that at this level, all delivery is based on the Ethernet number.

Normally, you will see frame headers only with a protocol analyzer or the `etherfind` command, and the numbers may be in user-unfriendly hex. In spite of their intimidating appearance, get to know the frame headers on Ethernet, 802.3, and OSI (which may use either) intimately, because they can help you troubleshoot your network by showing where the data are coming from and going to at the lowest protocol layers. Protocol analyzers work at this basic level, and hosts will give error messages relative to Ethernet addresses, particularly when they cannot resolve them. Fortunately, these lowest-level protocols are simple and easy to decipher, even in hex, so use protocol analyzers and simple diagnostic commands like `etherfind` to help analyze the frame header data.

ARP and RARP — Applied Addressing

Before a net can function, the machines need to know who they are and where everything else is. ARP and RARP protocols help machines find their own addresses or the addresses of other machines. For example, how does a router find the Ethernet address of a system when all it has is the system's Internet address? Any node can broadcast or multicast a special ICMP request for a system's Ethernet address. The requesting host sends an ARP (address resolution protocol) ICMP packet out on the wire, and all systems will ignore it except for the one that has that Internet address. When it responds, its address is the source address field of its datagram. Thus, when the host with the Internet number responds, its Ethernet address becomes known, and in this way any system with privilege to generate an ARP request can find another host's Ethernet address.

There are circumstances in which the reverse condition is true. A diskless workstation boots and has no idea who it is, for it has taken its kernel from a file server, and that kernel has no inkling of the workstation's hostname or Internet address. However, the workstation does know its own Ethernet address, because it is burned into a PROM on its Ethernet card or motherboard. When it sends a RARP (Reverse Address Resolution Protocol) request packet to its server, the server will reply with the workstation's Internet address.

Using the `arp` Command

When network administrators need to verify the numbers of their machines, there is a privileged command that will read the current ARP entries from memory (`/dev/kmem`), and this is particularly handy for finding a system's Ethernet and Internet addresses. First `ping` the system to get its network data into memory, and then run `arp` with the `-a` flag:

```
% su
password:
# ping conan
conan is alive
# arp -a
conan    (126.218.41.34) at 8:0:20:5:77:ea temporary
bombaata (126.218.41.84) at 8:0:20:5:77:1b temporary
akiro    (126.218.41.21) at 8:0:20:5:77:85 temporary trailers
malac    (126.218.41.85) at 8:0:20:5:77:f0 temporary
zula     (126.218.41.29) at 8:0:20:5:77:13 temporary
```

Here, a `ping` has been sent to the node `conan`, and then we did an **arp -a**. The ARP entries of that moment are displayed, with `conan` at the very top. This is a handy trick for getting addresses when you need them.

Is Ethernet Addressing Doomed?

Addressing is the key to the success of Ethernet-TCP/IP and, ironically, it will also be its downfall. The larger, 8-byte Ethernet number will be able to provide us with unique hardware numbers well into the the next century, but the smaller, 6-byte Internet address is already in danger of running out of numbers. The class A addresses are gone, class B addresses are very difficult to get, and all that are left are the class C addresses with their small host-part number. To aggravate the situation, organizations are grabbing blocks of class C addresses so that they can use them for subnetting. But it won't be too long before they are gone too.

Illegal Addresses

Thousands of organizations are using made-up, illegal addresses. Because they are not yet on the Internet, they create Internet addresses like 123.456.789.0. Of course, someone, somewhere, already has that address, but that is a problem everyone puts off until later.

However, eventually the day of reckoning will come. When these organizations join the Internet, they will discover that the Internet, and therefore the host numbers, have become imbedded in places they cannot even conceive. When they connect to the Internet, these bad addresses will go out into the Internet, resulting in a mixed-up mess.

Getting Host-Part Numbers with PERL

Administrators need to know about addressing because two of the most common administration tasks are adding new users and adding new systems. In order to add new systems, administrators need a listing of already used host-part numbers for the subnet on which the new system will be. Any error introduced at this stage will result in a duplicate Internet address error that is a nuisance to clean up. The following program in PERL shows you one way administrators use addressing, for it extracts the currently used host-part numbers from the NIS database and selects them by sub-network.

```perl
#!/usr/bin/perl
RETRY:
print  "Subnets 70  75  80  85  90  inout choice :";
chop ($_ = <STDIN>);
SWITCH: {
    /70/ && do {
        $sub = 70;
        last SWITCH;
        };
    /75/ && do {
        $sub =  75;
        last SWITCH;
        };
    /80/ && do {
        $sub = 80;
        last SWITCH;
        };
    /85/ && do {
        $sub = 85/;
        last SWITCH;
        };
    /90/ && do {
        $sub =  90;
        last SWITCH;
        };
    print "$_ is not a legitimate inputO;
    goto RETRY;
    }
open (HOSTS, "ypcat hosts |")
  && die "ypcat failed $!0;
while (<HOSTS>) {
    ($inetno, $hostname) = split(/);
    if (grep(/132.244.$sub/, $inetno)) {
        ($one, $two, $three, $hostn) =
        split(/./, $inetno);
        push(@hostpart, $hostn);
        push(@inteno, $inetno);
    }
}
$last = $#inetno + 1);
```

```
print ("$last host numbers used in $sub subnet0;
@std_hosts = sort numerically @hostpart;
print "host numbers used0;
for( $i=0 ; $i <=last ; $i++ ) {
    if ( $i % 4 ) {
        print $inetno[$i], "";
        }
        else {
            print inetno[$i], "0;
        }
print " host-part numbers0;
for( $i=0 ; $i <= $last ; $i++ ) {
    if( $i % 8 ) {
        print $std_hosts[$i], "";
    }
        else{
        print $std_hosts[$i],"";
        }
    }
sub numerically {
    $a <=> $b;
}
```

From Addressing to Protocols

Each of the three major protocol layers — transport, network, and
link — uses a different form of addressing. Understanding these
addresses is the key to understanding the protocols. As you break
down the protocols, you will see that there are lots of other fields
in the protocol layers besides addresses, and that's what we shall
discover in the next chapter.

CHAPTER

7

Ethernet-TCP/IP Protocols

What we perceive as magic is the art of the illusionist. "It's all done with mirrors," the saying goes, but for whatever reason our eyes are deceived, and it seems like magic. Getting data through no less than four levels of network hierarchy also seems like magic, but rather than using mirrors, network developers use something much more sophisticated — protocols.

It is important for UNIX network administrators to be able to see through the magic and understand protocols and how they are implemented in order to troubleshoot the network, understand all diagnostics used on UNIX systems, and run commercial network and protocol analyzers. The diagnostics and the network and protocol analyzers are protocol-dependent. They work at all protocol levels and frequently require that you read the protocol headers in raw hex, translating them as you go. For example, persistent ICMP error packets are traced backwards to their origin by reading the source address (in hex) from the frame's Ethernet header.

Getting data across any network is a tricky task, accomplished with a set of formalized procedures called protocols that segment the data and add routing and other critical network-specific information ahead of the data to guide its trip from host to host. UNIX networking relies on a combination of three protocols: TCP (and similar protocols like UDP and ICMP), IP, and Ethernet.

The Ethernet Protocol

Let's review the three network layers used in UNIX networking:

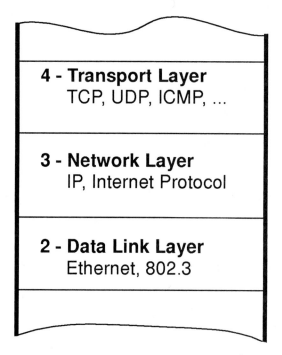

Figure 7.1: Second, third, and fourth layer

The Ethernet protocol is the simplest of the three, so we shall examine it first.

The Ethernet layer gets data on the wire and transmits data across the path created in the link layer, its home. It adds the 48-bit Ethernet destination and source addresses ahead of the data when it creates a *frame*, a method of encapsulation that allows data to go down the wire.

The frame is preceded by a *preamble,* a succession of ones and zeros used to synchronize the data stream, and just after the preamble but just ahead of the datagram's destination address is the start bit:

```
          1         2         3         4
012345678901234567890123456789012345678901234567

1010101010101010101010101010101010101010101011start
```

Figure 7.2: Frame preamble

Note the two 1s just ahead of the frame's start. The idle signal is a steady +0.7 volts. A quiescent line maintains a DC voltage of +0.7 volts and then signals the start of a frame by sending alternating 1s and 0s. In the Manchester encoding scheme, the line must shift from +0.7v to -0.7v or vice versa at least once every 100-billionths of a second:

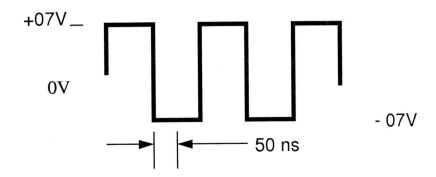

Figure 7.3: Manchester encoding scheme

Should the network catch the controller sleeping, there is enough preamble length for the device to wake up and catch the two 1s that form the frame start sequence, all typical activity at the physical layer.

Now let's go beyond the preamble to the frame format itself:

```
0123456789012345678901234567890123456789012345678901234567
```

destination address	
source address	
type	data
data	CRC

Figure 7.4: Ethernet header

The 48-bit Ethernet source and destination addresses are needed to get data on the wire to the nodes on the segment. At the hardware level there is no knowledge of ports or of Internet addresses. The 16-bit `type` field is passed to upper-level protocols to identify what type of packet (data segment) is being passed. The data can run as long as 46 to 1500 octets. (Recall that an *octet* is an Ethernet byte.) CRC stands for cyclic redundancy check, and it is also called a frame check sequence. It is compiled from all the data that go ahead of it, and the frame will be resent if the CRC does not match up on the receiving host.

Differences between Ethernet and IEEE 802.3 Protocols

Before we go any further, you need to know that there are two types of Ethernet protocols, Ethernet 2 and the older Ethernet 1. Naturally, they are not compatible. To add to the confusion, when the IEEE decided to create a specification for the Ethernet called 802.3, the Ethernet `type` field was changed into a `length count` field in 802.3:

```
0123456789012345678901234567890123456789012345 67
```

destination address	
source address	
length count	data
data	CRC

Figure 7.5: 802.3 header

Fortunately, TCP/IP will run as successfully above the 802.3 protocol as it does over either of the Ethernet protocols, but you must know which protocol you are using. For example, one characteristic of 802.3 is its absence of a "heartbeat" or SQE, so when you set your transceivers for the 802.3 protocol, you must be sure to switch or jumper SQE off.

IEEE 802.3 is as much a physical-level specification as a protocol. As network administrators you need to remember that its OSI-model link layer is divided into a link and MAC layer, so don't get upset when you see references to the MAC layer in some texts. IEEE 802.3 was intended to be an Ethernet specification, so Ethernet and 802.3 run on the same wire, but it is important that they are not compatible with each other when designing the network and specifying network components that operate at the physical level. Whether the hardware runs Ethernet or 802.3, it must comply with the 802.3 specification.

IP: The Internet Protocol

We saw that the Ethernet layer prepares the data stream for transmission on the physical network, but the IP layer above it prepares data for routing. Routing is accomplished by using the 4-byte Internet protocol (IP) address to get onto the network segment, to get off the segment, and to get onto another segment, subnet, or network.

IP protocols are not as simple as Ethernet protocols. In fact, there is a good chance that the IP datagram will not fit conveniently inside of an Ethernet frame, and consequently it must be fragmented. As a result, the IP protocol must therefore carry enough information to reassemble itself when it arrives at the destination:

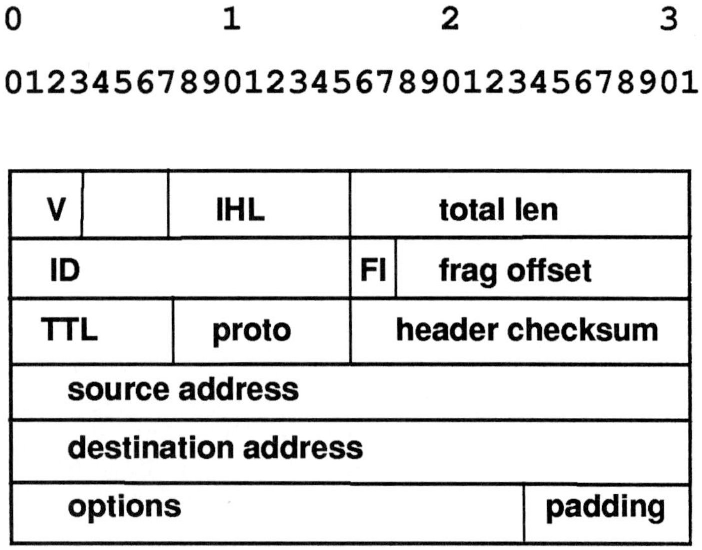

```
     0               1               2               3
     01234567890123456789012345678901
```

V		IHL	total len		
ID			FI	frag offset	
TTL		proto	header checksum		
source address					
destination address					
options				padding	

Figure 7.6: IP protocol header

Note how this datagram is made of 32-bit words. The largest members are the `source` and `destination` 32-bit addresses. Let's take a look at some of the fields.

V: Version Field

The version field contains whatever the current IP version is; at this writing, version 4.

TYPE: The Type-of-Service Field

The 8-bit type-of-service field tells what type of service will be used on the current datagram.

IHL: **The Internet Header Length Field**

This is the length of the IP header expressed in 32-bit words.

ID: **Identification Field**

A datagram can arrive broken or fragmented; that is a fact of network transmission. The IP header allows for rebuilding that data into an intelligent data stream by reassembling the datagram in sequence. The 16-bit identification value associates datagram fragments. It supplies the datagram number in order to permit the receiving host to reassemble the datagram in order.

FL: **The Flags Field**

This is a 3-bit field that passes one of two messages — *don't fragment* or *more fragments*. The first message prohibits IP fragmentation, and the second helps identify the fragment's position in the data. There are some versions of TCP that do not allow fragmentation, and the *don't fragment* flag negotiates requests.

FRAG OFF: **The Fragment Offset Field**

This is the field in which IP figures out where this datagram's data will fit relative to the rest of the sent data. The field size is 13 bits, and its range is from 0 to 8191, measured in octets.

TTL: **The Time-To-Live Field**

The TTL is an 8-bit field that gives the time that the IP datagram has to live on the wire. TTL is decremented as the datagram travels, and the datagram is gone when TTL hits 0. It is decremented on each hop, and the value is also decremented as it passes each router. Its maximum value is 255 seconds.

If there were no TTL field, a faulty packet could travel around the net forever.

PROTO: **The Protocol Field**

This 16-bit field tells which upper-layer protocol is to get the data contained in the datagram. Typical numbers and protocols are:

1   ICMP

6   TCP

17   UDP

These are read and interpreted by the transport layer, one layer above the IP layer.

HDR CHECKSUM: **Header Checksum Field**

The 16-bit checksum field applies to the IP header only. It does not checksum the data, because that job is reserved for the upper-layer protocol. Checksums are the results of error-detecting code used to test or compare blocks of data transmitted and received. One of the most often used is a polynomial code also known as a CRC, for cyclic redundancy check. This does polynomial arithmetic in modulo 2. The same check is done on sent and received data, and the results are compared.

SOURCE ADDRESS: **The Source Address Field**

This field is the source Internet address, such as

```
128.213.56.55
```

This 32-bit number is the address of the node where the datagram originated.

DESTINATION ADDRESS: **The Destination Address Field**

The 32-bit number destination address is the IP address of the datagram's target system.

OPTIONS: **The Options Field**

This field's size varies to allow for changes and expansion in the protocol. The current defined options are:

1. Security.

2. Loose source routing.

3. Strict source routing.

4. Record route.

5. Stream ID.

6. Time stamp.

The difference between strict and loose routing is the difference between following a defined path or taking certain defined subpaths on an overall source-specified route. The time stamp allows a time trace of the datagram through the network.

As each layer encapsulates the layer above it, there is no guarantee that the previous encapsulation will fit. Sometimes not all the data and the header can fit in one encapsulation. Thus, the previous encapsulation must be prepared to be fragmented. The datagram header allows for just that, reassembly of the datagram at the receiving system's IP layer.

The TCP Protocol

The first level of encapsulation of transmitted data occurs at the transport layer. In Ethernet-TCP/IP this layer is home to a number of different protocols, including TCP, ICMP, and UDP.

The TCP header and data segment is relatively large — 40 bytes (320 bits) at the smallest.

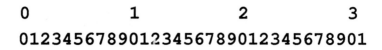

```
0                1                2                3
01234567890123456789012345678901
```

source port	destination port
sequence number	
acknowledgement number	

off	res	flags	windows
checksum		urge ptr
options		padd
data		

Figure 7.7: Transport protocol header

Transport-level data segments are not sent to IP addresses or Ethernet addresses. Rather, they are sent to a "well known port." The use of a standard number for each protocol is what makes the port well known. For example, `telnet`'s port is 23 (base 10), while `ftp`'s is 21. The port number is also a part of the socket number and can be seen on your system in `/etc/services` (manual section 5, `services`). The IP address and the 16-bit port number together form a *socket*, the entry point to a given service. The socket acts much like a file identifier for `open`, `close`, `read`, and `write` system calls. Let's take a look at some of the fields in this protocol.

SOURCE PORT: The Source Port Field

The first field is a 16-bit source port field. It identifies the sending system's application-level process.

DESTINATION PT: **The Destination Port Field**

This 16-bit port number identifies the receiving system's process.

SEQUENCE NUMBER: **The Sequence Number Field**

The sequence number relates to the position of the first byte of data in the total data stream over the life of the TCP connection. The maximum segment length is modulo 2 to the 32, but the total number of bytes over a connection is unlimited.

ACKNOWLEDGEMENT NUMBER: **The Acknowledgement Number Field**

This is a 32-bit number that shows the next segment number the sender expects to receive.

DA: **The Data Offset Field**

This short (4-bit) field indicates the number of 32-bit words that are in this TCP header. It is necessary because the options field length varies.

RES: **The Reserved Field**

Like many reserved fields, this contains nothing, but it takes 6 bits to do so!

FLAGS: **The Control Flags Field**

This 6-bit field is made up of control flags:

URG   This is the urgent pointer field. Set to 1, it indicates that the field is now used to locate urgent data. The urgent data is located by the byte offset from the current sequence number. Set to 0, it is simply ignored.

SYN   Set to 1, this request will establish a connection.

ACK   The acknowledgment field shows acknowledgment is significant.

PSH   Set to 1, it tells the receiving system to deliver the data of this segment immediately.

RST   Set to 1, the connection will be reset if duplicate SYNs are detected or a host crashes.

FIN   This terminates the connection when set to 1.

WINDOW: The Window Field

This 16-bit field is used to indicate the number of octets the sender expects to receive. The starting point is the byte shown in the ACK field.

CHECKSUM: The Checksum Field

A 16-bit checksum of all the 16-bit words in both header and data.

URG POINTER: The Urgent Pointer Field

A 16-bit indicator of the last byte of urgent data.

OPTIONS: The Options Field

As its name indicates, the options field is optional. If it exists at all, its length varies by a multiple of 32 bits. Each individual option with the field must be set on 32-bit boundaries.

Analyzing Protocol Layers

If you fail to understand the Ethernet-TCP/IP protocol stack, your network operation will be inefficient because you won't be able to analyze it. Administrators who cannot analyze their segments wind up throwing money away on questionable solutions, and upper management may never find out how many thousands of additional man-hours of work are lost because of inefficient networks.

Everyone knows that network delays are profit drains. They cause systems to repeatedly slow down and wait on the network, and every time that happens, engineers have to lean back in their chairs and wait, many times an hour. They can lose their train of thought when this happens, and the accumulation of time wasted is expensive for the company. On the other hand, efficiently run network operations result in minimal network delays, and that, in turn, maximizes employee work time.

Of course, network analyzers are expensive, so some organizations are hesitant to spend the money it takes to buy them. However, that's a mistake. Good network analyzers, such as Concord Scientific's Trakker, are worth the money. If you get one early enough, it can even help you determine how to build your network. On the other hand, if you wait too long, you can inadvertently build in some really bad design. Therefore, listen to the voice of experience: If your network is growing, you will need a network analyzer eventually.

Here's an example of how you can get yourself into trouble by trying to save money on network analyzers. Imagine that in order to gain speed on your subnetworks, you run out and buy Etherswitches instead of a network analyzer. However, you soon find out, to your dismay, that diagramming the paths between the concentrators and the file servers by way of the Etherswitches is a nightmare, because the Etherswitch paths criss-cross. Not only that, you end up buying so many Etherswitches, you aren't able to afford enough pods for all the lines running off the Etherswitches. Ironically, had you bought a network analyzer before you bought Etherswitches, you might have been able to avoid the use of Etherswitches altogether.

Solutions to network problems vary, depending on what the problem is. Therefore, identifying the problem is the first step, and network analyzers can help you do that. What protocols account for the bulk of your traffic? If you have a lot of TCP traffic on the lines dominated by the file servers, you have a problem because they use UDP at that level, and TCP is used for error-reporting NFS problems. But a network analyzer could figure out where the TCP traffic is coming from. The problem could be error messages, and an analyzer could pinpoint the location. On the other hand, if you don't have an analyzer, your servers and workstations will continue complaining, and nothing will be listening to them.

Are all your network services necessary? The time daemons that sync and skew the system clocks are constantly checking the time. If you are not running Secure NFS, the accuracy of a few hundredths of a second may not be important enough to take up 10 percent of your total bandwidth.

As you can see, without knowledge of all your protocols and without the equipment and training to analyze them, you won't know what is happening on the net. And you won't be able to find solutions to your networking problems unless you can pinpoint the problems.

Protocols and Routing

The importance of knowing your protocols cannot be overstressed. When Ethernet, TCP, and IP work together, they comprise a three-tier protocol relationship that moves data well with reasonable speed. Each protocol layer acts as if it were working with its corresponding layer on the destination system, and this seemingly independent peer-to-peer protocol method is the basis for all LAN data transmission. In short, without a knowledge of protocols, you will not be able to troubleshoot network problems, but with this knowledge, few problems are insurmountable.

So far we have learned about basic network devices and network media. We have seen how intelligence is passed electrically and how Ethernet protocols are used to get data from host to host. We've also taken a look at the IP protocol. In the next chapter, we're going to see how routers work with these IP protocols to achieve internetworking.

CHAPTER

8

Routers

Routing is one of the hottest areas in networking today. First-generation routers were ordinary computers running the router daemon and fitted with the system with multiple (usually two) Ethernet cards. Routing tables were created manually, and the routing tables were fixed, slow, difficult to maintain, and the biggest deterrents to subnetworking. But today's second-generation routers are dedicated multiprocessor devices that create their own routing tables dynamically, filter out unwanted traffic, and effortlessly handle multiprotocol traffic. Routers (as opposed to bridges) can deal with heterogeneous networks and bring together a mix of LANs and WANs. They are fast, easily able to keep up with an Ethernet or 802.3 line at normal loading, and able to do a fair job at peak loading.

Only the smallest single-segment local area networks can run without routing. The moment you have to reach a host on another network or subnetwork, you are *internetworking*, and that takes routing. To reach a system on your own network segment, the data rely exclusively on the Ethernet address in the frame header for delivery. In fact, the entire task is taken care of at the second protocol level (Ethernet); the third (Internet) protocol level is not even involved. If the datagrams have to pass through bridges, the entire transaction is handled in the MAC layer.

To get onto another network or subnet, the IP header must be examined, and a bridge cannot accomplish this. Only a router or gateway can do that, for they are special-purpose computers.

How Routing Is Done

Let's look at how two networks can be joined. We have two class B networks (domains) known as 125.213 and 125.218, joined by a router named after Hermes the messenger, son of the god Zeus:

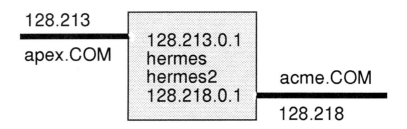

Figure 8.1: Joining apex to acme

The domains `apex.COM` and `acme.COM` are joined. The router called Hermes has two names and two Internet addresses in order to be able to reach either network. Datagrams sent to Hermes on the `apex` domain intended for the `acme` domain will get to their destination, but here's the catch. Any system in this simple internetwork must know about the routers `hermes` and `hermes2`, accomplished by having each system keep a routing table with the network's destination names, addresses, and the gateway name. Let's see how this is done.

Ethernet Interfaces

Each computer host, router, and gateway on the network must have one or more network interfaces. Nonrouting computers must have at least one, and usually will have no more than one. Routers and gateways must have at least two. This interface is an Ethernet card, the heart of which is an Ethernet processor like an Intel `ie` LAN controller. The access to the interface is built into the kernel and can be found in the kernel's configuration file. Indeed, if you add another interface, you must add the reference to the kernel. You will have to deal with the interface again whenever you use the `ifconfig` command, such as when you are configuring your `rc.local` or `rc.net` file.

The Routing Daemon

The routing daemon that handles static network routing is `routed` (also known by other names, including `in.routed`). `routed` is started by `rc` at system initiation when it looks for all the system's active interfaces marked `up`. At this point it is decision time: If only one interface is found, it assumes the system is an ordinary host computer and will take only a passive role in routing. If more than one interface is found, it assumes that the system is a router or a gateway. As the system comes up, `routed` broadcasts a *request* packet to each interface and then enters a loop while it waits (listens) for a *request* or a *response* from other hosts.

To see the active network router interfaces on a system, use `netstat -r`.

ifconfig

The `ifconfig` command is used to assign an address to a network interface and to configure network parameters, and it is called at system initiation (boot) time to define the network address of each interface on the system. Thus a router or gateway must have multiple `ifconfig` entries, whereas most ordinary hosts need only one. Here is the simplest kind of `rc` line for `ifconfig`:

```
ifconfig ie0 netmask +
```

This sets up the system's Intel-interface device number 0 (`ie0`) to access this system's one and only network. Rather than specifying a network mask, this command line uses a plus sign to signal `ifconfig` to look the mask up in the YP database for netmasks, `netmasks.byaddr`. If the system is not running YP, the look-up will take place in `/etc/netmasks`.

`ifconfig` can be used to shut off an interface. If an ordinary host has two Ethernet cards but is attached to only one network, the other interface is shut off:

```
ifconfig ie1 down
```

`route` — The Routing Command

`route` is used to manipulate the host's static routing table. If you want to add the host `stalker` to the system's routing table, you need to find out through which gateway it must be reached and through how many hops (routers, bridges, or gateways) it must pass to get there. Armed with this information, you can make an entry in `rc.local`:

```
/usr/etc/route add stalker hermes 1
```

The `add` command tells `route` to add the `stalker`/`hermes` information to the route table. `stalker` is the *destination*, and `hermes` is the *gateway*. The 1 is the hop count.

When using `route`, you can use an entire network as a destination:

```
/usr/etc/route c-net c-gate 1
```

You can also wildcard with `route`:

```
/usr/etc/route add 0 c-gate 1
```

The 0 adds a default route c-gate, used if no other destination is available.

Files Involved in Routing

The rc family of files are edited by the network administrator to set up routing on the system, and the command order is critical. The ifconfig command comes first, at the beginning of the rc networking section (a few lines after the port mapper, portmap). If YP services are used, they will be invoked first, before ifconfig. ifconfig is followed immediately by the route daemon, routed:

```
if [ "$NETWORKED" = yes ];then
   if ypwhich -m netmasks.byaddr>\
        /dev/null 2>&1
   then
        ifconfig ie0 netmask +
   fi
   if [ -f /usr/etc/in.routed ]; then
        in.routed && say ´ routed´
   fi
fi
```

The last command used for routing is the final command in local.rc. The route command is added at the very end:

```
#########################
# Append local commands to the
    end of this file
/usr/etc/route add 0 hermes 1
```

/etc/hosts

The `hosts` file and its YP database equivalent are used to list each host name and address on the network. Here is a typical entry:

```
stalker 128.213.35.55 # apex YP master
```

Without YP, every host on the network and every router and gateway accessed must be in this file. With the use of YP, `hosts` can be reduced to two lines — the loopback address and the network address of the system itself. The loopback interface must be set up on all systems. It delivers packets within the local machine.

`networks` or its YP counterpart supplies the domain names and corresponding addresses of every network likely to be accessed by the systems. The format is nearly identical to `hosts`:

```
acme-net     128.217
apex-net     128.215
apex-mfgnetm   128.215.69
```

Note that except in the case of a subnet, only the network part of the address is used. Here the subnet `apex-mfgnet` adds its subnet number, `69`, to the network address of Apex's network, `128.215`.

Setting Up Routing

To set up a router, you must first have the network addresses that will identify each interface. Make a physical connection to each Internet card for each network. There are no differences between a host connection for an ordinary host computer and a router. Typically, you come off the network medium (wire or fiber optic) to a transceiver, then through an interface cable, and into the network card's connector. Part of what makes routers special is that they have multiple network connections, and therefore multiple interface cards and cables.

A good software place to start is `/etc/networks` on all systems that will reach the router, since the systems can't route through that router unless they know about it. (The benefits of YP seem quite clear now.) Add an entry on each host system in the `/etc/hosts` files on all systems on all networks with which the router or gateway will interface. Remember to use the name that the router is known by on each network, in our example `hermes` on `128.213` and `hermes2` on `128.218`.

The `hosts` file on the server itself is unique since it will carry all network-interface addresses. Let's look at the host `hermes` again. Its `hosts` file has the following entries:

```
hermes     128.213.0.1
hermes2    128.218.0.1
```

It is a good convention to reserve the host number 1 for routers and gateways and to have all host names on the router be similar, such as `phobos` and `phobos-demos`.

You will also have to create a file on each system with the system's interface hostname and a name of the form:

```
hostname.interface
```

For the `hermes` interface, it would be `/etc/hermes.ie0` if that interface were on the Intel 0 internet interface. The contents of the file would be the host name, `hermes`.

Second-Generation Routers

Old-style routers did *static* routing by working off a set of fixed tables. The newest generation of routers generates their own tables from information gleaned from the net. A general-purpose computer with more than one Ethernet interface and a routing table qualifies as a router but is acceptable only for static routing, that is, handling minimal routing and few changes in network topology. However, a special-purpose, dedicated router is needed to handle the needs of most networked systems today. These routers are capable of handling a number of dynamic routing protocols to maintain routing tables that are constantly updated in order to cope with changes in topology and network conditions. You must program these routers to be able to accomplish any reasonable degree of filtering. Cisco routers are used for the programming examples in this chapter because of their high degree of flexibility.

Cisco Systems, Inc., uses a filtering mechanism called *access lists*, which they define as a sequential collection of *permit* and *deny* conditions that apply to Internet addresses. All routers have their own operating systems and command languages, and following is the `access-list` command syntax:

```
access-list nn [permit|deny] address mask
```

The `nn` is an integer argument that will tie together this statement in the access list with other access list commands. For example:

```
access-list 1 permit 128.213.0.0   0.0.255.255
```

This beginning of an access list allows all Class B network `128.213.0.0` traffic to get through. If you recall that 255 decimal is 1111 1111 base 2, you can understand that the all-ones part of the mask `0.0.255.255` tells the system to ignore the host bytes of the addresses from this nonsubnetted network.

You can get a little more exotic and extend the access list:

```
access-list 1 permit 128.213.0.0   0.0.255.255
access-list 1 deny 33.55.0.0   0.0.255.255
```

The list will still accept `128.213.0.0` but will immediately reject anything from Class A network `33.0.0.0`'s `33.55.0.0` subnet. Note that the router reads the access list from top to bottom, and as soon as it finds a condition that matches the address of the packet it's holding, it stops reading the list and processes the packet. Because of this you must order your listings carefully when creating an access list.

Extended `access-list` Commands

The `access-list` command uses that we've shown are simple
and easy to use, but unfortunately they lack some of the power
needed for tight filtering. Several attributes have been added to
cover extended use. Following is the list of protocol keywords
used by cisco's `access-list` command:

- `ip`
- `tcp`
- `udp`
- `icmp`

Naturally, `ip` covers all of the Ethernet-Internet protocols. The
address is *extended* by allowing both source and destination
addresses with their corresponding masks. The final extension is
an operator/operand pair to operate on transport/port addresses.
The syntax:

```
access-list [permit|deny] protocol \
source source-mask destination \
destination-mask [operator operand]
```

Now let's put theory into practice and allow IP connections for
ports on all networks greater than 1023:

```
access-list 45 permit ip 0.0.0.0 255.255.255.255 \
255.255.255.255 0.0.0.0 gt 1023
```

Bridges and Routers, Routing Algorithms, and Protocols

The days of simple routers and bridges are gone. Only simple networks can survive with nonadaptive bridges. Similarly, only simple internetworks can survive with a simple router using static
routing. Nowadays bridges come closer to router capabilities, and
they have new names like *brouters*. Routers are also advancing

with corresponding increases in throughput. They can be programmed to filter just about anything, and they can run with multiple routing protocols. However, the basic difference between bridges and routers still remains the same: bridges work at the *link layer*, while routers work at the *network layer*.

Transparent Bridges

Bridges are low-maintenance devices and should be able to run *transparently* after installation. The better ones are programmable and will do as good a filtering job as possible at the link level.

A transparent bridge easily lives in networks with redundant paths by *pruning* the network into a spanning tree. The adaptive bridge *learns* the locations of nodes on either of its interfaces by reading the *source* addresses in the datagram headers of incoming data, and it knows where a node is because the node has unwittingly told it of its location.

The down side to adaptive bridges is they can adapt to the wrong things. Since an adaptive bridge builds something like a routing table that associates the interface with the node's Ethernet address, it is critical that the bridge never see a datagram from a host on the wrong port (interface). Sometimes a *transient parallel link* is created, also known as a *bridge loop*, which is two active paths to the same location. If a datagram is received on an opposite port because of a transient parallel link, the bridge will adapt and try to reach that location through the wrong port. To circumvent this problem, adaptive bridges must either adapt quickly to changes in topology or deliberately wait on these changes to be sure that they are not transient.

There are other routing algorithms for bridges that are very interesting. Token ring uses a source-routing bridge that relies on routes contained in the data packets, and the routes are discovered and cached by stations. Are there any other UNIX versions that use token ring except for FDDI? It's a good idea to read up on everything about networking that you can. Networking technology is changing so rapidly, it's difficult to determine where we'll be in a few years.

Both bridges and routers work cooperatively. That is, both must work with their own kind to establish shared knowledge. For example, a group of bridges all exercising a spanning-tree algorithm must elect a unique *root* bridge. Checking with one another, they "elect" the one with the numerically lowest bridge number as the root, and then each bridge calculates the distance to the root. Each then elects a *designated* bridge, the one with the minimum *cost* to get to the root bridge. (Cost is figured differently by different algorithms, but one method is figured by the number of hops it takes to get from one place to another.) A *designated port* is also selected by each bridge. From time to time each bridge sends a message to all other bridges, called a Bridge Protocol Data Unit, BPDU, or *hello message*. The BPDU contains the bridge's identifier and port, the identifier of the bridge that it considers to be the root, and the root-path cost. Should the bridge tree get modified by the addition or deletion of a bridge, all the bridges communicate with each other to reestablish the root bridge, designated bridges, and so on.

Spanning Trees

Let's review what we've learned so far. Bridges operate at the link level, while routers operate at the network level. Bridges maintain a simple list of addresses and the ports to get to those addresses, and they will deliberately forget that information if not reinforced from time to time. Routers, on the other hand, maintain route tables that used to be created manually (static routing) but are now created dynamically (dynamic routing).

Routing protocols are used to create the router's tables. We've seen simple fixed routing, where the system administrator creates the routing tables. Static routing cannot adjust to changes in topology and is suitable only for the smallest internetworks.

Today's truly sophisticated routers will communicate with all adjacent routers and, as part of a community intellect, create a map of the current internet, immediately sensing which interfaces are directly attached to which networks. Next, they will find adjacent gateways and their addresses. Ultimately, they have a map of nearby gateways and networks relating to their own interfaces.

There are numerous routing algorithms, and no one routing algorithm is clearly superior to the others; rather, the choice of algorithm depends on many factors. We will look at a few currently in use on UNIX-dominated networks.

Let's start with the *spanning tree*. Here we have a simple internetwork with networks A, B, C, and D, all joined by a single path. Network C must be accessed to get from A or B to D or vice versa:

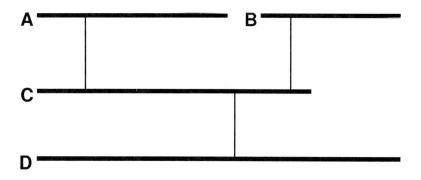

Figure 8.2: Simple spanning tree

Now let's complicate the problem by making a direct path from B to D.

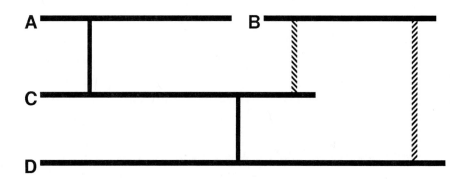

Figure 8.3: Spanning tree with redundant route added from B to D

The newly created problems are severe. In this network loop, information going from D to B will duplicate itself, and first-generation routers and simple bridges will become hopelessly confused. Only second-generation routers and adaptive bridges can cope with this situation.

Let's join the networks with intelligent, adaptive bridges. They share their concept of the Internet with one another and all know the routing map:

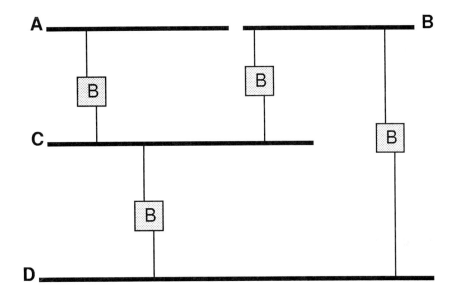

Figure 8.4: Spanning tree with adaptive bridges

The routing map for this little four-banger internet shows a B to D connection with a hop-count metric of 2 and another with a hop count of 1. If the hop count is considered the *cost* of routing, the single-hop B to D route will win every time. The bridges are in effect blind to the route through network C, thus, a *spanning tree* is set up with one virtual route from any one point to another. However, more sophisticated protocols can take advantage of both routes.

RIP and IGRP Protocols

The spanning tree algorithm is the basis of the XEROX and Berkeley Routing Information Protocol, RIP. RIP uses UDP packets between routers. A fancy name for a hop-count mechanism protocol is *vector protocol*, and RIP limits the number of hops to 15. RIP has limitations: It won't work very well if there is any level of complexity in the Internet. Picture the line from B to D as an asynchronous 9600 baud line and the lines from B to C and C to D as 100,000,000 bps FDDI lines. By hop count alone the direct route will be chosen every time, even though it is significantly slower.

Each protocol uses similar simple mechanisms for dynamically updating the routing tables for router information. With RIP they *advertise* every 30 seconds by sending routing information updates to the current routing table. If one router fails to receive an update from another router for 90 seconds or more, it considers that router unusable and will not use it. After 450 seconds, an eternity in computer time, it removes the router from its routing table. IGRP uses a similar algorithm.

IGRP was created with a broader set of design goals than RIP:

- Stable routing with no loops.

- Quick response to changes in topology.

- Low overhead.

- Traffic-splitting ability over parallel routes.

- Compensation for line-error rates and traffic.

- Ability to handle multiple types of services.

Like older protocols, IGRP is also a vector protocol, but it has more sophistication in measuring distance. It takes into account not only line speed but also the actual delay time of the line, the bandwidth of the narrowest part of the line, how much of that bandwidth is in use, and the current reliability of the line. IGRP knows of multiple routes and will use them if traffic gets too heavy, as long as both are equal or nearly equal in *cost*.

The most important point is that IGRP allows the routers to build their own routing tables with the help of other routers and gateways. At initiation, the router takes all the entries from the routers that are on the network segments to which it is *directly* connected and gets to know them, effectively cascading network information in defining paths. A *path* is the next router or gateway on the way to some specific destination, along with the associated cost and conditions.

With IGRP, routers and gateways quickly gather enough *metrics*, information about path costs, line quality and delays, hop count, minimum packet size, minimum bandwidth, and traffic. Armed with all this information, the router not only selects the best route but can also select a second-best route if it must split the traffic between two roughly parallel paths because of excess traffic.

Contemporary Network Technology

Router technology has accelerated rapidly in the last few years, What administrators are setting up as "routers" are also capable of working as bridges and gateways. They are capable of using multiple protocols, work with a variety of media types, and get their high throughput by way of multiple processors.

The router may join you to another part of the network or to another network altogether, but at the same time it can be a bastion against unwanted intrusion into your world. The device's ability to disallow specific types of traffic has earned it the nicknames "choke" and "firewall." No one would think about designing a network without putting in a firewall between their network and the outside world, because minimizing unwanted traffic is the name of the game. Traffic slows down machines, so you want only what is relevant to your site. It goes without saying that any unwelcome intruders pose a severe security risk, so they need to be prevented from coming in.

Speaking of unwanted intruders, here too is an important point to ponder. If you have a number of chokes between your domain and the world, do you want them all from the same vendor? From a security perspective, the answer is no. If they are all the same, a cracker who figures out one has figured out all of them!

Specialty Routers

How do you join packet-switched lines with circuit-switched lines? ISDN could be the way of the future. The need for a multimedia network has existed for a long time, and its implementation is well underway in Japan, France, Germany, and North America. To join them you will need a different kind of router with two interfaces — one for each. An example is the Cisco 3000 for multiprotocol connection to TCP/IP and ISDN.

Another special-purpose router is one that does FDDI-to-Ethernet. The creators of FDDI saw it as an all encompassing technology that would replace the Ethernet, but it hasn't replaced the Ethernet yet, nor does it appear that it's going to. Most designs call for fiber optic cable between all network junctions, closet to closet, and from the closet to the computer room. The installation of the fiber optic cable and the cable itself are the major costs. However, once the cables are in, why not take advantage of the 100,000,000-BPS capability by using FDDI across these major points and conventional Ethernet from the routers to the concentrators and on to the nodes? This creates an FDDI backbone while keeping your initial investment in your Ethernet safe on your local segments. You do this with FDDI-to-Ethernet routers.

Multimedia is shaping our networking future. The rule for network packet size used to be the longer the packet, the more size-efficient the protocol. Typical Ethernet-TCP/IP packets are 250 bytes. It makes sense because of efficiency — the header information is all overhead, and the less we repeat the overhead, the less space it takes up. Multimedia is an entirely different problem, because it is timing-dependent. If a packet arrives a few seconds sooner or later, it will not change your view of a file over NFS, but let a packet arrive a bit late as the raster of a video display is being constructed, and you will have CRT garbage. ATM is for real-time transmissions that are delay sensitive.

ATM uses a switch technology. To make it work, it uses a very small packet size — 53 bytes. Of that, only 5 bytes are header. Current transmission rates are 52 megabits per second, and much higher rates are expected.

Routers like the Cisco 7000 work out optimal paths through the ATM network, form ATM encapsulation, and define ATM virtual circuits. This router and routers like it route Ethernet, token ring, FDDI, and ATM. To create routers of this type, their manufacturers had to overcome the major axiom that switching and routing are mutually exclusive.

Making Your Network Decisions

It's not enough to know that routers and bridges exist when you design them into your network; you must know their full capabilities. Then once the net is designed and the routers are in place, you must choose which protocols to run, for modern second-generation routers run more than one protocol.

We have looked at how data get on the net and how they get off the wire to their destinations. Now let's see how network data are handled on servers and workstations.

CHAPTER

9

File Servers

Servers are the center of networked systems. If we say that the servers are the vital organs of a network, then the network cables are the arteries of the system, and the protocols the blood. As long as we're using this metaphor, we might as well take it one step further and say that workstations and other clients are the appendages of the network body.

Users' computers are called *clients* because they are consumers of resources, such as files, printing, mail, and YP (NIS) services. *Servers* are the systems that provide all these services for the clients. There are many kinds of servers, but the most common are:

File servers: File servers provide their client systems access to files.

YP servers: YP servers provide YP domain services, and the two types of YP servers are domain masters and slaves.

Print servers: Print servers are systems dedicated in whole or in part to spooling files and sending them to their own locally attached printers. They get most or all of their jobs from remote hosts.

Mail masters: Every machine within a domain is capable of sending and receiving mail by using `sendmail`. They do a reasonable job, but sometimes they can't deliver the mail, and when that happens, they send the undelivered mail to the mail master, a system that has the job of delivering the mail when no other system can.

DNS servers: DNS servers provide BIND name resolution. With DNS, host names outside of the local host table can be resolved.

More kinds of servers are emerging, such as the *work server*, also known as the *compute server*, used to offload CPU-intensive work from the workstations. Users who have work that is beyond the capacity of their own workstations can send it to a large work server to handle the job. That's about as precise a definition as we can give at this time, because the software to make this happen isn't generally available yet. At this writing, on UNIX sites all over, users are currently experimenting with using high-end machines to function as work servers — that is, they are in the process of defining what work servers are going to be. There have been several schemes to allow UNIX batching from one system to another, some of them quite complex, but none have shown any signs of becoming standard just yet. However, IBM's AIX is one of the first to have a product offering for job scheduling for this type of system.

The method of requesting a service and supplying that service depends on the service itself and how it is implemented on the server. Some services, such as mail and printing, are triggered by the transfer of data. Others, like NFS (network file service), have special mechanisms called RPCs (remote procedure calls).

File Servers and NFS

In this chapter we shall concentrate on file servers, which are made possible by Sun Microsystems' NFS. NFS stands for networked file systems, and it is a remarkable achievement. It permits files on one host to be shared by any other host on the network; in other words, all computers within a network can access each other's files. NFS has changed computing forever.

Imagine a computer without any secondary storage. They not only exist but are commonplace, and are called *diskless workstations*. They rely entirely on file servers to provide them with disk space for all needs, even their swap partitions. At boot time, even their kernels are served by the network from a file server.

When a specialized system exists exclusively to serve files, users no longer need to use mainframes and high-end minis to access common data. Whereas 370 mainframes get their power from multiple processors, each capable of about 13 MIPS, only one processor can work on any one job at a time. High-end workstations are capable of 100 MIPS and over, and if one of them could be benchmarked against a 3090, in terms of *wall* time, high-end workstations will outdistance a working mainframe. Thus, smaller and less expensive desktop and deskside computers can provide the computational power for each user, while all users can share the data by NFS networking.

The members of an engineering group developing a product all need to access the same files in order to create their product, so everyone on the project will be working from the same database and using the same tools. In fact, I've been on sites where the tools alone take up as much as 2 gigabytes. Duplicating the files and tools on each machine would be a waste, but putting them on a machine that exists only to serve these files is the innovation offerred by NFS. It would be a nightmare to try to back up hundreds of small systems, but with NFS only the file servers have to be backed up.

The combination of all the network parts working as a whole is what makes them competitive with the mainframes of older days. Back in 1980, it took a $10 million mainframe to satisfy the needs of 100 engineering users, but 10 short years later 100 workstations varying in size from 20 to 55 MIPS can provide an average aggregate of about 5000 MIPS for a tenth of that investment. Maintenance costs and support staff size are proportionally reduced.

Files can be served from one client system to another, or even from a client to a server, but the classic model is a dedicated file server serving files to workstation client systems. The mechanisms for this service are the remote procedure calls, known as RPCs, which make your requests for remote services *seem* like local system calls. An RPC has another system execute a local system call and then gets the results back to your system. Under NFS, requests for basic system calls like `open`, `read`, `write`, and `close` are handled by RPCs that yield results similar to local system calls. There is an entire repertoire of remote procedure calls, and NFS is the sum of these capabilities that allow systems to share each other's file systems.

For example, when you need to read a file on another system in your network, say a file server, a need for a `read` is sent by your system to the file server by a daemon on your system. The corresponding daemon on the server replies by initiating a `read` on the server and sending the data back to your system. The daemon on your system initiates the RPC for the `read` and receives the data when they arrive.

Here's another example: If a host system, `stalker`, wants to access X Windows tools from a server, `sparkey`, it accesses them by mounting the server's X Window file systems as if they were its own. An entry is created in its mounting file `/etc/fstab`:

```
sparkey:/usr/386/x11 /exports/x11 nfs ro,soft,bg,intr 0 0
```

This entry tells the system that upon going to multiuser mode it should mount `sparkey`'s `/usr/386/x11` disk partition to its own `exports/x11` mount point. The mount is of type `nfs` and is read only (`ro`), a `soft` mount, background (`bg`), and interruptable (`intr`). This mount can also be done manually with the NFS version of the `mount` command:

```
# /usr/etc/mount -o soft sparkey:/usr/386/x11 /exports/x11
```

To allow the mount to occur, the server first must have the `/u/project` directory in its `/etc/exports` file. `/etc/exports` is read at boot time by a process called `exportfs`. It is not read again unless `/usr/etc/exportfs` is manually invoked: This is NFS's form of access control. The simplest way is to see the file system in `sparkey`'s `/etc/exports` file:

```
% grep x11 /etc/exports /usr/386/x11
```

It can also limit its access:

```
/usr/386/x11 -access=cj:farside:stalker
```

These entries advertise that they are mountable. At boot time one of the many daemons and programs started is `exportfs`, which looks at `/etc/exports` when it is invoked and places its information in the system's kernel. A client requesting a mount from a server does so in a universal network language called XDR, for external data representation. Once a legitimate request has been made, the server permits that mount. All of this is done with remote procedure calls. An RPC works between systems the way a system call works locally.

Once the mount is complete, it acts no different than a locally mounted partition. In fact, many users are not even aware that their files are mounted from another machine. The advantages of remote mounts are that all authorized workstations can access them, and they can be backed up from a single system rather than attempting to run a backup from 50 to 100 desktop and deskside systems.

A few surrogates for local services must be provided in order to get remote files to act as if they are local. There are no `inodes` across systems, so `gnodes` take their place. There is no mechanism for mounting a remote file directory on your machine, so your machine makes a request to the mount daemon on the server, which in turn responds by sending back a file handle. Now whenever your machine wants to do any kind of operation on that file, it uses that file handle so the server knows what file your machine is talking about. In other words, when file operations are done on remote files, the kernel of the client system sends the `fhandle` to the server, and the NFS daemon `nfsd` will process the request — with a little help from its friends, that is.

Internals

Understanding the internals of NFS mounts or requests is not particularly difficult. We already looked at `exportfs` reading `/etc/exports` for the kernel. This simple act initiated at boot time from `/etc/rc.local` sets the stage for every NFS mount to follow.

All of the daemons required for ordinary networking must be present for NFS networking, starting with `portmap` (the RPC port mapping daemon) and `biod` (which handles block I/O similar to the way the kernel's own buffer cache does). These pave the way for the small army of daemons that are invoked next, including the `exportfs` daemon (which, along with the file `/etc/exports`, handles the servers making directories available to clients) and `rpc.mountd` (which takes care of the actual mounting).

The `nfsd` and `biod` daemons must be added to the system's `rc` files in order to bring up NFS. When the server boots the daemon, `rcp.mountd` is started. Immediately, four to eight `nfsd` daemons will be started. The server's NFS mount daemon is `rpc.mountd`, and it answers all mount requests. Filling all client requests is the job of `nfsd`.

The `nfs` and `biod` daemons have a unique feature: They create multiple instances of themselves to ensure that all requests are taken care of at all possible speeds. (The manual says that they are "invoked multiply.") It takes several of each to make NFS work well, so they both have an argument that specifies how many server daemons to invoke. A moderately busy workstation needs about eight NFS daemons and four block I/O daemons, as typical lines from `/etc/local` show:

```
if [ -f /usr/etc/biod ];then
    biod 4 && echo -n '    biod'
if [ -f /etc/exports ]; then
    /etc/xtab
    exports -a /dev/cons
    nfsd 8 && echo -n '    nfsd'
```

Lines like these can be seen in `rc.local` after the `portmap` daemon invocation.

Systems that serve files with NFS must know which files they are allowed to serve, and systems mounting NFS files must know which files to mount. This information is needed in conjunction with the server's `/etc/exports` and the client's `/etc/fstab` files. When the client system boots, it reads its `/etc/fstab` file and makes the local mounts first. Then it makes the remote mount requests, and the server's `rpc.mountd` daemon handles the mount requests from the clients.

The `/etc/exports` file is a list of directories that are exportable; in other words, they can be mounted by other systems. The `exportfs` daemon makes these local directories available for mounting. The following lines from `/etc/exports` show that `/usr/system`, `/usr/users`, and `/usr/tools` are mountable by all systems:

```
/usr/system
/usr/users
/usr/tools
```

You can add options to each entry, such as making a file system *read only*, allowing `root` access to a specific host, and adding security extensions. Here's how you make the tools directory read-only with access only to engineering:

```
/usr/tools -ro,-access=eng #read only access to engineering
```

Note the comment line for easy readability.

One caveat: You cannot export file systems that are part of other file systems. For example, if `/usr/tools` is listed as exportable, it would be illegal to export `/usr` or `/usr/tools/cad`.

You also need to understand another related file called `/etc/fstab`, which tells the system what to mount and whether to mount it local, remote, or loopback. However, to understand `fstab` you must first be able to do a simple mount of an exported file system.

Recall the way a local mount is done:

```
mount /dev/hd2/usr
```

The first argument is the device that the file system lives on, `/dev/hd2`, and the second is the mount point name, `/usr`. It has the same form, whether or not you have NFS.

Contrast that with a remote mount:

```
mount -t nfs server1:/usr/cae /usr/cae
```

The `t` flag is for the type of mount, here specified as `nfs`.

Here is the same mount in `fstab`, also known as 4.2 mounts:[1]

```
server1:/usr/cae /usr/cae nfs rw,soft 0 0
```

The `rw,soft` are *options* specifying that the mount is read, write, and soft. (Note how the mount type must be called out on 4.2 mounts.) The two zeros are for *frequency* and *pass*: The zero frequency is for zero days between dumps, and the zero pass signifies that *fsck* file checking is turned off.

Following is what a typical workstation's `fstab` file looks like:

---

1. The 4.2 is a reference to BSD 4.2.

```
/dev/roota / 4.2 rw 0 0
/dev/rootg /usr rw 0 0
/dev/rootg /files 0 0
 .
 .
 .
server.a:/usr/cad /usr/cad nfs ro 0 2
server.b:/u/users /u/users nfs soft,rw 0 2
```

Each entry is a mount request. The first three are local files (to be mounted locally), and the last two are remote files.

Again, as each mount request is honored, the mount daemon sends off a special identifier called a *file handle* to the client system. The client's kernel stores the file handle and will reference it again if there is any doubt of the legitimacy of the file mount. When a client makes a request for any file operation, it sends the file handle back to the server where the server's `nfsd` acts on the file request. The daemon already knows how to process the request from the information it got from `/etc/exports` by way of `exportsfs`.

Back at the client, the `biod` daemons handle all asynchronous block I/O requests. Like any block mode handling, this buffering improves performance, and it is similar to the system's buffer cache for regular disk I/O.

Because it's so important for network administrators to fully understand, let's go through the sequence one more time:

1. The server's `exportfs` file reads `/etc/exports` and stores what is mountable.

2. The client mount program reads `/etc/fstab` and requests the server to mount the file systems it finds there for `nfs` mounts. The server's `rpc.mountd` daemon makes the mount.

3. The server sends back a unique identifier to the client to be used for all future transactions, called a *file handle*.

NFS Administration

Now to look at what we've learned from the network administration perspective. Administering a new file server starts with modifying its `/etc/rc.local` file. Be sure that all relevant daemon lines (invocations of daemon processes) are present and uncommented. Be especially sure that `biod` and `nfsd` are there in sufficient quantity to handle the server's business. No less than four of each daemon should be initiated:

```
if [ -f /usr/etc/biod]; then
    biod 8
if [ -f /usr/etc/nfsd]; then
    nfsd 8
```

Even workstations should have at least four of each initiated, just to be on the safe side.

Next, edit the server's `/etc/exports` file to include the names of the file systems it will allow to be mounted. If any access control is to be enforced, here is the place to do it.

The next step in setting up server-client relationships is to go to all of the systems mounting from the server to create the necessary mount points. Next, edit their `/etc/fstab` files to include the file systems they want mounted from the server. There is a simple way to debug new `fstab` entries. Make your modifications and double-check them visually. Exit the editor, and from single-user mode do a

```
# mount -at nfs
```

Any errors will immediately appear on the console. The error messages start with `giving up on` ... . The `mount` program will attempt to make the mount, fail, and complain. Go back into the file and clean up your mistakes. Some mistakes that the `mount` command will find fall outside of `/etc/fstab`, like when you fail to create the mount point and when the file server doesn't have permission to export the file system.

Once up, NFS servers and clients go about their work with little attention on the part of the administrator until the network gets overloaded with traffic. The NFS system is robust. If an exported file system on the server is unmounted and remounted, there will be `stale file handle` complaints from all the workstations accessing the server.

The largest problem in managing a busy NFS system is the traffic it imposes on the network. Fifty workstations using NFS to access two to four file servers will bring the traffic of a network segment to the end of its comfortable limit, collisions and runt packets start to show up with reasonable frequency, and you will learn about the headache of timeouts.

Timeouts are not only an incredible nuisance, but they are also the number one problem on most NFS networks. New NFS installations start out small, say one or two file servers and a dozen or so workstations. It takes the users a while to get the hang of the network, and for a brief sweet period, the word *timeout* is unknown. Then the net grows, the users learn how to squeeze the life out of the network, and the word `timeout` appears onscreen more often than the name Smith in a metropolitan phone directory.

Timeouts can come from one or all three of these places:

• the wire (the network media itself)

• the NFS file server

• the client itself, such as a workstation

The wire is the most obvious source of timeouts. Everything goes bad on you if there is too much traffic on the wire, and you start losing data when network traffic hits somewhere between 20 and 30 percent load average. UDP packets will resend, and they will make it after some delays. TCP sends its data in streams, and if pieces of data are missing, the entire stream must be sent again, making the network load even heavier and starting an unhealthy network cycle. To add insult to injury, errors created on the wire, such as collisions and runt packets, cause ICMP error-handling packets to be sent, adding further to the network load.

Another common performance problem is caused by insufficient NFS and block I/O daemons. To look for this problem, run **nfstat** with the **s** flag and look at UDP socket overflows. If socket overflows are reported, you have insufficient buffering and need to increase the number of server daemons.

NFS Administration for System V

System V Release 4 for both monoprocessor and multiprocessor machines is somewhat different from the simpler versions of installed NFS we have talked about so far. Most of us were introduced to NFS on BSD-based systems like SunOS and ULTRIX, but the SVR4 versions are extended from BSD versions. They have more files involved in their operation, and they use different files than the simple `/etc/fstabs` and `/etc/exports` of the BSD versions. Another major and welcome difference is Secure NFS. Original NFS versions became notorious for their openness, but Secure NFS can be set up to verify both the user and system accessing files, and it will deny access to anyone not specifically permitted to have access to them.

System V Initiation States and NFS

If you have never worked with System V, the first big difference that you will notice is that System V does not have the two traditional states, single-user and multiuser. Instead, it has many initiation states, **s** and **S** states for single-user, and many numbered states for multiuser. SVR4 lists seven defined states, **0** through **6**. `init` **0** is the power-down state, while `init` **1** is SA mode. `init` **2** in System V Releases 2 and 3 were standard for most operations. Now `init` **3** is the state in which NFS goes active. If the system leaves `init` **3**, NFS exits. The mechanism is the SVR4 NFS command in `/etc`'s `init.d` directory.

```
sh /etc/init.d/NFS start
```

The `stop` option will halt NFS activity.

```
sh /etc/init.d/nfs stop.
```

Sharing and `share`

NFS is all about sharing — sharing disk volumes with client systems, even sharing other file servers. Early NFS required only that the server's `/etc/exports` file listed the file for exporting (remote mounting) and that the client system had the file system in its how-to-mount file, `/etc/fstab`. Both the server's `exports` file and the client's `exports` file gave a degree of access control by specifying if mounts were read-only or read/write, and the exports file could allow or disallow clients by name or netgroup. Beyond that, all these versions needed was that the `nfsd` and `biod` daemons were enabled in sufficient quantities to give good service.

System V takes sharing seriously enough to have a share command. The `share` command makes a single resource available, while its sister command, `shareall`, shares a group of resources. Put in the manner of the manual, share makes local NFS resources available for mounting by remote systems. Their counterparts are `unshare` and `unshareall`.

The `share` command adds a level of access control to NFS previously provided by the server's `/etc/exports` file. The mutually exclusive options `ro` and `rw`, which allow read or read/write access of exports, are given by share options. Read-only access works well with tool directories that should not be "improved" by the users and for true read-only access like a marketing group's access to active engineering files. The option can be applied to specific clients (in a colon-delimited list).

```
share -F nfs -o rw=eng ro=mkrg:mfg root=jaeger /eng
```

In the example above, we also see that `root` (UID 0) access from jaeger is allowed. All other UID 0s will become nobody (UID -1) with less privilege than a VMS supporter at a UNIX convention. The files involved with the `share` command are in `/etc/dfs` and are `dfstab`, `sharetab`, and `fdtypes`.

The `secure` Option of `share`

One of the `share` options is `secure`. If the secure option is used, clients must use DES authentication for all their remote procedure calls.

Secure NFS

The old NFS security was limited to how cleverly the administrator could create the lines in `/etc/exports` on the file servers. If a system called `stalker` was listed in the options as

```
access=stalker:jaeger:...
```

the server gave it access. There was no way for the server to test to see if it really was `jaeger`. There were practical limitations as well. It is a lot of work to add each client to the server's `exports` file. `netgroups` makes it easier, but then again, `netgroups` must be maintained. Because of the extra work involved, some administrators wouldn't bother, preferring to sacrifice security in order to get increased accessibility. But with liberties like this, anyone could mount a disk from the client. As a result, NFS gained the (underserved) reputation of not being secure. To gain maximum security, a scheme was created using user and client authentication with the U.S. Data Encryption Standard (DES) to encrypt a pair of keys, a public key and a user key.

Secure NFS authentication is relatively involved. It starts with all systems having the same time, and therefore the time daemons must be run.[2] A pair of keys are maintained for each transaction.

---

2. If the time daemon is not running, secure NFS will use the time from the server.

A public key is kept to authenticate both the user and the system. Both the sender and the receiver must use the same key. The sender encrypts the current time, and the receiver decrypts it, checking the time against its own.

Thus, RPC authentication uses two keys and two key concepts, *credentials* and *verifiers*. They are similar to an industrial ID card. The card is your credential, and the photo is the verification of your identification. State drivers' licenses are similar because they are credentials to drive, and the photo ID verifies that the license is really yours.

The UNIX NFS credentials contain the client machine name, the user's UID and GID, and group access list. The authentication is the exchange of time encryptions using the same encryption key.

Secure NFS Administration

Systems using secure NFS must be within an assigned domain and must have a hostname. It is easiest done on systems with NIS (YP), and some form of mail delivery service, like `sendmail`, since to run mail you have a domain, and all systems have a name. DES authentication uses these to form a netname, which looks like this:

```
unix.2000mfg.acme.com
```

The name of the OS comes first (`unix`), the user's ID number (`2000`), the domain name (`mfg`), followed by the Internet name of the organization (`acme.com`). This produces a truly unique name. Netnames are used for both systems and users. The system's netname is

```
unix.jaeger@mfg.acme.com
```

Public and secret keys are created with the `newkey` command. Users can do their own with the `chkey` command. Store the public key in the `publickey` database. The secret key is stored in `/etc/keystore`. The administrator's key (root's) is kept in `/etc/.rootkey`.

Users must add the `keylogin` command to their `.login` or `.profile`. The `keyserv` daemon must be running, so install it in the proper `rc` file. Add the `secure` option to `/etc/dfs/keyserv`. Finally, edit each client's `/etc/vfstab` to add the `secure` option to all mounts.

Wire Contention

The number one cause of wire contention at most sites is unwanted traffic. On a Mr. Potato Head network, you plug anything and everything into the same network backbone and try to go with it.

Meanwhile, on the enterprise network you have 3com, Banyon, Novell, DECnet, and UNIX traffic all sharing the same Ethernet or 802.3 wire. In time you learn how to filter and isolate or watch the net die before your very eyes.

Excessive broadcasts are another form of wire plague. Recall that a broadcast is a transmission sent to every machine on that network, and every machine will respond. Machines can ignore most mutant packets, but they can't ignore broadcasts, so systems sending runaway broadcasts need to be located and fixed. Broadcasts that generate broadcasts are the most virulent type. Conflicts between Ethernet 1 and Ethernet 2 can put you into a broadcast storm that will stop the wire cold.

Performance Balancing for NFS Servers

NFS servers have as many problems as the network media do. Most servers are general-purpose computers that have enough hardware to be called a server. Like any general-purpose computer, the CPU keeps track of everything the machine is doing and does most of it, including NFS traffic. When there is not enough CPU to go around, NFS work slows down, and bingo, you have timeouts on your hands. UNIX has old-style disk access and buffering algorithms that favor local disk read/writes rather than NFS read/write requests. Since the read/write mix is different for NFS than it is for local access, systems that are not specially optimized for NFS traffic will become too slow.

NFS Timing for Client Systems

Client systems add to the problems created by the wire and the servers. If they are not properly configured for the sort of NFS business that each `nfs` mount must handle, they will give up too quickly and create a timeout error. Conversely, a system that is set up to try excessively hard for access will increase the load on the wire way too much and will also cause a timeout error. You can see how it goes around in circles sometimes.

Fixing Timeouts

How do you stop or at least slow down timeout problems? Start with the wire. Bridge each segment so that segments will not send local traffic to the next segment or out on to the backbone. Some bridges can also filter incoming traffic to some extent. Because this is the traditional role of the router, it may be time to go to router isolation if your bridges can't stop junk traffic from the outside.

When you have totally isolated the network segment so nothing goes out except whatever has to go out and nothing comes in except whatever has to come in, you will have some delicious moments of peace and quiet. Savor them while you can, because the more your network grows, the more legitimate traffic will come on the wire, and you will have to deal with timeouts again.

Now the only option you have is to place logical work groups on their own subnetworks. Subnetting appears to be an expensive proposition at first because you need a server, a router, and a cable for each one just for starters; but if your servers have the capacity to handle multiple subnetted work groups, use multiple Ethernet interfaces on one server to deal with as many subnets as it can take. However, by putting multiple interfaces on the server itself, you transform it into an entirely new beast, a server/router, and new sets of problems evolve.

Replacing existing hardware with new hardware is sometimes the way you have to go, but throwing out a server and getting a better one is a bit costly. Upgrading your hardware whenever possible is easier on the pocketbook. For example, NFS accelerators like the Legato product favor NFS read/write mixes (approximately

80/20), and they do their own caching. They march to a different drummer than the UNIX CPU, for the card and the patches put in algorithms are specific to NFS. Major upgrades (like going from a Sun 4/390 to a 4/490) are not too costly and can double some types of performance.

Should you opt to replace the hardware with a new system, look at some of the new machines out there, such as a dedicated, functional, multiprocessor system like the Auspex 3000, 5000, or 6000. With an Auspex, you attach each network segment to a different Ethernet port. Then the general purpose computers you have that are functioning as file servers can go on to find new, useful lives as compute servers.

But before you rush out and spend any money, perhaps you should review your systems' tuning, starting with the configuration of each workstation's `fstab` file. There are three mount options that are critical to timeout performance:

- `soft` vs. `hard`

- `timeo`

- `retrans`

Mounts must be `soft` or `hard`, the latter the default. Try mounting infrequently accessed, read-only file systems `soft`, because if they fail to make contact, they try a few times and give up, resulting in timeout errors that you can live with. Critical file systems like the users' work areas and the tools they use are good candidates for `hard` mounts. This kind of mount will hang on tenaciously, for it never stops trying to connect. Obviously, should a mount fail for any period of time, other systems with `hard` mounts to the same file system will also flood the wire with requests, and that's trouble. Acquiring the best balance between your `hard` and `soft` mounts requires judicious planning.

`retrans` is the number of times NFS will retry. The next time you have persistent problems with timeouts on a soft mount, try extending `timeo` to 10 or more.

`timeo` is the number of one-tenths of a second that the system will try before timing out. When you are plagued with timeout problems, try extending `timeo` to 2.5 seconds (`timeo=25`). Here is a `/etc/fstab` file for a die-hard mount:

```
svr04:/usr/eng /usr/eng nfs hard,timeo=25,retrans=10 0 0
```

Don't forget to make critical mounts `hard`.

In order to test all this, you will have to make do with `nfstat` if you don't have your own specialized NFS analyzers, monitors, or managers:

```
% nfsstat
calls   badcalls ...
0       0          ...
 .
 .
Client rpc:
calls   badcalls  retrans  badxid  timeout  wait  newcred
760     0         6        0       6        0     0
 .
 .
```

Notice that the six timeouts match the number of retransmissions. This is your main source of information, lacking more sophisticated, specialized tools.

Network tuning will help you avoid system timeouts, but, like system tuning, it's something that must be done repeatedly for optimum performance.

How Many Server Processes on One Server?

Fully understanding the functions of your servers is paramount to having a successful network. You want all of your servers, workstations, routers, and bridges to function as a single efficient piece of hardware. If your main file server goes down, do you want mail to stop too? It will if you have made that server mail master and the home of the shared mail disk as well. Is that system also the DNS server? It doesn't have to be.

What makes a good server? You don't use the same sets of guidelines for choosing servers and workstations. A high MIP rate is good for workstations, but not necessarily for servers. If a machine has a high MIP rate but only one Ethernet port, it won't be able to handle much traffic, so how could it be a good server? On the other hand, a relatively slow CPU that only has to loosely coordinate a fully multiprocessed server is well worth looking at because it has the data throughput. These systems are busless, using multiple channels and having a separate processor for their Ethernet interfaces, disk interfaces, and memory. They take the NFS traffic which normally do synchronous writes and do mass buffering so disk writes can be asynchronous the same way that local disk writes are.

Your use of the server has as much to do with its efficiency as its design. The fastest processor on earth won't do you a bit of good if you have it tied up all the time with user processes. Servers are for serving, and workstations are for user work. Don't allow users to log on to file servers.

There are systems available that favor high reliability as opposed to speed or fast network interfaces. These are good choices for DNS and mail servers. Any application that is truly mission-critical requires a high-reliability system, and disk mirroring[3] is a given.

From NFS to YP

More than one kind of server exists on the net. In this chapter we learned how NFS serves files, but in the next chapter we'll discover the importance of YP servers and the look-up services they provide.

---

3. Mirroring is the automatic copying of one disk's information to another as an always ready backup.

CHAPTER

10

YP Servers

NIS stands for Network Information Services, a distributed network lookup service developed by Sun Microsystems, Inc., that maintains a set of files accessible by machines on the net. This service used to be called Yellow Pages, or YP for short, and although its name has been changed to NIS, the original name was firmly established on UNIX sites, and many people still call it YP. The impact of YP can't really be appreciated unless you understand what it would be like without it.

Because computer sites grow and change with the passage of time, some workstations are more powerful than others. Even if today you buy the most powerful workstations made for each user on your site at $35,000 a shot, in a few years your latest-and-greatest workstations will be considered slow and outmoded, the number of users may have increased by as much as 50 percent, and the kind of work you do may have changed, requiring different kinds of workstations. Thus, most sites have quite a variety of machines accumulated over a long period of time.

Imagine that you have a network domain of 100 systems consisting of multi-user systems, personal workstations, file servers, departmental workstations, and stand-alone UNIX micros. Your typical users will work on their own workstations, but they also might log on to one of the multi-user machines because of a few tools located there that aren't available elsewhere. Whenever they need extra horsepower to do certain jobs, they may also need to go to the powerful compute server. In other words, users aren't limited to one workstation; for various reasons, they log on to different machines all over the net. When users request logins on these machines, the system administrator will give them the next available ID number. But what happens when their files have to be transferred from one machine to another? If their user-ID numbers are different from machine to machine, and they will be, they won't own their files anymore when they are transferred to another machine.

Without YP, systems administrators would have to constantly exchange their user lists to coordinate user-ID numbers. To prevent duplicate user IDs, user-ID numbers would have to be drawn from a pool, and one individual would work full-time maintaining it. And that's just one list that would need to be updated and maintained. You wouldn't want two hosts with the same name, so a pool of network host numbers would have to be maintained for new systems. Lists of node names and their corresponding host numbers would also have to be maintained and exchanged. Printers are shared, so `printcap` files would need the same identity from machine to machine. Network files, such as `/etc/services` and `/etc/netgroup`, would have to be shared as well. You can see how time-consuming it would be to coordinate all this. Even ace administrators would make some mistakes. Eventually, different users with the same user-ID number would wind up on the same machine, and when the transfer of their files occurred, the wrong owner would have ownership. That's trouble you want to avoid.

That is what life would be like without YP. Now let's see what a difference YP makes.

Yellow Pages — An Overview

Under NIS, common system files are stored in a database of information accessible to all users and all systems. Just as the average driver isn't aware of air/fuel ratios in carburation, the average user isn't aware of YP. System and network administrators access the databases constantly, and although users are free to examine the individual databases with the `ypcat`, they seldom do.

The domain master is the repository of all database source files within the YP domain. The database source files usually reside in the master's `/etc` directory, and systems needing information stored in the YP database will access the master's database.

Network administrators have to deal with computer site jargon, and when a machine is deemed *mission-critical,* that means it cannot be allowed to fail — if it goes down, the cost to the company is too great. Since you cannot afford to be without YP servers, *slave servers* can be created that receive copies of the database when they are *pushed* to them by the master. Computer site people would say that you need YP slaves for *mission-critical redundancy.*

The master maintains a YP directory in which you will find YP's `Makefile`, the key to the whole system. You will also find the domain's database files, called *maps.* They are not ASCII files in the usual sense, and you need the `makedbm` command to read them. The database is stored in a directory named after the domain, so an engineering domain might exist in `/var/yp/YP.eng`. All machines using the same YP database are in one domain, and normally a domain will have the same boundaries as a network segment. Usually there is one domain, but there can be more.

How does YP work? When a user logs on to a workstation, for example, the system looks for the user's logname in its own `/etc/passwd` file, reading to the bottom until it encounters a plus sign, the signal to look in YP's `passwd` file. It knows to look to the server, because the system is running a daemon called `ypbind` that *binds* it to YP and the YP domain servers. The workstation uses a remote procedure call to access the server and get a copy of the password file, which it then reads as if it were a local file.

Although you usually want one of your best file servers to be the YP master, almost any machine can be a YP slave if it runs a daemon called `ypserv`. Often administrators make their own personal workstations YP slaves because they know their own machines will not be CPU-bound with demanding applications; thus, their CPUs will be available to respond to YP requests.

YP's Makefile

You might think that looking through Section 5 of the manual or doing a **man -k** on **yp** would help you find that magical file of files from which YP gets its information for setting up database maps, but you would be wrong: All the files and dependencies are hardcoded into the **/var/yp/Makefile** script.

Many UNIX administrators don't have to worry about what goes on inside of YP's **Makefile**, because it works fine most of the time. All they have to do is go to a YP database source file, most of which are in **/etc**, make their changes, and move off to the YP database directory (**/var/yp** or **/etc/yp**) to run **make**:

```
# cd /etc
# vipw passwd
.
# cd /var/yp
# make
updating passwd
pushing passwd
```

Here we see that the **passwd** file has been modified and that **make** has been run. The **Makefile** creates the YP **passwd** data base files and then pushes them to the slave servers. The **make** command lets you be specific about which target file you wish to update by passing it the name of the file as an argument:

```
# cd /var/yp
# make passwd
updating passwd
pushing passwd
```

Everything seems so easy until one day, when you set up a new YP master, the **Makefile** doesn't work. What do you do when it spits out some error messages and hangs?

There are makefiles all over UNIX, including the one for the kernel, but the YP **Makefile** is one of the largest. It is so long that even though you may be a whiz at debugging a C program or a shell script, wading through that entire `Makefile` looking for problems is a mighty discouraging proposition the first time you do it. And yet you must do it. There is no other way.

After you have more experience, you will discover that more often than not the problem is too much code. Like a GENERIC kernel, YP's `Makefile` has code to cover every possibility. For example, it references target files that don't exist in the `/etc` directory for your machine.

The cure is the same used to generate a lean, mean kernel. Either comment out or remove all the code that is not germane to your current configuration. Naturally you save the original first, copying it to something self-documenting like `make.GENERIC`.

The `make` command and makefiles are generally used to create and update software and software systems. One use is to make an executable program from C code and the related libraries. `make` tests the modification times on the files; if it finds any of the constituents of the code newer than the final product, it will remake the final program using only the components necessary.

A makefile uses the following format:

> *target: dependencies ; commands*

or

> *target : dependencies*
> *commands*

The *target* is a label, and the *dependencies* are usually file names, since it is the files that will have to be checked for modification times. The *commands* are the ones that will be executed if the `make` times warrant it. Here's another way to look at the format:

> *label : file1 file2 fileN*
> *command1 command2 ... commandN*

Targets can be preceded by MACRO definitions, which are usually no more than the setting of constants:

```
CC  =    cc
DIR =    /usr/etc
```

How to Modify YP's Makefile

The YP `Makefile` is much more complicated than the makefiles just described. Laid out in sections, similar to the way kernel code is, the first section is macro definitions, with a *THIS = that* form:

```
DIR =      /etc
DOM =      `domainname`
NOPUSH =   ""
```

Read the constants and note what they are, because here is where you find out where your YP files and commands are hidden:

```
YPDIR = /usr/etc/yp
YPDBDIR = /var/yp
```

The `YPDIR` constant is set to the directory, in which the YP executables are kept, `/usr/etc/yp`. The `YPDBDIR` constant is set to `/var/yp`, the directory, in which NIS keeps and maintains the database files.

The next section of YP's `Makefile` consists of the MACRO definitions of group targets. The definitions start with the files needed for the YP database. Here, also, is where all the files that are not needed for your installation are mixed in with the ones you do need. On our site, these are some of the "good" guys:

```
ALL_TARGETS = \
    group \
    hosts \
    netgroup \
    passwd \
    printcap \
    rpc \
    services \
    ypservers
```

These are the "bad" guys:

```
auto.home \
auto.master \
bootparams \
bootservers \
ethers \
ext_ports \
     .
     .
```

If any of these files are not precious to your installation, shovel them into the bit bucket.

Now go to the section immediately following the MACRO definitions for individual files, the REQUIRED_FILES section. Every file target you deleted has a matching directory entry here that needs to be removed:

```
REQUIRED_FILES = \
    ${ALIASES} \
    ${DIR}/auto.home
         .
```

The rest of the YP `Makefile` follows the standard form:

targets : dependencies
    commands

but they are a bit more complex than most makefiles you might have seen for creating programs from C code and libraries. Here's an example:

```
bootparams: bootparams.push
bootparams.push: bootparams.time
  -@if [ ! $(NOPUSH) -a -f $(DIR)/$(@:.push=) ];\
    then\
    $(YPPUSH) bootparams;\
    touch $@; echo "pushed $(@:push=)";\
  fi
```

In the first line, `bootparams` is the target and `bootparams.push` is the dependency. In the second line, `bootparams.push` is the target and `bootparams.time` is the dependency. The rest until the `fi` are the commands. This code is similar to Bourne shell, with some additions and restrictions. Find the sections that match the files and directories you removed in the MACRO definitions section. Then wipe out the section you want, from the first line with the name of the target you want to delete all the way out to the ending `fi`. *Remove it all*, because you made a copy of the entire file called `make.GENERIC`, remember?

That should complete your cleaning job. Now to see if it works. Touch the `group` file and run `make`. If `group` is updated and pushed, you're home free. If not, note all error messages. For example, a common error message is `usage`. If your YP masters and slaves are not running the same UNIX version, and YP's `Makefile` comes from a later release, a command may use a flag that is deemed "illegal." That's why YP masters and slaves should always run the same UNIX version at the same release level. If there are no error messages, but the machine still hangs, you have a larger problem. The `make` command has no less than four debug flags, so use them one by one to find out what the problem is.

When you are done, and it can take a few hours, you will have a faster and more reliable `Makefile`. Then in the future, as you extend your YP's database capabilities, you can go back to your original `Makefile` and get the lines you need. Should you get adventurous and add a database not covered in the original file, you can use the rest of the `Makefile` as a cookbook for your addition.

Setting Up a YP Domain Master Server

Now that YP's `Makefile` is taken care of, you can create your YP master. The first decision is what machine to use for the master. When networked systems are recovering from a power hit, they can get deadlocked in the boot process. The necessary boot sequence is to bring up a YP server first, then the file servers, and finally the workstations, because only the YP servers can supply critically needed information like hosts tables to the file servers. If the workstations come up ahead of the servers, they will flood the Ethernet with RPCs requesting file handles for remote mounts, and when they don't get that information, they become hopelessly confused. The wire is peaked, and the servers drown while trying to come up because they can't handle that many requests.

In the trade, we say we need "YP server redundancy." One way to achieve this is to put a very small system like a workstation or even a UNIX PC on an inexpensive UPS and make it a YP slave. It can double as a system's or network's group machine, as long as it isn't expected to handle CPU-intensive tasks. If it is on the same power as the other workstations, it will recover from a power hit at the same time as the workstations, which is generally before anything in the machine room. Dedicated file servers are usually kept in a machine room and fed via a motor-generator set. They are more resistant to power ripples, but they are much slower in recovering from a power outage. In addition, most machine rooms will not power up their systems until the air conditioning is up, another delay in coming on line. These are all factors to consider for YP server placement.

You can put YP slaves and masters on file servers, you can put both on workstations that belong to the systems group, or you can use any other combination that works for you. The most functional solution we have found at our site is putting the YP master on the fastest dedicated file server, having one slave minimum per subnet on another dedicated file server, and having one slave server on a UPS (first choice) or line power (last choice) located with all the workstations in case of a power outage.

The YP master server knows it is a server when it boots because it sees the `ypserv` daemon uncommented in its `rc` file. It was set up as a master server by the administrator using `ypinit` `-m` which creates the database from the source files, typically files found in `/etc` like `passwd`, `group`, `hosts`, and `printcap`. Slave servers are created by `ypinit`; the `-s` flag makes them slaves. YP slave servers have no `Makefile` and receive their database files by having them `pushed` from the master.

Once you have selected a system to be YP master, you must create a YP-domain name. As mentioned earlier, it's helpful if you make the YP-domain name reflect the group name. For example, if the working group is a manufacturing group, a name like `YP.mfg` may be appropriate as well as self-descriptive. The process that sets up master and slaves is `ypinit`, an interactive utility that asks you many questions. If you get stuck, you can bail out and initiate `ypinit`. You will be asked the names of your YP slaves, so be prepared with the answers.

Before running `ypinit` you must be sure that all the files you are going to need as YP maps are present on the master-to-be, such as:

- `passwd`
- `group`
- `hosts`
- `networks`
- `protocols`
- `services`
- `ethers`
- `netgroup`

You may not consider `netgroup` a candidate, but you will need it for NFS security and the `rwall` command, if nothing else. Set it up before making your YP domain.

If you have created a domain name, set up `netgroup`, selected your slaves, and created or updated all YP map source files, you are ready to run `ypinit`. Run it first on the master with the `-m` option, and second on the slaves with the `-s` option.

Migrating YP Domain Servers

Once you have the YP master installed, why would you ever want to change its location? Most administrators of NFS and YP systems tend to put the YP domain master on one of their major file servers, and although this may be a "best choice," there are still a few problems to work around. When you put the YP domain master on a server, eventually you find out that it leaves your file server vulnerable to remote or local logins. The master server has the source file to create all the YP maps, and the password file is what makes the server vulnerable. The last thing you need is users logging on to a server. One way around this problem is protecting `/etc/passwd` by creating a separate password source file other than `/etc/passwd`, perhaps an abbreviated password file that only allows the system staff to log on to the machine. But don't be surprised if your strategy for the location of the YP master has to be revised a few times before you are satisfied.

Actually, after you've been administering a network for a while, you discover that there are several reasons for moving YP. Sometimes you need to replace the original server or augment it with a newer or more reliable machine. What if your original server is running BSD 4.2 or a derivative (like ULTRIX), but you now have systems running BSD 4.3 like SunOS? BSD 4.2 isn't compatible enough with BSD 4.3 to push the data files, and that's a problem. Whatever the reason, moving the YP domain master is something you will have to do eventually.

You can study theory all you want, but nothing will help you more than going through an actual YP server migration. Imagine this scenario: Your original YP slave and master are on 4.2 Berkeley-based systems. Several times these systems have come down while all the workstations, running a 4.3 BSD version, stayed up. This problem needs a solution, so you decide to move the YP master to your (administrator's) SPARC workstation. You only use the workstation to log on to other machines, so it is never CPU-bound and doesn't load its Ethernet port. Let's say that you also have a couple of new-and-improved file servers to replace the old, clunky ones, so you decide to make the fastest new file server the slave so all YP systems are running at the same Berkeley release level. The new server, a Sun 4, has the undocumented trick of getting back on the Ethernet ahead of all other systems when collisions occur.

It sounds easy enough when you plan it, but you are cautious because you know that if two systems claim to be YP master, you will be deluged with error messages, and you'll have a big cleanup job on your hands. You also know that if both YP servers leave the net, the system will be in even worse shape because there will be no source for YP information. And trying to `yppush` the database from the old 4.2 systems to the new 4.3 won't work, because the two versions of UNIX are incompatible in that area. The database will have to be remade from scratch; that's all there is to it. The key files will have to be copied from the old master to the new, and a new YP domain master must be created as if the old one never existed.

Copy the Old Source Database

Copy the key YP source files like /etc's `passwd`, `group`, `hosts`, and `services`. One trick to circumvent problems with a foreign `root` accessing a system is to log on to the new master-to-be system as yourself, not as `root`. Then when you `su` to `root`, your effective user ID will be 0, but your user ID will be that of an ordinary user, yours. Change directories to /etc. Be sure to `ftp` to the old YP master, not `rcp`. Then `mget` the files you need, and they will overwrite the ones in /etc. Naturally, you do a backup or create backup copies on disk before all of this happens. Otherwise, your backout plan is shot.

On old Sun SPARC systems, don't forget to copy `passwd` to `yppasswd` and `group` to `ypgroup`. The SPARC machines have alternate `passwd` and `group` files. This condition permits one of the files to be in the database file and the other to be in the **passwd** or **group** file, preventing conflict between the YP domain source's files and the login files, reason enough for trying to use a SPARC for a domain master.

Uncomment rc.local

Move to */etc/rc.local* on the new master-to-be. Uncomment the lines for **ypserv** or add them if necessary.

```
if [ -f /usr/etc/ypserv -a -d /var/yp/`domainname` ]; then
    ypserv && echo ` ypserv`
fi
```

Comment Out ypserv on the Old YP Systems

Go to the old YP master and slave systems and comment out the **ypserv** lines shown above, but don't kill the **ypserv** daemon yet.

Warn the Users

If you haven't warned the users yet, don't waste time — do it now. You should have sent them mail at the beginning of the day with **rwall**, but there's no time like the present:

```
% rwall -n Agroup
YP services will be interrupted briefly at 1700.
The interruption to service will not take long,
but a server and/or workstations may have to reboot.
^D
```

Tell them like it is; with luck they will only feel a small hiccough.

Zero Hour

When it's time to complete the final switch, timing will be everything. You cannot have two active masters, not even for a second. The only choice is to be without a master and slaves for a minute or two.

Run `ypinit` on the Master-to-Be

Move to `/usr/etc/yp` and execute `./ypinit -s` to create the new YP database. The command is interactive. You will be asked a few questions and given the choice of a graceful bailout if you ask for it. If you can't find your YP directory, look in places like `/var/yp` or `/etc/yp`. Once you find it, look at its `Makefile` and it will tell you the names of the YP executables and database directories, such as:

```
YPDIR=      /usr/etc/yp
YPDBDIR=    /var/yp
```

When the program completes, everything is ready for the final transition from one master to another. If you reboot or execute `ypserv` you will have a new master server on line, but don't do it yet.

Kill `ypserv` on the Old YP Systems

Go to the YP domain master and each slave and kill its `ypserv` daemon. If you `grep` the `ps` output on the string `ypserv`, you will have its process-ID number.

Enable `ypserv` on the New Master

Now go back to the new YP Master and reboot it or start `ypserv`. There will be a small rumble on the net. A few systems will complain, and one or two may even reboot. It is the only YP domain server now, and there will be delays until you bring a slave on line.

First test to see if your systems recognize the new master. Move to a few systems and execute `ypwhich`. The name returned will be that of the new master.

Create Your New Slave

When creating a YP slave server, a really fast file server is a good choice. It will be fast enough to even preempt the master. Go to the YP directory and execute the following command line:

```
# ./ypinit -s YP_master_name
```

There will be a lot of yppushing, and then the new slave will be nearly ready to go. Now start its ypserv daemon. Double-check its rc.local and see if you have uncommented the ypserv lines.

Testing It All

One last test before going home and calling it a day. Make a quick and dirty test for all hosts to force them to look for the new YP domain master or slave.

```
#
for name in stalker cj huey dewey louie daisy donald
  do
      echo $name
      rsh $name ypwhich
  done
exit 1
```

Some will respond quicker than others. Some will give the name of the master, others the name of the slave. It's good if you get a mix of names, because that means they're all responding rapidly.

Troubleshooting YP

YP is robust and relatively trouble-free, but occasionally you will have some problems. Since YP is daemon-driven, most of your trouble will involve the daemons in some way. For example, any system that cannot get YP information is probably missing a daemon at the server's or client's side. Like NFS, YP is dependent on RPCs and will not function if they lose track of RPC port information, controlled by the portmap daemon. Let's look at some specific problems.

Server's `ypserv` Daemon Is Not Stable

When a YP slave server's YP maps are not up to date, executing **ypwhich** will not show you that the server is responding. Logging on to the server and doing a

```
% ps -ax|grep yp
```

will show that **ypbind** is running but that **ypserv** has gone away. If you restart **ypserv**, you may find it dead the next time you check it.

Clearly, the problem is not **ypserv**. The prime candidate is `portmap`. First check to see if the `portmapper` is alive:

```
% ps -ax|grep portmap|grep -v grep
```

If there is no response, restart `portmap`. If `portmap` seems alive, check the quality of its service with `rpcinfo`.

```
# rpcinfo -p hostname
```

Typically, you will see four lines returned for **ypserv** if it is healthy. All the **ypserv** entries will have the same program number, with two version numbers each for `tcp` and `udp`:

```
# rpcinfo -p stalker
program vers proto port
   100000  2   tcp    111   portmapper
   100000  2   udp    111   portmapper
   100004  2   udp    642   ypserv
   100004  2   tcp    643   ypserv
   100004  1   udp    642   ypserv
   100004  1   tcp    643   ypserv
   100007  2   tcp   1024   ypbind
   100007  2   udp   1024   ypbind
   100007  1   tcp   1024   ypbind
   100007  1   udp   1024   ypbind
   .
```

The crudest way to fix the problem is to reboot the server, but killing the daemon and then restarting it has more class because the machine stays up with no loss of service to the users.

Server Not Responding

The message

```
yp: server not responding for domain server_name.
Still trying.
```

is accompanied by a loss of service. This error is caused when the `ypserv` and `portmap` daemons are dead or disabled.

If the server is dead, restart it. If it is a daemon problem, follow the steps for fixing a broken daemon.

Loss of YP Services

One system in particular cannot get YP services, while other systems on the same wire can get the same services. Commands like `ypcat` fail to work. Long listings of the user's directories show user-ID numbers instead of user names. The problem is at home, for you will find your `ypbind` daemon dead. `grep` for the presence of `ypbind`:

```
% ps -ax | grep yp |grep -v grep
```

If `ypbind` is gone, restart it. Recheck the system after a while and if the daemon has died again look for the cause. Of course, `portmap` is a good candidate. If all else fails, reboot.

ypwhich

The `ypwhich` command tells you which YP server is responding at the moment. It is a handy command since, if it shows the same server serving continually, there is a chance the alternate YP server is in trouble. Executed rapidly several times in succession, `ypwhich` should show both the YP master and slaves.

Another Kind of Server

NFS and YP servers are the main types of servers used in UNIX distributed computing, but we mustn't forget that distributed computing results in distributed printing. Thus, print servers are the subject of the next chapter.

CHAPTER

11

Print Servers

Every time you pick up a network magazine, you read about another kind of server. As new network applications evolve, new types of specialized servers are created to accommodate them, such as PC NFS servers and X terminal boot servers. We can't hope to cover every kind of server in this book, so instead we'll talk about one specialized server that most sites will have, a print server.

Printing was easy in the old days of standalone machines: The printer was attached directly to your computer, you invoked the printer command, and the file was printed. However, it's a different story on the network. If the printer isn't directly attached to your machine, the only way you can get something printed is through *remote printing* by invoking the standard command on your workstation and giving it the name of any printer that is accessible on the net, and the print servers will spool your files for printing. In fact, a dedicated print server does little else than spool print files and send them to directly attached printers, and some systems are manufactured specifically for that purpose, such as the DEC PrintServer 20.

At first remote printing may not seem like much of a trick, but as administrators you soon appreciate the subtleties involved because you must delve into how it works. The first thing you discover is that the ability to do remote printing depends on the UNIX version. Berkeley-based UNIX systems have had *built-in* remote printing capabilities through print servers the longest. AIX now does remote printing to another AIX server, but this feature is a recent addition.[1] Until recently, AT&T System V made no provision for remote printing, so you had to create a script to do an `rcp` (remote copy) to another machine, `rsh` to have it print the file, and then `rsh` to remove the file, and this kludge worked well enough, to be sure.

The Berkeley UNIX mechanism for remote printing is the `lpr` spooler system and `printcap`. Under BSD, local print files are sent directly to a print server, where they are spooled before being sent to a printer. The mechanism is interesting, because the print server treats the job as if it were received locally.

Two things are required for remote printing: 1) specifying the name of the remote printer and its host in the local client's `printcap` file, and 2) putting the name of the client in the print server's `host.lpd` file. The network administrator has to create a `printcap` entry on any local machine that will direct printer requests to a print server. Let's see what a `printcap` entry for a remote machine looks like:

```
lp3|remote2:\
    :lp=:rm=dec20:\
    :sd=/var/spool/lp:\
    :rp=fx850:
```

The `lp3|remote2:` is a label, and it shows two printer names, `lp3` and `remote2`. The users think that they are sending files to these printers, but what actually happens is that their print requests are forwarded to the `dec20` print server.

---

1. AIX also can do remote batch work not specific to printing.

These are the entries that enable remote printing:

lp
: This sets `lp` equal to null, telling the system that there is no local printing device by the name `lp3` or `remote2`.

rm
: Note that `rm` is set to the name of the remote machine, `dec20`, a dedicated DEC PrintServer 20.

rp
: Here `rp` holds the name of the remote printer, in this case an `fx850`.

Note that there is no port setting. If this were for a local printer, a port would have to be assigned, but `lp=` means that there is no physical device and thus no port.

The network administrator must also write a corresponding `printcap` entry on the print server, but that's easier because it is a conventional `printcap` entry:

```
lp|fx850:\
:lp=/dev/pp0:sd=var/spool/lpd:\
:lf=/var/adm/error_log:\
```

Nothing is out of the ordinary except that the `rs` flag is not set, but after all, if `rs` were present, no remote user would be able to access the system. Of course, `lp=/dev/pp0` is the printer name, `sd=var/spool/lpd` is the spool directory, and `lf=/var/adm/error_log` specifies the error file.

Note that, typical of `printcap` entries, the `lp|fx850` label has two printer names. The entry following is for an `fx850`, but it also happens to be the default printer because the first name listed is `lp`.

The only remaining task you have to do on the print server is setting up access control for the remote system, which is accomplished by putting the system's name in the print server's `/hosts/lpd` file:

```
% cat /etc/hosts.lpd
stalker
folsm1
folsm2
folsm3
    .
```

You may also need to have the system's name in `/etc/hosts.equiv` for access control through the Berkeley R protocols, such as `rsh` (remote shell), `rcp` (remote copy), and `rlogin` (Berkeley remote login).

Accessing Remote Printers in AIX

Since AIX is rapidly becoming a major system in distributed computing, and since on many sites AIX machines must coexist with Berkeley UNIX machines, we're putting in a few comments about remote printing with AIX.

AIX systems can't act as BSD print servers, but they can send print requests to them, so UNIX network administrators must learn how to interface with AIX. However, configuring an AIX system is a completely different experience from UNIX System V or BSD UNIX, so don't rely on past experience with other UNIX versions.

To get an AIX machine set up to send files to a Berkeley server, start with the `/etc/qconfig` file. AIX configuration files are made up of *stanzas*. For the sake of a known reference, here is a BSD `printcap` entry that takes files sent to `hp2` on the local machine and directs them over to `laser2` on the `stalker` print server:

```
hp2:\
  :lp=:rm=stalker:rp=laser2:sd=/var/spool/lphp:
```

The `hp2` is a label, and `lp=` means no local print device. That the print server is `stalker` we can deduce from `rm=stalker`, and `rp=laser2` tells us that `laser2` is the printer wanted. The `sd=/var/spool/lphp` is the name of the local machine's spool directory.

Compare that to the AIX `/etc/qconfig` entry:

```
hp2:
     device = lph2
     host = stalker
     rq = lp
lph3:
     backend = /usr/lpd/rembak
```

Note that `hp2:` is a label, like a `case` in C. There are a couple of other obvious similarities: The `device = lph2` corresponds to `printcap`'s `rp=laser2`. It's also clear that `host = stalker` is equivalent to `printcap`'s `rm=stalker`.

Clients — The Reason for Servers

We've looked at several different kinds of servers, and print servers may be the most unglamorous of the lot. After all, they are usually nothing more than ordinary hosts with printers attached, to which remote hosts can spool their files. In fact, most of the network administrator's print server setup work is actually done on the `printcap` file of each host that will be sending to the print server.

Since we have seen a small piece of the network setup work required for these hosts, also called *clients*, why stop there? In the next chapter, we shall see precisely what these clients require for their piece of the net.

CHAPTER
12

Clients

Servers are an interesting, integral part of the network, but *client* systems are the reason servers exist on the net in the first place. A client receives services from other systems. X terminals are clients, and so is a server that takes YP services from another server. Even an otherwise freestanding system that takes mail service is a client. Of course, the most well-known client is a workstation, which consumes more services than any other client.

Getting each workstation up and ready to run on the network is a big job, and network administration tasks are intermixed with system administration tasks. First you need to get its Internet number, give it a host name, and put it in all the system's host tables. You must put in the network connections, partition the drives, install or reinstall the entire operating system, bring it up to the latest revision levels, power down, remove the tape unit, and bring it up on its own. Now the work *really* begins. The `/fstab` file must be modified to write to `/usr`. Then a ton of work is done in `rc.local`. Permissions must be changed in some of the files in `/etc`, and then you need to reboot the machine to make it all take. Next you must put in all the needed directories, edit the file system table, put in all of the mounting points needed for this particular machine, mount the directories, copy in the local software, copy in `printcap`, create all the spooling directories for the printer system, modify `motd`, modify the `crontabs` file, install `sendmail`, and set the machine up for remote administration. Only after all that is a workstation up, running, and network-ready. Fortunately, most clients are fairly easy to set up. (Workstations are a notable exception.) Clients consume one or more of the following services provided by servers:

- General network services such as Berkeley R protocols (`rlogin`, `rsh`, and `rcp`) and heterogeneous commands (`telnet`, `ftp`, and `tftp`).

- NFS remote procedure calls (RPCs).

- Compute serving.

- Network mail service, such as `smtp` and `sendmail`.

- Remote printing through (`lpr` via `printcap`).

- Remote batch processing on compute servers.

It is up to the network administrator to configure clients in such a way that they avail themselves of these services.

General Network Services

In order to set up a client for networking, you must locate and understand all of the client files that make networking happen. Many files are read during the initiation sequence (boot) in order to get pertinent information, and the kernel holds the information in its data structures. Let's follow a typical client's networking sequence.

The client receives general network services by invoking `inetd`, the Internet services daemon invoked from `rc.local` at boot time. This daemon looks up the services it will run in the `inetd.conf` file, whose records have the following format:

service_name socket_type protocol
  wait_status user_ID server_program server_arguments

The `/etc/services` file must be consulted for the additional data (notice the form: *service_name port_number/protocol aliases*):

```
% head /etc/services
# services
# network services
echo            7/udp       ping
echo            7/tcp       ping
discard  9/udp        sink null
discard  9/tcp        sink null
systat   11/udp               users
.

.
```

The *service name* is the Internet service name, the *port* number is the port number of the service, and *protocol* signifies one of many protocols, such as `tcp`, `udp`, `stream`, or `dgram`.

The `/etc/protocols` file is also read, so let's take a look:

```
% head protocols
# protocols
ip        O           IP
igmp            1           ICMP
igmp            3           IGMP
igmp            6           IGMP
```

Note that the file's form is *protocol_name protocol_number aliases*, referring to Internet protocols and the numbers assigned to them. The most commonly used protocols are `tcp`, `udp`, `ip`, and `icmp`.

Before we go on, let's stop a moment and review how all these files are linked together: The `inetd` network services daemon is invoked at boot time from `/etc/rc.local`. It looks up the services to provide as well as the port number and protocol from the `/etc/services` file, and it learns the protocol number from the `/etc/protocols` file. Then, from `inetd.conf`, it determines the rest of the network information.

Boot Time Initiation Files in `rc`

So much for some of the things the system does at boot time to reach out to the network. What do you, the network administrator, have to do to the machine in order to get it network-ready? The tasks are varied, but a lot of real work is done in relevant `rc` files by activating the appropriate code.

All unconfigured, fully networkable UNIX systems have their `rc` files ready to be configured as server or client by having all the pertinent lines of code commented in `rc` files. The art of setting up either as client or server is knowing which lines to uncomment. Although most of the work will be done in `/etc/rc.local`, it depends on the system you have. You will also do some work in `rc`, `rc.boot`, and possibly other files as well.

The first network requirement is to set the system's host name, either in `rc.boot`, or in `/etc/net/conf` from a *call* from `rc.boot`. You don't always have to do this, but if the machine is new or has been used before with another host name, often you must set the system's host name yourself.

Once that's done, go into `rc.local` and feast your eyes on one of the longest scripts you have ever seen. Essentially, `rc` scripts are a bunch of executable lines, and many of the commands mentioned are daemons. As network administrator, your job is to skim through this script and stop at network-related portions where you will add, comment, uncomment, or leave the code alone, depending on what condition it's in when you find it.

On systems like SVR4, Solaris, and AIX you have multiple `rc` files to configure, such as `rc.net` and `rc.nfs`. With AIX, you must also set up the ODM (object data manager) with the aid of SMIT, the AIX system management tool.

Your first stop in `rc.local` will be `portmap`, which must run on clients and servers, so make sure that its lines are uncommented. This daemon assigns the transport-level ports, the first part of network readiness. When you've found the port mapper, you've located the place where the network code starts.

Next stop are the `ypserv` and `ypbind` daemons.

```
if [ -f /etc/ypserv -a -d /var/yp/`domainname` ];
  then
    ypserv && echo -n ´  ypserv´
fi
if [ -f /usr/etc/ypbind ];
  then
    ypbind && echo -n ´  ypbind´
fi
```

These lines look for the existence of the executable files for the daemons and, on finding them, execute them. Don't be surprised if the lines in your script are a bit more complex.

A client system needs ypbind uncommented and ypserv commented, but *be careful*. Once we hung up our system during the boot process because we did this:

```
# if [ -f /etc/ypserv -a -d /var/yp/`domainname` ];
#    then
#       ypserv && echo -n ´  ypserv´
fi
if [ -f /usr/etc/ypbind ];
  then
    ypbind && echo -n ´  ypbind´
fi
```

We had a terrible time finding the error, that first uncommented ending fi. Commenting one line too many is equally fatal.

Ever since that disastrous day, we have made any commenting obvious by using white space and putting in our own comment descriptions:

```
#
#    ypserv commented out 9/16/93 BHH
# if [ -f /etc/ypserv -a -d /var/yp/`domainname` ];
#    then
#        ypserv && echo -n `  ypserv`
# fi
#
if [ -f /usr/etc/ypbind ];
   then
   ypbind && echo -n `  ypbind`
```

This removes all the necessary lines, and it leaves an audit trail that is easy to find.

Move on to `ifconfig`. This daemon must be present for both servers and clients, and you must be sure that it has the right interface number. Any machine that is on the net has one network interface, number 0, and if it's an Intel device, it will be `ie0` and the executable line of the `if` statement will be:.

```
      ifconfig ie0 netmask +
```

You must either provide the network mask or have it in the YP database. In this example, the `+` points to the YP database.

If you don't have YP, the executable `ifconfig` line for a nonsubnetted class B network is

```
      ifconfig ie0 netmask 255.255.0.0
```

Time to move on to the `rpc.statd` and `rpc.lockd` daemons. If your software does not need them, comment both of them.

Cruise on to the NFS daemons, `biod` and `nfsd`, stopping to be sure they are there, have large enough arguments, and are uncommented. `nfsd` should have an argument of 8 to 16, while `biod` should have an argument of 4 to 6. You will probably want to stop at `rwhod` and comment it so it won't be active, for this daemon draws heavily on resources. You don't need it; instead, have your users use `rsh` to execute a `who`.

The last stop in `rc.local` will probably be the `route` command, which may not be present. If it isn't, you'll have to add it whenever the client will do any routing or even if it simply needs to manipulate the routing tables. When would that happen? More often than you might imagine, if your machines are subnetworked.

On a subnet, it's a distinct possibility that a client will have more than one Ethernet port. If it does, technically it's a router, and you'll need the `route` daemon and `route` tables set.

Client systems don't normally do routing, but if a client has a single interface port, then it will need to modify the routing tables to pass routing information. For example, if there is a router on the network that the client must access, the router must be in the client's `route` table. The way you `add` an enhanced router called a gateway to a client's `route` table is by putting the following entry at the end of `rc.local` (the gateway's name is `hermes`):

```
/usr/etc/route add 0 hermes 1
```

The information in this entry will be added to the `route` table in the client's kernel. Note that the hop count is `1`, and the `0` in the destination field wildcards the destination.

Adding a Gateway

If your site is like most other networked sites, your networking needs have grown more quickly than you ever anticipated, and you must subnet to relieve the load. You also may have already discovered that you must access other networks sooner than you realized. For both of these reasons, you might as well plan on learning how to install routers (for homogeneous systems) and gateways (for heterogeneous systems). We're going to add another gateway, called `mfg-gate`, for practice.

Whenever a subnet or gateway is added, you must update every host on your piece of the network. We've seen how to add some pertinent information to a client's `rc.local` file when adding a gateway, but that's not quite enough. There's a bit more to do in each client's `/etc/hosts` files. If you have YP, count your blessings, because you can do all of your workstations' `hosts` files in one shot from YP's source file.

The `hosts` file is a long, continuous list of addresses and host names. There's nothing executable here. What you want to do is add the name of the gateway and its Internet address to the `/etc/hosts` table so that the information gets into the kernel. Then whenever the kernel sees the name `mfg-gate` in its internal host tables, it will know its Internet address.

A *gateway device* is well named, because it actually is a gateway to another network. Let's imagine that you were given the `mfg` network name from the *manufacturing* group, and you must do whatever is necessary for your users to access it. Go to your piece of `/etc/hosts` and insert the network name and Internet address as a comment so that you, the human being, can easily find it again in this long file. Then add the actual `mfg-gate` gateway entry immediately following.

```
128.213.58.136    gaff
#
# 133.250.0.0      mfg-net
133.250.0.1       mfg-gate
```

If you are lucky enough to have YP, all you need to do is to `make` YP so the network knows about `mfg-gate`. If you are not running YP, you may have to make this addition manually to every host in the domain.

Now you add the router information to every client's `rc` file at the end of `rc.local`. Let's put this addition at the end of `rc.local`, right after `hermes`:

```
        .

        .
/usr/etc/route add 0 hermes 1
# mgf gateway added 9/21/90 BHH
/usr/etc/route add  mfg-net mfg-gate 1
```

sendmail

One of the last things you do to set up the client system for networking is prepare it to bring up `sendmail`. However, this subject is so complex, we gave it a chapter of its own. Please refer to
Chapter 16.

A Special Kind of Client

In this chapter we saw how clients compare with the rest of the
machines on the network, but in the next chapter we shall look at
the most demanding client of all — the workstation.

CHAPTER

13

Setting Up a Workstation

Workstations were created in the early 1980s, and they singlehandedly created what we now call distributed computing. Their rapid popularity made fortunes for both Sun and Apollo, and soon heavyweights like Hewlett-Packard, DEC, and IBM got into the market. This resulted in a proliferation of various UNIX versions for workstations, including SunOS, ULTRIX, HPUX and AIX.

All these UNIX versions were a mixed blessing for the people who administer their systems. UNIX versions might look more or less the same to the user, but to the system administrator they are very different, and the more versions of UNIX there are on the network, the more administration work there is to do. Then when networks started to proliferate, system administrators also had to become network administrators, and their workloads increased proportionately. Today's UNIX administrators may be expected to run all the different UNIX systems on the net as well as take care of the network itself, and setting up various workstations is something they do quite often.

Setting up workstations is an ongoing job. You set them up when they arrive, every time a new operating system release comes out, whenever there is an update tape for the operating system, each time the systems are moved or transferred, and whenever they lose a hard disk. At first, setting up a workstation is rather intimidating, but after a while you can do it in your sleep.

Workstations used to have two common configurations, diskless and dataless. The diskless workstation had no disk of its own and relied on a server, and therefore the network, for all of its needs. It even had to boot from the network. The dataless workstation had its own disk for the system, the swap area, and /usr, but relied on the file server for most of its other needs.

The workstations coming out today are quite different from the older ones, and you rarely see a new diskless workstation anymore. In fact, IBM recommends that its RS/6000 550 be configured with three disks, because it runs better if the swap area is *striped* across the center of all three disks. Most sites have a combination of older and newer workstations, and the older ones are gradually being phased out. The latest desktop and departmental workstations are larger, much more powerful, and have more processors and more memory than ever before.

Workstations used to run Berkeley-based operating systems exclusively, because of BSD's built-in Ethernet and NFS features and dependencies. For example, DEC's ULTRIX (BSD 4.2) and Sun's SunOS (BSD 4.3) were two common workstation systems, and they are running on systems to this day. Then along came AT&T's System 5 Release 4 and AIX, which incorporate most of the Berkeley networking features. UNIX systems continued to evolve, with OSF/1 trying to join the list of UNIX variations, while Sun's software division successfully marketed its own version of SVR4, called Solaris, to attempt unification. (Solaris is not only for the Sun SPARC platform but for the Intel X86 family as well.)

Because there are more workstations than any other type of machine on the network, their configuration warrants separate discussion. After all, part of any system configuration is hooking it up to the network, and you do more workstations than any other machine. We're going to look at how to hardware-configure a single-disk Sun workstation first, and then look at some of the differences in installation for an IBM AIX system. These should provide maximum contrast.

Sun and IBM currently share over 60 percent of the workstation market. They are an interesting contrast. Sun practically invented the

market, and their systems are a do-it-yourself affair to set up. Some
systems ship with the frame buffer and memory cards separate, and you
do the installation. IBM also ships their 5XX workstations as an erector
set, but a field engineer will either do the installation or complete the
installation.

Out of the Box

If this this is your first workstation installation, open the manual
set before unboxing the workstation components, and find the
installation instructions. Then roll up your sleeves and take the
system out of the box. The CPU box is the first piece of hardware
to be worked on.

On any system where you have to install cards or populate them,
such as memory cards, be sure to ground yourself to the system's
frame with a grounding cuff and wire before touching any boards
or SIMMs, for electrostatic discharge kills ICs. SPARCstations have
everything on one card.

Now take the monitor from its box and *carefully* put it down
where it's going to live. Don't drop, skid, or bounce the monitor,
or you may wind up with a black screen and a narrow stripe for an
image. Plug the monitor cable into the frame buffer port at the back
of the CPU box.

Suns are frequently purchased with several peripheral boxes for
add-ons, such as tapes or CD drives. The users decide how they
want them put on the desktop. Most users will stack each peripheral on top of the CPU box and have the monitor put on top of
the whole stack, putting the screen at eyelevel or slightly above.

Attach the keyboard to the monitor cable and anchor the cable
to the monitor's base. Attach the mouse to the keyboard, and put
it on the right or the left, depending on the user's hand of choice.
Attach the Ethernet cable to the DB-25 on the top back of the CPU
box, and lock it. If a printer is to be installed, cable it to the CPU
box's parallel port now. If a tape-cassette/disk expansion unit is to
be added, remove the expansion-port terminator from the CPU
box's back, and attach the expansion unit's cable. Keeping a spare
terminator handy will save time if you plan to do a lot of these.

Now all that you need to do is attach the power cables — one to the monitor, one from the wall to the CPU box, and another from the optional expansion unit to the CPU box.

Smoke Test

According to an amusing legend in the trade, there is a small puff of smoke deliberately trapped in every integrated circuit, and the unit will fail if it ever gets out. Thus the name "smoke test," where you let the system come up and sit on its prompt for 24 hours for a burn-in. If everything is installed properly, there will be no smoke. If not, you will become well acquainted with your area field engineer or service rep.

If you have enough room in your own office to set up the workstations, attach them to a spare Ethernet port to configure them. This way you can do other work in the comfort and convenience of your own office while the tapes are being read in.

Configuration

Factory disk partitioning is supposed to cover the needs of most sites, but you can never count on it. At some sites, workstations run memory-intensive jobs on desktop units, and even when you have small drives, 50 megabytes of a 91-megabyte drive can be devoted to the swap area. When you are forced to live with older, smaller workstations, you must use creative disk partitioning until you can move up to larger workstations with 128 to 512 megabytes of RAM, but even then you can expect to do some disk partitioning, because large, real memory demands large, multiple swap disk areas and disk access schemes like striping.

When software is unbundled, only the essential stuff goes on the machine, and the rest, sometimes referred to as *cluster* software, is usually put on one of the domain's major file servers. After all, it doesn't make sense to store distribution software on each system when it can be served from a file server. Instead, you install a minimal /usr and mount it read-only. However, you have to watch its size, because people are always putting things in there. Even vendors suggest that you install software there. Paring down /usr saves an lot of local disk space that can be used for something else.

In order to repartition a workstation's disk, it must be booted from tape or diskette to run under a memory-resident version of UNIX. Other options are loading the operating system from the network or booting from a "shoebox" resident disk drive.

There have been many advances over the years to make repartitioning easier and faster. Larger Sun systems use SMD or IPI drives and controllers, not SCSI drives, so partitioning can be done on the live system in multi-user mode; only the root disk requires that the memory-resident version of UNIX be used. Larger AIX systems, such as RISC 6000s, have multiple disks, so only the root disk needs repartitioning. Also, disk space is dynamic on AIX, so expansions should not come up too often. However, smaller units like SPARCstations do not have these luxuries, so they must be done the hard way. Use the OEM's format utility to repartition, for it allows the disks to be selected and current disk partitions to be displayed, resized, or reformatted.

When repartitioning, create a map of what the partitions are going to look like when the partitioning is completed, especially when you are making up a partition table. Wouldn't it be easier to visualize how much space is used if you could see the partitions in graph form? That is precisely what dedicated file servers like Auspex's NS servers do with the format command.

It takes a little math to divide the disk into the clean, even cylinder boundaries required. The initial output of format's partition option will show you the disk layout in number of sectors, writable surfaces (heads), and cylinders. From there you can calculate the remaining figures. Following is a partitioning table that gives the system 50 megabytes of swap at the cost of reducing all other partitions: It is the layout of a Wren II as shipped by Sun and as seen from the Sun format command.

```
partition a - start cylinder 0, #blocks   10500(60/0/0)
partition b - start cylinder 318, #blocks 99925(571/0/0)
partition c - start cylinder 0, #blocks  178500(1020/0/0)
partition d - start cylinder 0, #blocks  0(/0/0)
partition e - start cylinder 0, #blocks  0(/0/0)
partition f - start cylinder 0, #blocks  0(/0/0)
partition g - start cylinder 60,#blocks  45150(258/0/0)
partition h - start cylinder 889,#blocks 22925(131/0/0)
```

Since all partitions must fall on even cylinder boundaries, there can be nothing but 0 for head and sector. The notation (60/0/0) is track 60, head 0, sector 0, and the 10500 is 10,500 blocks. On this particular drive there are 175 blocks per cylinder, and each block is 512 bytes (plus overhead), so you can save time by typing in 60/.

Many workstations have conventions that should be known before partitioning them. For example, DEC and Sun systems have partitions A through H, and both traditionally use the C partition as an overlap that encompasses the entire disk. Sun uses a G partition to straddle the E and F partitions, and the B partition is used for the swap area on the root disk. It doesn't have to be this way, but it's traditional.

Disk management systems are one of the new trends in workstation computing. For instance, AIX uses a disk management system called LVM (logical volume manager) that allows up to 256 partitions, a far cry from the eight traditionally provided by most BSD-based systems. Similar virtual disk systems are provided by Sun and Auspex. In time, virtual disk management should be available for most systems.

Reloading the System

If you are repartitioning, you have a problem once a full repartitioning is complete: The interactive installation software has allowed you to repartition all of the available disk partitions, A through H, and now there is no system on disk. So when the installation software asks you if you want to reinstall the system, naturally the answer is yes. You can load about 12 diskettes, or you can use tape and let it go, stopping by from time to time to type in `yes` to the occasional `do you want to continue?`: prompt. Loading the system over the network or via a disk-to-disk copy is even faster.

Repartitioning

You will often need to repartition a system that is already in use, such as when you need to expand the swap area or the `/usr` partition. Part of the reason for this is that you don't size the swap area correctly on the first try. Since most of the time the sizes of the swap areas are determined from past experience, you *hope*, but don't necessarily *expect*, them to work right away. Experienced administrators know that since networked systems are used more heavily than standalone machines, the sizes of their swap areas need to be changed often until they are the best size. In fact, it's not unusual to have to change them more than once before you get them right.

You find out about missized swap areas after you set up your machines. Usually, users wander into your office complaining that their jobs don't run well. A little work with `vmstat` reveals the problem: The machine is out of swap space again. If you're running AIX on an RS/6000, you can increase swap space dynamically, but if not, you will have to repartition.

Why not increase your swap area as much as possible with a little forethought and planning? You can start by laying out your disk for expandability when you first create the system. Locate the swap partition in the middle tracks for efficiency and miscellaneous file systems like Sun's `/files` at the outer edge for convenience. In the middle tracks, the heads will have the least movement, and any requests for disk access will move the heads a minimum amount. Excessive head movement is called contention and is to be avoided at all costs. If you also locate swap at the next-to-last group of cylinders towards the outer edge, then you can steal from the last partition on the track when you need to expand.

Single-disk workstations use the following default locations:

Inner (center) tracks	`root`
Tracks next to center	`/usr`
Middle tracks	Swap area
Tracks on outer edge	Miscellaneous, like Sun's `/files`

A suffix is added to the disk's name so you know which partition you're dealing with, but don't let the disk suffix fool you. They may be in alphabetical order, but their actual *layout* is

`a`	`root`	Inner (center)
`g`	`/usr`	Next
`b`	Swap	Middle
`h`	Files	Outer edge

Just for clarification, partition `c` is the whole disk, and `e` and `f` are not used for default partitioning.

The OEM's disk layout is not exactly something that someone thought up in the shower one morning. There are good reasons for what they do. However, if you are expanding a user's swap area, you might not have thought about disk swapping much, and you may start from scratch and repartition the whole disk, and then read in the entire operating system and other software. But that could take an entire day! The time can be improved if you do it with tape and are using a good installation script, cutting down the process to three or four hours, two from the network, but that's still an awfully long time. Fortunately, disk swap repartitioning can be easier yet.

Picture the disk as a slice through an onion. If you leave the inner rings (cylinders) alone, you can peel off the outer two sets of rings (cylinders) and put them back. One slip of the knife, however, and all you have is minced onion. Likewise, if you screw up the partitioning job, the disks must be repartitioned from scratch, and the operating system must be read in again. How do you avoid this problem?

Start with your system's disk formatting and partitioning utility, probably called `format`. Have it give you the current partition layout: Note that `root` is at the center, `/usr` is next to it, and swap next to that. Calculator in hand, create a map of the current usage by cylinders. Don't bother with heads, tracks, or sectors, since file systems can only be created on even cylinder boundaries. Here is a typical entry for the `root` partition:

```
part    start    size    [blocks(cyls/tracks/sectors)]

a       0        10764   (26/0/0)
```

The worst kind partitioning utility asks for the start cylinder and the number of blocks it will be in length. You can tell it the start cylinder easily enough, but how can you tell it the exact number of cylinders? It's too easy to end up losing part of a cylinder. The best partitioning utilities allow you to give the size in blocks or cylinders, like `26/0/0`, so you are sure of even cylinder alignment. You can even shortcut the process and enter `26/`. Be sure to enter the slash, or it will think you mean blocks, and you will get absurdities like having a 26-block `root` partition on which only the world's smallest operating system will fit.

By recalculating the partition table so that `root` and `/usr` are left untouched, you avoid having to read in either, and if all you destroy is the `/files` partition, only the contents of transient files like `mail` and `/tmp` will be lost. Have the users read their mail or copy it to the file server's partitions, and then make your move.

Boot the system from the first installation diskette or tape, and repartion swap and `/files`. Now go to the software installation part, skip `root` and `/usr`, and just read in `/files`. The whole process (minus planning) takes about 15 minutes.

Swapping Multiple-Disk Systems

Multiple-disk systems take an entirely different approach. Ideally you would stripe your swap partitions across three disks, and these multiple swap partitions reside at the disk's track center. Current disk partitioning technologies allow disk *striping*, the creation of identically sized and located physical partitions on multiple disks that are treated by the system as a single virtual disk. This is available from many OEMs, including Sun, IBM, and Auspex.

When you have this sort of swap layout, you increase swap by adding partitions to the swap "pool." On a system like UTS, you can use the `pagdev` command to dynamically add another swap partition. However, you can't take a swap partition away dynamically on any system.

Additional swap partitions can be brought on line with commands like Sun's `swapon` command. Typically, `rc` will do the following to bring up all swap areas on boot:

```
swapon -a >/dev/null
```

Thus, if you care to hold any swap areas in reserve, you will have to change the lines in `rc`, and one particular swap partition can be enabled with `swapon /dev/dsk3b`.

Initial Configuration

Now the new system is booted for the first time from its own disk. Write down the workstation's host ID number, because Sun ships it as the system's initial `root` password. (Other OEMs have no `root` password as shipped). The first screenful of information will repeat the host-ID number and give you the Ethernet address that is burned into a very small PROM on the motherboard. Write them both down and keep them handy.

A workstation must be on the Ethernet when being configured; therefore, the installation cannot go beyond this stage until it contacts the network. It must verify that you have given it a good YP-domain name and a unique Internet number when going through the network part of the installation.

The system's `boot` program will run you through an installation procedure that will alter `/etc/net.conf`, but don't change the file directly unless you are skillful as an administrator.

The network installation software will ask if the workstation is to be *diskless, networked,* or *standalone.* "How can a workstation be a standalone machine?" you may ask. After all, a workstation's ability to be on the local net is one of its principal design features, along with being intended for use by one person and being graphics-oriented. But there are several conditions in which a workstation can stand alone: the user is an individual consultant working at home; the department has one person; the user is not on NFS or YP but accesses the organization's network via `ftp` and `telnet`; and the users access the Internet but are not part of a network domain. However, most of the time you will pick *networked* as your category.

When the network software asks for the time zone, give it a simple answer like `pst` for Pacific Standard Time or the number of hours away from Greenwich.

It will ask for the Internet number, which you get from the administrator of Internet numbers at your site. You will be asked the name of the system (`hostname`) and the name of the YP domain by which it will be served. The software must modify `/etc/net.conf` and `/etc/rc.boot` before it will allow the boot process to continue, but once the system puts itself on the net, you can continue with the system installation.

Set up your system with the greatest of care, for if you upset the new system with bad information, you will have a long evening, because it will not let you proceed until the answers are right. Also, a badly set-up system will flood the network with extraneous packets that cause further error generation.

At the end of the question-and-answer session, change the system's `root` password to something other than the system serial number, or create one if the system came from the factory without a password. Now reboot the system. By the way, if you are going to reconfigure the kernel, now is as good a time as any.

Not all installations are clean read-in-one-tape affairs. All too frequently, the installation must be augmented by an additional tape to bring the system to a desired release level. A case in point was SunOS 4.0.2 from 4.0. You had to load the 4.0.1 installation tape and get a system going before you could read in a 4.0.2 `tar` tape on top of the original 4.0.1. That installation was tedious from tape, and from diskette it must have been a nightmare. Most of the time you end up working off releases with a patch tape.

Kernel Reconfiguration

A poorly configured workstation kernel reacts badly with the net, causing time-outs and unnecessary retransmissions, but most sites don't reconfigure workstation kernels because of the inconvenience involved. Often you *can't* create a kernel on old workstations because they lack space for cluster software. This is unfortunate, because the tables are sized on the small side, and increasing `maxusers` could increase performance. Thus, administrators who are able to take this parameter from 8 to the system maximum of 128 can get a process table size that is workable. So even though it's easier not to reconfigure a system, reconfiguring is just plain practical, because the GENERIC kernel's tables are too small for most applications, and the size of its devices section is probably too large for the devices that currently run on the machine. Besides, undersized kernel tables beat up the network.

A workstation's configuration file is taken from places like:

```
/usr/cluster/devl/config/share/sys/sun/conf/GENERIC
```

There is only one configurable parameter in the file, `maxusers`, the multiplier for most of the system's tables. For sizing anything else, look to files like `param.h`. The biggest workstation configuration task is stripping the GENERIC file of unnecessary devices, requiring an intimate knowledge of the bus and the hardware.

When you have removed all devices from the configuration file that you neither own nor ever expect to own, and you have sized the system tables so that they will not rob memory needlessly but will allow the system to do its work without thrashing, `make` the kernel, install it, and see if it works. Rename the old kernel just in case so that you will have a working kernel to fall back on.

If you installed the system with a portable shoebox, shut down the new system, power it down, and remove the expansion unit. (If you try to remove it under power, you may well burn out internal fuses, wreck a hard disk, or worse.)

rc

We've seen the `rc` modifications that are required for client systems in Chapter 12, but here is a short review with specifics for workstations.

Almost everything you will need in the boot file `/etc/rc.local` is uncommented in the file, and you modify it by judicious commenting. You can get rid of unnecessary system overhead by commenting the `rwho` daemon. If your software doesn't need file locking, comment `lockd` and `stat`. For a workstation, you comment `ypserv` and uncomment `ypbind`. At the end of the file you add code for things like adding a `route` daemon or adding all of your network gateways.

Be sure that you have a reasonable number of `biod` and `nfsd` daemons. You can increase the number of `nfsd` daemons to get better network performance, but don't be overgenerous with `biod` daemons, for too many will defeat your purpose by flooding the net. To handle a minimum of network traffic, you need four `biod` daemons and eight `nfsd` daemons.

On the other hand, the number of `nfsd` daemons can get much larger on high-end systems like departmental workstations, because they need higher NFS throughput.

The network administrator's place to configure the workstations is `rc.local`, so don't be afraid to get in there and work with it.

Configuring for Use

With the system up and on the net, but still in single-user mode, it is time to ready the system for its intended work. The `/usr` directory is normally set up as read-only, so you need to change it to read/write while you add mount points. Change it back to read-only when you're through.

While you're at it, make /etc/utmp and /dev/kmem writable as well, because Sunview and X need to write to them. Reboot the system after altering /etc/fstab to make /usr writable.

/etc/fstab

It is important to modify the fstab file, because workstations mount from servers here. Following is a typical entry, which mounts the tool area with a soft mount:

```
svr2:/usr/tools /usr/tools nfs rw,hard,noquota,bg,intr 0 0
```

Here is where the mount of the user's file system is made to happen. Be sure to mount read-only all systems that do not require writing. Users may want cluster software mounted as writable, but be aware that they may need the write link only to use fortunes. Is the access of games worth risking an unauthorized write? It's your decision, because it affects the configuration of networked machines. Some games intended for multiple players utilize broadcasts, which really beat up the network because every machine has to respond.

Setting the mount options allows you the liberty of increasing performance. Increasing timeout and retry parameters will keep the workstation trying harder and reduce the number of timeout errors. Adding noquota will speed up booting. Soft mounts, on the other hand, increase timeout errors and should only be used on small, quiet networks if at all.

Make all fstab files the same, if possible, because maintenance will be easier. Much confusion is saved if both sides of the mount have the same name, such as having /usr/users on the workstations mount to /usr/users on the server. The exceptions are system-specific directories on the server. For example, /usr/tools/sun4 on the server will be mounted simply as /usr/tools on a Sun workstation.

For sites with many workstations, you will save a lot of time and eliminate errors if you have a single distribution of `fstab` to install. Simply keep it in your system distribution directory on the file server, and mount it early in the installation. However, if you decide to use a generic `fstab` and distribute it to all workstations, you must comment out or delete entries that will not be used on each workstation.

You may also want to automate the installation with a script stored in the same area. Automated installations can save you two to four hours on each workstation, and with 50 workstations on a site, the total time saved will be considerable. Automated installations also allow you to give the task to less skilled people, like your operators, and that leaves you free to go on to something else.

After putting file systems in `fstab`, don't forget to create the mount points. On rare occasions, you may have to create symbolic links, such as when you are unable to mount to wherever a user's software expects to find a file. Don't get carried away with symbolic links, though, because they make archives a nightmare.

YP

Doing user maintenance without YP is hard to imagine. Its convenience is wonderful, but the files affected by YP must be modified in order to take advantage of it. For example, `/etc/passwd` must be cleaned out of everything but nonhuman entries in the YP version, and a jump point must be added to get over to the YP version.

Perhaps the most critical file for YP conversion is `/etc/hosts`. If the workstation version does not jump to the YP database version of `hosts`, the system will never get off the ground. Under YP, the `hosts` file is short and sweet. It contains only a `loopback` entry with the standard address `127.0.0.1` (reserved for this purpose) and the system's name and Internet number:

```
128.213.58.55       stalker
127.0.0.1           localhost
```

The /etc/passwd file is just as short with YP, containing only root and daemon and the + entry, a kick-off to YP:

```
root:i2s3WD40dRaNo:0:1:Super User:/:/bin/sh
daemon:*:1:1:System Daemons:/:
+:0:0:::
```

/etc/crontabs

You will want to add or remove accounting commands from /var/spool/cron/crontabs/root. Most workstations do not run accounting, so you should add your own line to flush /tmp and clean out core files.

```
13 0 * * * find /tmp -mtime +3 -exec rm -f {} \;
16 0 * * * find / -type f -name core -exec re -f {} \;
```

/etc/printcap

Workstations share printers as well as files, and most sites will have one or more systems set up as print servers. Since few workstations will have locally attached printers, the local printcap file must be changed to access the remote printers. Try keeping a copy of all common files like printcap in a system group directory on the server so you can copy it to the workstations when you are setting them up. The printcap file could also be put into the YP database as well, but remember that you must create an empty printcap file in /etc if printcap is to be served by YP. A typical printcap entry for a remote printer looks like this:

```
laser1|hp1:\
    :lp=:rm=psvr2:rp=hplaser:st=/var/spool/hp1:
```

Recall that `lp` is the device name of the printer (always set to null for remote printers), `rm` is the remote machine name, and `rp` is the remote printer name. For further details on `printcap`, refer to Chapter 11.

YP Access Control

Without setup, the system won't allow access to other systems, so now is the time to make access happen. You must modify `/.rhosts`, `/etc/netgroup`, and `/etc/hosts.equiv` so that YP can serve these files. The `hosts.equiv` file consists of one line containing a single character, a `+`. We'll see how to do all this in Chapter 14.

Server Modifications for Workstations

You must tell the server about the addition of a new workstation. At the very least, the workstation's host name and Ethernet address will have to be added to the YP master's source file, `/etc/hosts`. If the YP master server is separate from the file server, wherever the YP master is located is where the change must be made. If the workstation is mounting a unique file system (unlikely but possible), the server's `/etc/exports` file will also have to be modified. Usually, all workstations in a group will be the same, so if you know that you are going to add 15 workstations in the next three months, add their host names and network addresses to the YP host file all at the same time.

sendmail

The last step is to be sure that `sendmail` is functional. For a workstation client, you will want to create a symbolic link from `/etc/sendmail.cf` to `/usr/lib/sendmail.subsidiary.cf`. Take little for granted. Be sure the `host` file makes the name of the mail master known and that the workstation's `sendmail.cf` file reflects the same system name.

The last touch will be to add the workstation's and user's names to the mail server's `aliases` file, such as:

```
bob:rfriedmn@csus
```

AIX

Originally, all workstations were BSD-based, because only Berkeley UNIX was network-ready. At that time network administration duties were less complex, mainly knowing the differences between BSD 4.2 and 4.3. The differences were significant. For example, YP was different on each version, and the two YP versions were not compatible at the server. Also, files and directories were different. For example, 4.2 still had `/bin`, but by 4.3 `/bin` was gone, and `/var` was present.

However, that kind of simplicity was too good to last. Just prior to this period, there were only two main versions of UNIX, BSD UNIX and AT&T UNIX (System 5 Releases 2 and 3). Everyone was waiting for AT&T to come out with System V Release 4, and many UNIX people hoped it would tie divergent releases of UNIX back together again under one super-enhanced version. That would have made life easier for the people who have to administer the machines. Sun Microsystems pioneered the workstation/server technology using BSD-based UNIX on their systems, and they spent a lot of time and effort with AT&T to make System V Release 4 a viable super-release. However, alarmed at the prospect of a powerful alliance between Sun and AT&T, other major players in the industry made a move to wrest control of UNIX away from AT&T, and the Open Software Foundation was created. A UNIX-like operating system was created called OSF/1, and although most of the original OSF members eventually backed out of using it, the move away from a single version of UNIX was begun.

The Intel X86 family shaped UNIX to some extent as well. These processors created the personal computer market. In time, these PCs became quite powerful. The 386SX and 386DX were more than powerful enough to run a non-Windows version of UNIX. Think about it; XENIX was created on the 286. The 486 had the power needed for the X Window System. The Intel Pentium is more than capable of being the heart of a high-end workstation with its near-RISC performance added to DOS and Microsoft Windows capability. It was natural, therefore, that UNIX systems on the X86 finally became workstation-capable.

Meanwhile, IBM, an OSF member, was busy creating its own niche in the UNIX workstation market. After one or two false starts, it hit the marketplace with a winner, its RISC/6000 line. These systems are powerful and have an innovative UNIX-variant operating system, AIX. AIX is POSIX-compliant, meaning that it is like UNIX in some ways. From the users' point of view, everything except the printer queue is the same. There are even front ends to their `enq` and `qprt` queuing system to make it look like `lp` or `lpr`. Users don't feel the difference until they need to see the queue or remove files from it.

However, to administrators there is a world of difference between AIX and UNIX. AIX has everything that you expect of a fully networked UNIX system, and it is interesting, but it isn't really UNIX. There are significant differences in the spooler, the disk management system (called LVM for logical volume manager), and the system database manager, the ODM, for Object Data Manager.

The ODM is capable of loading every known IBM driver. It stores most of the system's configuration in its database. The system will consult the ODM before the configuration files. In fact, it will frequently consult the ODM and ignore the configuration files. For example, at boot time it looks at the host and network information in the ODM, completely ignoring configuration data in the `rc` files.

Picture this scenario, found in early AIX 4.X releases. The system boots but fails to contact the network. It hangs in there, trying to bomb the net with all kinds of requests, and complains with the message `YP server unreachable`.

Reboot and halt the initialization process just before it contacts the network daemons. When you doublecheck `rc.nfs` and `rc.net`, everything is in order. It has the right netmask, host address, hostname, and everything else. Now you bring up `smit`, the IBM system administrator's do-all-fits-all program, and see that it does not know the path to the router and has the wrong netmask. It was put in as `255.255.255.0`, and now it's `255.255.0.0`! How it changes that information in the ODM is unknown, but it does it. If you administer these machines, then you need to be aware of this problem.

Frequently, the system fails to bring up the network interface as well. You have to manually bring it up with the command

```
ifconfig en0 up
```

and then manually run `rc.net`, followed by `rc.nfs`. Last, you have to run `rc.local`, and the system will be up. This problem is prevalent after a power failure. The ODM must be manipulated with `smit` because manual editing of the system configuration files will not update the ODM.

The next mystery of AIX is LVM, the Logical Volume Manager. AIX places a virtual layer of disk management between the OS and the physical disks. The disks are remapped into virtual disks which can mirror any disk, exceed the capacity of any one physical disk by concatenation, or strip a virtual disk across several physical disks. Disks are dynamically expandable as long as there is reserve space. Its management can look complex, but `smit` does a good job of covering the implementation details.

Installation

The first system install on an AIX system will have to be a scratch install. It is possible to install AIX by taking an image of a system across the network, but obviously you have to start somewhere, and the first install is by tape. If you already have AIX on the system and are doing an update, you will want to save files like

```
/etc/filesystems
/etc/qconfig
/etc/hosts
/etc/rc.net
/etc/rc.nfs
```

If the tape drive has not been installed yet, install it as /dev/rmt0. AIX will ignore it unless it is attached; you cannot install or preinstall any device that is not attached physically.

AIX machines have a key, just like an automobile. Turn the key from *normal* to *service*. Put tape 1 in the drive and power up the drive first, then the AIX system. The drive will read for a while, and there will be no sign of life from the console. AIX does not turn control over to the console when either loading or booting. If the system has anything to say, it will do it to the digital display of the front panel of the CPU box. Finally, it will contact the CRT and ask if you want to continue. Hit the F1 key to acknowledge. You now have a memory-resident UNIX system.

You will have several options to deal with. Select a complete install (versus preservation). Pick your language (English, or whatever). Pick your install device — tape. Once past this phase, you are partially loaded. Shut down the system and key over to the "normal" position, and then let the system boot by itself.

Reload tape one and run a **smit** install. You will have to walk through the **smit** menus, moving from software product to install software to update software. You will now be faced with the monumental task of selecting the software products you want to install. It's a long list and will take up a lot of room if you take it all. Use F4 to get a long list and F7 to select your options. You can use all defaults, but be sure to take the option

```
COMMIT=yes
```

Post Install Customization

If you manage to live through all that, you now have to make a real system out of what you got from tape. There may be a single-user mode available at boot, but none that we know of. Watch the console carefully as the system boots, and just before it starts the network daemons, kill `rc` with a ^C.

smit

Configure the network interface with `smit`. You will not boot successfully if you bypass this step; only `smit` can change the ODM database. Select the network interface from `smit`. The interface for the Ethernet is `en0`. There is a separate interface for IEEE 802. Set the network mask, and give `smit` the system's Internet number, the router's Internet number, and the network mask.

It is handy, after your first install, to make a floppy disk of the files that you need to modify, like `filesystems` and `qconfig`.

Now is the time you can modify any partitions. Perhaps you will want to create a `/usr/work` area. If the file system already exists, use `smit` to remove it. The long-hand commands used are

```
unmount /usr/work
rmfs /usr/work
rmlv/lv00     # remove the logical volume
```

Now the deed is done. Add the new file system (or enlarge it) by following this path in `smit`:

    smit -> physical devices -> file systems -> add/change/show \
    -> JFS (Journaled File Systems) -> add a JFS

If you want to change the size of the page disk, and most sites will, use `chps` with the `-s` option. If you want to enlarge volume group `myvg` and add four logical partitions, use

```
chps -s'8' hd 6
```

Change protections wherever necessary. For example,

```
chmod 4755 /etc/swcons
chmod 644 /dev/kmem
```

Before leaving the configuration process, be sure to use **smit** one more time to check the ODM. Follow this **smit** menu path:

smit ->communications-> TCP/IP->mun config->en0->NFS->NFS ->conf

Be sure the system knows its

- Host name
- Internet number
- Network mask
- Network interface
- Gateway (router) address

Network Image Installs

If you have many AIX workstations, you will probably want to do your remaining installs over the network. Create an image on your existing system. It should be an archetype system, because you will rubberstamp it all over your domain.

Once you have your image on your donor machine, write down the donor system's Internet number. Add to your notes the information you will want to put on the new workstation. The information needed is

- The image server name and Internet number

- The netmask

- The router's Internet address (if you have to pass through the router)

- The name and Internet number of the new system

You will need a set of three floppy disks from your IBM SE to start the net install.

Since this is an install, you will have to have the AIX system keyed to service mode. Power the system on and insert the first floppy. The first two diskettes will run without accessing the console. Only the LED display will show any signs of life. Code C09 shows it's reading the floppy, and C07 is a demand for another diskette. At the end of floppy 2, you will go interactive as the control turns over to the CRT. Hit F1 to go interactive.

Install diskette three, set your time zone, and change the installation mode from floppy to the network. You will be asked for the client IP address, the server IP address, and the netmask. You will also be asked to respond Y or N if you want to use a gateway. If the answer is yes, you need to give the gateway (router) address and, believe it or not, the type of interface connector (such as DB15). The install will take about 20 minutes over a moderately loaded network.

Remote Administration

As you read these lines, workstations are being set up somewhere to take care of new kinds of tasks, and new kinds of servers are being created to handle them. As always, network administrators must be able to adapt to each new wrinkle and addition. Being prepared for change is an administrator's survival skill.

One area of development that relates specifically to network administrators is remote administration, and new developments will be forthcoming. For now, implementing remote administration requires special work on all workstations, involving access control. We'll see how to do that in the next chapter.

CHAPTER
14

Security and Access Control

In previous chapters, we have seen how UNIX networking requires a lot more than knowing about network media and network protocols. You must also have an intimate knowledge of UNIX commands and files that are pertinent to networking. Also, if you are going to control access to computers on a UNIX network, a knowledge of certain key files is vital.

A lot of research has been done on UNIX security. Kerberos, from MIT's Project Athena, is one development that focuses on network security, and some UNIX versions, such as ULTRIX, have strengthened their security by including it. Secure NFS is its counterpart. System V R4 and AIX releases strengthen UNIX by using a *shadow file* — the password encryption in `passwd` is hidden from the users. In addition, both SunOS and AIX have made their systems more secure. Still, a lot more research and development needs to be done. Under current UNIX networking schemes, if someone is logged on to one machine, he or she can log on to, copy files to or from, or perform remote shells on any machine he or she is allowed to access. Of course, you never want to leave an open login unprotected, because even if you go away for a few minutes, anyone can sit down in your chair and take advantage of your login if they know your environment well enough.

Login Access Control

Current provisions for access control on UNIX are somewhat limited, and the only way you achieve the highest possible degree of access control is by both knowing and understanding these important files. The system's bastion of access control is the same for network access as for direct access, the `/etc/passwd` file. In almost every case, if there is no entry in the password file, there will be no entry to the system; it's that simple.[1]

The second line of defense is the `/etc/hosts.equiv` file, which lists hosts that are trusted by the system. In other words, the local system will allow access only to the machines listed in `/etc/hosts.equiv`. However, in each entry you can add user names that are allowed access. The file entry form is

```
hostname [username]
```

as in

```
stalker
cj scott
archer
linus chad
```

In the last entry, `linus` is the name of the machine allowed entry, and `chad` is the user on that machine.

Thus, to get into a remote machine you must be on the remote machine's `passwd` file, and the machine that you're on must be on the remote machine's `host.equiv` file.

When a Berkeley R command is issued, such as `rlogin`, `rcp`, or `rsh`, there are several conditions possible:

---

1. There are a few ways to get around the password file to get into the machine, but normal access is through `passwd`.

- Users and systems in both `passwd` and `hosts.equiv` can `rlogin` without password checking and use `rcp` and `rsh`.

- Users and systems in `passwd` but not in `hosts.equiv` can `rlogin` but must supply a password. However, they won't be able to do an `rsh` or `rcp`.

- Users and systems that are in `hosts.equiv` but not in `passwd` cannot `rlogin`, run a remote shell, or do a remote copy. Access is denied.

- Users and systems that aren't listed in either `passwd` or `hosts.equiv` cannot `rlogin`. Access is denied.

Furthermore, the access control given by `hosts.equiv` is extended with the `.rhosts` file, which can be located in every user's home directory. (Even `root` has one, called `/.rhosts`.) This file does for individual users what `hosts.equiv` does for the system, and its format is identical to `/etc/hosts.equiv`. Let's see how it works.

Let's imagine that user Joanna has a local machine called **popeye**, and she wants to log on to a remote system called **wimpy**. First **wimpy** checks its own `passwd` file for Joanna's listing. If a listing for Joanna is not found, access is denied. However, if it is found, **wimpy** checks its own `host.equiv` file to see if **popeye** is in there. If **popeye** isn't listed, **wimpy** goes to Joanna's home directory (if she is on **wimpy**'s `passwd` file, she has a home directory on **wimpy**) and looks in her `.rhosts` file. If **popeye** is listed, access is accepted, but if not found, Joanna will be asked for a password, but she won't be allowed to do an `rcp rsh`.

Thus, with a `~/.rhosts` entry but no entry in `/etc/hosts.equiv`, a user can `rlogin`, because they have an entry in the `passwd` file. In effect, `.rhosts` is an extension of `hosts.equiv`.

An additional protection in `hosts.equiv` is the ability to include or exclude entire groups of users. Groups are defined in `/etc/netgroups`. Once defined, they can be included in `/etc/hosts.equiv` with an entry like `+@groupA` or excluded with `-@groupB`.

The `/etc/netgroups` file shows each group by its name and its members with the following form:

group_name member1, member2, .. memberN

The *member* entries consist of a triplet of the *hostname*, *username*, and *domainname* enclosed in parentheses. Often only the *hostname* is used, and the other two are left blank:

```
design (stalker,,) (cj,,) (scooter,,)
```

This method saves you the time of typing in every user in the domain.

One or more groups can also be included in a group, and you can even create a group that wildcards all users, all machines, and all users:

```
all (,,)
```

However, if you have a single plus-sign entry in `host.equiv`, you accomplish the same goal.

The use of `netgroup` is also necessary for using `rwall`, the network version of `wall`, the user warning system.

Remote Printers

Dealing with printers on the net is not difficult, but it's not a piece of cake either. Normally, system administrators don't allow user access to system files on workstations unless they trust users to administer their own printer access, and then `/etc/printcap` is made writeable. The reason for this precaution is simple — any user with *write* access to the `/etc/printcap` file can create an entry that will allow remote access to any printer on any machine in that machine's `hosts` file. Since the `/etc/hosts` file contains the node name and IP address of every machine likely to be contacted in the local domains, if Eric had *write* access to

/etc/printcap, without further access control he could send a
100-page file to Joanna's dot-matrix printer without Joanna's
permission. The noise alone would irritate everyone in the
immediate vicinity.

Fortunately, printer access is controlled in the
/etc/hosts.lpd file, because only the hosts named in this file
can access the printers on the local system. Thus, any machines
listed in popeye's /etc/hosts.lpd file can access popeye's
printers, and Eric wouldn't be allowed access. Naturally, if you
want everyone to print on the print servers, you give unlimited
printer access on the print server's /etc/hosts.lpd file or
/etc/hosts.equiv by putting everyone on it.

Moreover, the local printer's /etc/printcap file offers further
access control methods by using mnemonics. For example, by
adding the mnemonic rs to a printer's entry, the printer is
restricted to users with local accounts only.

```
lp|epson|dot:\
  :lp=/dev/pp0:st=/var/spool/lpr:rs:
```

Note that rs is a Boolean, and thus it need only be present to be
active.

NFS Access Control

NFS has few defenses against unwanted access. Its first line of
defense is the server's /etc/exports file, whose primary purpose
is to list the directories that host systems may mount. If a file system is not in exports, it is not available for mounting by a remote
system.

A basic /etc/exports looks like

```
# exports - server1
/export/tools
/export/X11
/export/X10
/u/users
    .
    .
```

but the directory entries can be modified with options that specify precisely what may be mounted and how. A few of the most important mount options are:

ro
: All mounts are read/write unless the `ro`, the read-only option, is used.

access=*host*
: The `access` option is used to limit access to a single client, clients, or `/etc/netgroup` member.

root=*hostname*
: `root=` gives `root` access only to the host named as *hostname*.

Here's a more typical `exports` file:

```
# exports server2
/usr           ro,access=clients
/usr/tools     ro,access=cadgroup,root=stalker
/usr/system    access=stalker
```

The `access=clients` option leaves mounting open to all clients. Note that `/usr` and `/usr/tools` are *read-only*. NFS access can be controlled through *netgroups*.

fstab **Access Control**

A workstation's `/etc/fstab` file was never intended to be used for access control; in fact, this file is a mount file used to mount both local and remote files. However, interestingly enough, it does offer limited security potential. Primary control can be exercised by confining the `root` password to the systems staff, and then restricting `fstab` to `root` only. Naturally, this won't work on user-administered machines.

The only mounting attribute that offers any protection is the *read-only* (`ro`) mount option. When creating mount attributes, think carefully about the use of each file system and directory being mounted. Users' file systems and their work and project areas must obviously be *read/write*, but does a game directory have to be *read/write*? Most games are *read-only*, but `fortune` needs to be *read/write*, and there's the rub. On big servers the `games` directory is hidden away on the bottom of the `clusters` directory, which needs to be mounted *read-only*.

UNIX evolves and changes constantly, and in the latest versions there is a new paradigm of directories. `/bin` is gone, and there is a new directory called `/var` is intended for file structures that grow and shrink, such as `spool`, `log`, and `adm`. The purpose of creating `/var` was to remove all the *read/write* files from `/usr`, and now `/usr` is a fixed size, located in a directory that is usually 99 percent full. The `clusters` directory is also fixed in size and always mounted *read-only*, even on a server. Therefore, alas, even a historic, amusing UNIX whimsy like `fortune` has to be sacrificed for today's optimum network performance unless you take the time to move `fortune` to a directory like `/usr/local`, mounted *read/write*, where it will be in the user's path.

Thus, if you want to retain control of your network, you must retain control of all the `fstabs` files. Your network will run better, and that is why your job was created.

Router Access Control

Dedicated routers can maintain access control across networks in a way that no other mechanism on servers or clients can. Operating at the IP level, the router examines each IP address and compares it against an access list. If the address is found, there are two conditions, *permit* and *deny*. Beyond that, the access list's entries can include wildcard masks that tell what can be done with the transmission.

The significance of the 32-bit wildcard mask depends on whether the bits are set to zero or one. Every address going through is compared against a mask. Wildcard mask bits set to zero are *used* in a comparison, but wildcard mask bits set to one are *ignored* in a comparison.

Let's look at some concrete examples. Following is an example allowing traffic from the network `128.213.0.0`'s subnet `55`:

```
access-list 1 permit 128.213.55.0  0.0.0.255
```

The first two zeros in the mask let network `128.215` be used. The third zero lets the subnet `55` be used. However, the final `255` (eight binary ones) in the mask ignores the host part of the address, which in effect allows all hosts on that subnet.

Access lists can grind as fine as a single machine

```
access-list 1 permit 128.213.55.56
```

which is the same as

```
access-list 1 permit 128.213.55.56  0.0.0.0
```

Or access lists can stop access from a single machine:

```
access-list 1 deny 128.213.55.21
```

Access lists can be used to block subnets. In the following example, a subnet of a class A network is blocked:

```
access-list 4 deny 12.122.0.0  0.0.255.255
```

Line Access with Routers

Router access control can be tuned more finely than the examples shown so far. For example, the router can be used to control incoming and outgoing connections for virtual terminals. Consider the following access list number, `13`:

```
access-list 13 permit 198.41.55.0  0.0.0.255
```

This line is used in conjunction with another line with the same number to get incoming remote terminals on network `198.41.55.0`:

```
access-list 13 permit 198.41.55.0  0.0.0.255
line 1 9
access-class 13 in
```

Extended Access

The router's ability to control access is extended by the ability to do *extended access*. The `access-list` command is also extended syntactically to filter specific types of transport-level protocols. For TCP, the following protocols are recognized:

- `ip`
- `tcp`
- `udp`
- `icmp`

Note that the key word `ip` is not a network-level filter but a catch-all for any Internet protocol, *including* `tcp`, `udp` and `icmp`.

Putting extended access to use, here's how all TCP connections to anywhere from the local network `128.213.0.0` on a DDN interface are opened up:

```
access list 37 permit tcp 128.213.0.0 0.0.255.255\
        0.0.0.0 255.255.255.255
```

Note the address/mask pairs — both source and destination addresses and their masks must be included.

Ethernet interfaces require port number considerations. The following example allows all TCP connections for ports greater than 1023:

```
access-list 38 permit tcp 0.0.0.0 255.255.255.255 \
        0.0.0.0 255.255.255.255 gt 1023
```

By judicious mixing and matching of router access list attributes, traffic across the network interfaces can be controlled very closely.

The Bottom Line to Access Control

Access control methods are scattered and inconsistent. It takes a great deal of time and diligence to maintain tight security through access control, not to mention dedication to the task. Augmenting your internal access control and security with random security audits will put a lid on internal tampering, but only the strictest access control enhanced with every available security feature — such as call-back devices on modem connections — can stop external tampering.

From Security to Diagnostics

Maintaining optimum access control is one vital area of networking that you must master, and the more proficient you are, the safer your network will be. After all, distributed computing depends not only on the health of every system on the net, but also on the health of the network itself. However, without the ability to do network diagnostics, there is no way to ascertain the health of either. In the next chapter we will look at some of the built-in network diagnostics available on UNIX as well as some of the network hardware and software you can buy to help you diagnose the ailments of your network.

CHAPTER

15

Monitoring and Diagnostics

It isn't necessary to constantly monitor a tiny network, such as two PCs joined together, but anything larger requires constant vigilance with diagnostics and monitoring tools, which take header data from the data stream and make that information human-readable. You need all the help you can get to discover what is happening on the net, but be aware that any in-depth analysis of network transmissions requires a working knowledge of protocols, because you will be breaking down up to three layers of protocol headers in order to analyze the data.

There are numerous tools that help you watch the network, and many are built into the UNIX distribution. Others are particular to the OEM, and still others are specialty software and hardware items.

Examples of resident tools are:

- `ping`
- `vmstat`
- `netstat`
- `rpcinfo`
- `spray`
- `pstat`
- `nsfstats`
- `etherfind`

None of these commands were intended to give you a complete analysis of the network. Indeed, some of them weren't designed to work with the network at all, such as `vmstat` and `pstat`. Nevertheless, each of them can give you a tiny view of the node activity on some part of the network. On the other hand, you can't rely on the distribution tools entirely, because they may not be adequate for all your network needs. Eventually, you will need the help of commercial network managers, network monitors, network analyzers, protocol analyzers, and dedicated special-purpose computers and software intended exclusively for network diagnostics and monitoring.

Definition of Terms

Let's look at the differences between a *protocol analyzer*, a *network analyzer*, a *network monitor*, and a *network manager*.

A *protocol analyzer* is a special-purpose computer that is designed to break down packets at the Ethernet (Level 2) protocol layer. It can also work at the higher protocol layers, but not as effectively. One of the earliest network diagnostic tools available, it captures a piece of the transmission for you and shows you the pieces of the puzzle, but it's up to you to put the pieces together. Some, like the HP network analyzer, have their own operating systems. Most others are built on small PC-AT-type systems and are DOS-based, but in time we shall see more protocol analyzers running UNIX. Protocol analyzers do have some built-in network analyzer functions, but the information does not come easily, for they must be programmed for almost every application.

A *network analyzer* is a special-purpose computer that is more comprehensive, for it can operate at higher protocol levels and look at the network as a whole, giving information about the total level of traffic, the percentage of the network utilized, the total collision rate, the number of sent packets per second, and so on. You need to program it, but it knows its piece of the wire, and it may create a map of that piece partly from information you give it and partly from the information it gleans from the wire. A network analyzer is well equipped to deal with special applications, like NFS and mail. The Network General Sniffer is a network analyzer that also has network monitoring and protocol analyzing capabilities.

A *network monitor* is special software that usually runs on a PC-type machine with a specialized network interface. It allows you to look at upper-level protocols and overall networking, and most of the information it gives you does not require programming; rather, you can get it by selecting some menus and answering questions.

A *network manager* is in a class by itself, for it is specialized software that watches the entire network. Some are concentrator-oriented and can't see other devices except bridges, because they rely on hardware devices in the concentrators and bridges for feedback. Others are highly sophisticated, and they can track the condition of the network and report overall use, such as peak traffic and traffic per node. Major components of the net can be watched, and some can be regulated from the console. For example, ports can be seen and turned on and off. Some are so advanced that they can create a complete map of the LAN simply by analyzing network transmission. They can zero in on activity at any one node, bridge, router, concentrator, or port, and they can also be programmed to warn you when certain high-water marks appear, such as a specific collision rate.

The functions of these tools overlap, so you can do packet analysis with a network monitor, for example. However, each tool has its own special strengths, and you will be fortunate indeed if you are lucky enough to have one of each on your site.

Standard Diagnostics

Without the ability to watch the network and gather statistics, you quickly become a victim of network loading, imbalance, and inefficiency. For example, imagine two servers side by side serving engineering groups of approximately equal size. Both servers are the same architecture, but whereas one server has compute servers and workstations, the other has only workstations. Imagine that the compute servers are new, you're not sure how they will affect the network, and you don't have any network analyzers, protocol analyzers, or network monitors yet.

Although you may not have access to sophisticated network diagnostic tools, simply examining the network activity on both servers with `netstats` will be a revelation. In fact, you may well decide to revise your network strategy, because the server supporting the compute servers will have four times the amount of network activity. In other words, the network load imposed by a machine is roughly proportional to its MIPS rate. Of course, it's obvious that the 90-MIPS compute servers would make more demands on the network than the 4-MIPS workstations, but without network diagnostics, some time may have passed before you would realize how much the compute servers add to the network load. With network diagnostics, you can see the difference in precise, quantitative terms, and you can redesign the network layout and correct the condition.

The `netstat` command is standard UNIX, used on all systems running NFS. The moral of this story is, don't wait until you can afford a network analyzer or a network monitor to analyze the state of your network. Use the tools at hand.

Let's take a look at some of the network tools available on UNIX.

`ping` and `spray`

The `ping` command sends out a packet that must be returned, verifying whether or not a machine's Ethernet card is functioning, and you use it over the net to see if a machine is "alive." The `spray` command, on the other hand, is used to check the effect of short bursts of heavy traffic on the wire. If the wire is near its threshold and `spray` sends out 600 packets, you know it's time to take further action if only 15 percent of them are received.

`vmstat` and `pstat`

These aren't dedicated networking commands, but I'm including them here to make a point: If you want to tune the network, each machine must be tuned as well. Only when every machine is in top running order will your network run at optimum efficiency, and these commands will help you see how your machines are responding to the net.

For example, not infrequently, a machine's inode tables will fill, typical of today's distributed computing NFS machines with their huge numbers of files and windows. The machine will page the inode table if an inode table fills, which keeps the computer from blowing up, to be sure, but also considerably slows down the overall speed of the machine and thus hampers its ability to handle network functions. However, the `pstat` command checks table sizes, and if you use it periodically to check machine tables, you'll prevent the inode table from filling.

On the other hand, machines page memory in two directions. Paging memory *in* is a normal computer function, but paging memory *out* means that the computer is short of resources and is a bad sign, especially on a server. After all, if a server slows down, the net will slow down. Luckily, the `vmstat` command checks memory functions, including pageouts.

netstat

The `netstat` command shows the status of the network, and it has over one manual page of options. Because it was created at Berkeley, it is socket-oriented and will display all the active sockets for each protocol. It is equally adept at breaking down and displaying network data structures, but perhaps its most useful function is reporting packet traffic statistics. To a limited extent, `netstat` does some network analyzer and network monitor tasks.

Socket States

The first use of `netstat` is to show the state of network sockets. Used with the `-a` flag, `netstat` generates a list of protocols, receiving queues, sending queues, local addresses, remote (foreign) addresses, and protocol states. Here is some typical `netstat` output (display truncated):

```
# netstat -a
Active Internet connections (including servers)
Proto Recv-Q Send-Q Local Address    Foreign Address
  tcp    0      0    localhost.2027   localhost.111
  tcp    0      0    localhost.2026   localhost.111
  tcp    0      0    stalker.login    folsm1.1019
  tcp    0      0    stalker.login    folsm1.1023
  tcp    0      0    stalker.login    folsm6.1027
  tcp    0      0    stalker.1457     fmw18.smtp
    .
  tcp    0      0    *.111            *.*
  udp    0      0    *.789            *.*
  udp    0      0    *.616            *.*
  udp    0      0    *.603            *.*
  udp    0      0    *.1015           *.*
    .
Active UNIX domain sockets
Address    Type     Recv-Q Send-Q   Vnode    Conn   Refs
fc71220c   stream     0      0      fc073e8    0      0
fc713a8c   stream     0      0      fc71210c   0      0
    .
fc70a28c   dgram      0      0      fc0ee55c   0      0
    .
```

The first field is the protocol field, and it shows the transport layer
protocol. This protocol will most often be `tcp` or `udp`. The
second field is the receive queue, the third the send queue, and
both queues have their sizes shown in bytes. Next comes the local
address, followed by the remote address or node name/address
combination. Finally, the last field[1] (the protocol state) shows the
state or condition of the socket.

---

1. Not shown. Truncated due to space limitations.

Following is a brief explanation of some of the words you might see in the last field of this `netstat` output.

CLOSED	The socket is unused.
LISTEN	The socket is listening for incoming connections.
SYN_SEND	A connection is being attempted.
SYN_RECEIVED	Connection synchronization is underway.
ESTABLISHED	The connection has been made.
CLOSE_WAIT	Waiting for the socket to close.
FIN_WAIT_1	The socket is closed, shutting down the connection.
CLOSING	The socket is about to close.
LAST_ACK	Closed on remote shutdown waiting acknowledgement.
FIN_WAIT_2	Closed socket is waiting on remote shutdown.
TIME_WAIT	Wait after close for remote shutdown.

Now let's break down this `netstat -a` output further. To start, two sockets are waiting to be closed:

```
tcp  0  0  localhost.2027  localhost.111  TIME_WAIT
tcp  0  0  localhost.2026  localhost.111  TIME_WAIT
```

Their queues are empty (0), and both are addresses to `localhost` at both ends of the connection.

These entries are followed by a series of remote logins on open established connections:

```
tcp  0  0  stalker.login  folsm1.1019  ESTABLISHED
tcp  0  0  stalker.login  folsm1.1023  ESTABLISHED
tcp  0  0  stalker.login  folsm6.1027  ESTABLISHED
```

Note the mail socket, `fmw18.smtp`, which is using a simple mail transport protocol sitting on a closed socket waiting for a remote shutdown from the system `fmw18`:

```
tcp  0  0  stalker.1457    fmw18.smtp    FIN_WAIT_2
```

The rest of the sockets are *listening* to their ports.

```
tcp  0  0  *.111      *.*       LISTEN
udp  0  0  *.789      *.*
udp  0  0  *.616      *.*
udp  0  0  *.603      *.*
udp  0  0  *.1015     *.*
```

They will become active when they receive a connection, but until then they patiently wait. Note that the `Foreign Address, *.*,` is a wildcard.

The UNIX domain sockets at the end of the output are stream and datagram connections for NFS and YP (display has been truncated):

```
Active UNIX domain sockets
Address    Type     Recv-Q Send-Q   Vnode    Conn   Refs
fc71220c stream     0      0      fc073e8    0      0
fc713a8c stream     0      0      fc71210c   0      0
.
fc70a28c dgram      0      0      fc0ee55c   0      0
```

Note the `Vnode` numbers, in effect remote inodes used by NFS.

Network Data Structures

The `netstat` command shows network data structures and their states. Using the `-i` flag, for example, shows the *interface* structure and state, on UNIX systems the system's Ethernet card and the supporting software. While most systems use one interface, multiple interfaces are provided for. Imagine a system that doubles as a server with four Ethernet ports and as a router. It must be attached to at least two network segments, and therefore must have two node names and two Ethernet devices. In network terms, it has two interfaces.

If you want to display the interface structure and state, use `netstat -i` (display has been truncated):

```
# netstat -i
Name Mtu  Net/Dest    Address    Ipks    Ierrs Opkts
ie0  1500 128.213.0.  stalker    3668545 258   281247
lo0  1536 127.0.0.0   localhost  24353   0     24353
```

Here one interface is supported by a device, `ie0`, an Intel interface device found at `/dev/ie0`, and `lo0` is the loopback device. This host, `stalker`, is on a class B network address `123.213.0`, and the loopback device, `localhost`, uses the universal loopback address `127.0.0.0`.

The `Collis` column (display has been truncated), is the number of collisions, and a high collision rate is indicative of a crowded network. On the other hand, the term `mtu` is the maximum transmission unit, the largest allowable datagram at 1.5 kilobytes. With "I" standing for input and "O" for output, `Ipkts` are input packets, `Ierrs` input errors, and so on.

Another example of the formatting capability of `netstats` is the `r` option for routers (display truncated):

```
# netstat -r
Routing tables
Destination      Gateway    Flags  Refcnt  Use
default          masada     UG     0       2364
221.255.10.0     janus      UG     0       0
apex-net         stalker    U      46      255223
127.0.0.0        localhost  U      12      21215
```

The flags are `U` for up and `G` for gateway. `Refcnt` is reference count, the active uses per route.

Statistics

The third form of `netstat` is cumulative statistics. Let's say your users are being plagued by timeouts. Are they threatening your network performance? How often do they occur? You may think that isolating portions of the net is imperative, but you will have to get some hard statistical data before anyone will give you $100,000 for bridges and routers to do the isolation.

A little over a page of stats will be generated with `netstat` `-s`. Here is an abbreviated example of its output:

```
# netstat -s
ip:
      407513 total packets received
      0 bad header checksum
            .
      2883 fragments received
            .
      6 packets not forwardable
      0 redirects sent
icmp:
      11 calls to icmp_error
      0 errors generated 'cuz old massages too short
      0 errors generated 'cuz old massages was icmp
      Output histogram:
            destination unreachable: 11
      0 messages with bad code fileds
            .
      Input histogram:
            echo reply: 2
            destination unreachable: 49
      0 message responses generated
 tcp:
      182753 packets sent
         48054 data packets (5128376 bytes)
         167 data packets (2872 bytes) retransmitted
         128423 ack-only packets (4059 delayed)
         13 URG only packets
         47 window probe packets
         189 window packets
         5860 control packets
      184794 packets received
```

```
          49871 acks (for 5132283 bytes)
          117455 duplicate acks
          0 acks unsent data
          47108 packets (2867123 bytes)
                received in-sequence
          115592 completely duplicate packets
                (151761 bytes)

                .

      2204 connection requests
      1022 connections accepted
      2901 connections established (including accepts)
      3219 connections closed (including 2 drops)
      325 embryonic connections dropped
      4097 segments updated rtt (of 52021 attempts)
      932 retransmit timeouts
          1 connection dropped by rexmit timeout
      0 persistent timeouts
      94238 keepalive timeouts
          1487 keepalive probes sent
          252 connections dripped by keepalive
udp:
      0 incomplete headers
      0 bad data length fields
      0 bad checksums
      0 socket overflows
```

Although you always want to keep an eye on disk usage, if you don't use any other network diagnostics or monitors, at least run netstat -s.

Look for fragments that are the result of collisions:

```
      2883 fragments received
```

When a network segment gets too crowded, collisions are the result.

Look for too many timeouts, another result of the same ailment.

```
932 retransmit timeouts
1 connection dropped by rexmit timeout
0 persistent timeouts
94238 keepalive timeouts
1487 keepalive probes sent
252 connections dripped by keepalive
```

Watch for any disproportionately large errors or imbalances. In the `netstat -s` output, the `tcp` packets data shows less than ideal conditions. For example, there are a lot of duplicate packets:

```
115592 completely duplicate packets (151761 bytes)
```

and too few packets received in sequence, `47108` out of the total `184794` packets received. This network segment could definitely use a higher degree of isolation.

The `netstat` statistics are accumulated since the last reboot or running of `netstat`. If you rely on `netstat` for daily information, run it from `cron` at a certain time each day. For statistical purposes, run it on every file server and on at least one workstation on each network segment. If your YP server is a separate server, as is recommended, run `nfstat` there as well, in order to get some NFS statistics. Gather your information daily so that you can compare the output from day to day.

Unless you have a dedicated network analyzer, the `netstat` command may be the best tool you have. When its output becomes sufficiently grim, buying a dedicated network analyzer is the next step.

etherfind

The `etherfind` command operates at Protocol Layer 2 and prints out Ethernet headers that match Boolean expressions given to the command as arguments. The command has enough knowledge of the IP layer and its protocols to give the Ethernet packet information needed to transmit an IP datagram.

Be prepared for a little pain, because `etherfind`'s command syntax is about as arcane as `find`'s. For example, if you want to capture all of `stalker`'s packets, either coming or going, you need to do this:

```
% su
password:
# etherfind -src stalker -o -dst stalker
```

The `-src` and `-dst` flags are for source and destination, and the `-o` flag is the *or* operator. Thus, the arguments read *source stalker or destination stalker*.

The key to using `etherfind` is understanding how to use its flags. The basic options are:

`-n`	Don't convert host addresses and port numbers to names.
`-p`	Don't go into *promiscuous mode*.
`-r`	Treat each packet as an RPC (remote procedure call) message.
`-t`	Time stamp each packet listing.
`-u`	Buffer the output line.
`-v`	Print some of the TCP and UDP packet fields. This flag is useful for debugging.
`-x`	Dump the header in hex.
`-c`	Exit after *count* packets.

If you don't have outside network firmware and software such as dedicated analyzers or monitors, rely on `etherfind` for low-level protocol breakdown and monitoring until you can purchase some.

rpcinfo

Imagine that a user calls you to say she cannot get her workstation to mount files from a file server. You move to the window on your workstation that is logged on to the server, do a `df`, and discover that the server is alive. But when you log on to her system and do a `df`, none of the files on the server in question are mounted. A `ping` from her workstation to the file server shows that the server is alive, her `fstab` file is OK, and the `/etc/exports` file on the server is OK, also. Now what?

You could log on to the server and test the networking daemons one at a time with `ps`, but there is a much easier way. From any system on the net, execute an `rpcinfo` to exercise the daemons. In effect, you are generating an RPC call both to and from another system in order to test that system's ability to handle RPCs. Let's try the mount daemon:

```
# rpcinfo -u server4 mountd
program 100005 not available version 0 not available
```

This shows that the `mountd` daemon is not running on the file server. If you don't know which daemon is in trouble, use `rpcinfo` to test them all:

```
# rpcinfo -p server4
program   vers   proto  port
  100000   2      tcp    111      portmapper
  100000   2      ucp    111      portmapper
  100007   2      tcp   1024      ypbind
  100007   2      ucp   1026      ypbind
  100007   1      tcp   1024      ypbind
  100007   1      ucp   1026      ypbind
  100029   2      ucp    663      keyserv
  .
  .
```

However, in the case of the unresponsive file server, you are more interested in what you don't see, `mountd`.

Now you can use `rpcinfo -p` as a probe method, or you can look for a specific daemon, but there are several other `rpcinfo` options. You can search for TCP (`-t`) or UDP (`-u`) exclusively, or you can search by way of a broadcast (`-b`). The command can also be used to delete (`-d`) a specific version or `program` listed by both name and number in `rpcinfo`'s output. Most will exist in a `tcp` or `udp` protocol version.

Network Managers

Eventually, your local area network will need extensive monitoring tools that are beyond the scope of built-in UNIX network commands or the monitoring capabilities of protocol and network analyzers. Then it's time to think about a network manager that can watch the entire network at all protocol-layer levels. However, before you run out and buy one, be aware that most of them work best only with their own software running on their own hardware.

SunNet Manager

SunNet Manager is a marvel of software engineering that created a large installed user base quickly because, like X Windows, it is more than a piece of network software — it is a software and development tool suite and platform. The word *platform* is key here, because offering an open platform for other vendors to build upon allows vendors to shortcut their development cycle. In a sense they become VARs, and we who administer benefit by having a familiar and uniform interface. In short, the first thing to understand about SNM is that it's an open, heterogeneous platform on which you can build. However, the sum of SNM's base software and software tools is a tool set that monitors and analyzes the network automatically. Through programs, it has the capability to warn the system's caretakers when it detects any condition or high-water mark for which it has been set.

To learn SNM you must plan on spending at least one week at school, and here is a sample of some of the new words you will have in your vocabulary:

element   Any active device such as a host or server, a
                          bridge, concentrator, or router.

objects   Application and network services, operating
                          system resources, and interfaces.

agent   A program that collects and reports data.

proxy agent   An agent that translates or works between
                          elements (devices).

Sun has many programs (agents) to manage network services
(objects) found under SNM. An agent is required to look at
anything on the network. What is fascinating is that so many
agents are provided by other vendors, and agents can be written by
users. Even a new network manager can be written with this
platform, if you are adventurous and talented enough. A few of
the agents provided include Ethernet, FDDI, X.25, device support
for routers and MAC bridges, and statistic services.

Thus, SNM can run with almost any device that you have an
agent for, and if you don't have an agent, you can build one.
Finally, because so many vendors are building on it, it's a relatively
safe software investment and will be around for quite a while.

If you were working on SNM right now, the first screen you
would see is an overall look at the LAN or WAN, starting with the
buildings that house the network segments. From there, you could
pull down a separate window of each network segment. The
individual elements of the network are graphically displayed, and
the usual mouse *point-and-click* manipulations on any element
bring in all sorts of useful information about that device.

SNM works in two modes, either tracking data or being set to
trigger on events, called *alarms*, which can be set for any
programmable condition. What is delightfully different about
SNM's alarms is its wide array of notification choices: it can buzz,
beep, or flash you, but it is also capable of paging your beeper,
sending mail, flashing an icon, or talking to you with voice
messages or preselected sounds. Now that Sun has a speaker in its
workstations, libraries of sounds are building up, and they are
changing the way a computer site sounds.

Features offered by SNM as managed resources are:

- network devices

- system resources

- protocol layers and interfaces

- application, database, and network services

It's important to note that all of these services can be extended by the administrator or programmer to add managed objects, additional analysis, and automation. Custom logs can be created, and all of this can be integrated with existing Sun management programs, X Windows, or a variety of terminal emulations, including IBM 32XX or DEC VT terminals. This is significant because it means that it can be run with terminals from two proprietary platforms.

Most UNIX network sites are local, highly networked, and run with a fair degree of autonomy; because administrators have their own way of doing things, a network manager must be flexible enough to work in benevolent dictatorship environments. To answer this need, SNM is extended for Internet-type (Ethernet-TCP/IP) local area networks, and soon Sun will be providing the protocols for enterprise-level systems to operate with OSI.

Event Reporting

SNM is designed to report predetermined events to the administrator: The administrator sets the sampling interval, selects the conditions that will trip the alarm, and then walks away from the tube, safe in the knowledge that the event will be reported every time it happens. Events include fault notification, configuration management, warning notification (such as a specific disk reaching a high-water mark), security violations (such as a suspected break-in), accounting (billable resource usage), and configuration changes. Note that these functional areas of network management comply with OSI protocols.

Setting Up and Customizing SNM

Setting up SNM involves more than setting up a piece of software, for you are providing a software analyzing base for your network. It can take anywhere from a week to a month of work to get the system going, for the learning curve is high. Like setting up UUCP, `sendmail`, YP, and NFS, the first time is a bear, but each successive time thereafter is easier. It may take a day to write an agent for SNM, but you can save time by cookbooking the agent from an existing program.

SynOptic's Network Manager

Let's compare SNM with another network manager, SynOptic's LattisNet Network System. LNMS is not an open system, but rather it is specifically intended for use with SynOptics' concentrators, and it is created to to let you watch the network for:

- data flow

- topology (configuration)

- network components (concentrators, bridges, and cables)

- segment monitoring

- performance

Notice the absence of routers. Concentrator monitors watch concentrators; they study port activity and deduce the amount of traffic to the devices attached at the other end of the wire on the port. This software is concentrator-oriented and can't really monitor anything else, such as workstations, but you can gather a great deal of information about the data coming and going to the devices attached to the concentrators. In use, the network is shown on the screen of a PC-type system running MS-DOS, and the screen display is created and updated automatically. You use the mouse to select a concentrator from the display and then choose from menu commands to observe performance and statistics.

LNMS allows alarms to be set for a wide variety of conditions, like selecting the threshold, the parameter, or a high-water mark.

Notification is automatic. This feature allows you to find network faults quickly, and you can also isolate them if necessary.

One of the best benefits of LNMS is that you can enable or disable a concentrator from your monitor. Imagine that you have a system filling the net with trash like continuous mutant ICMP packets. You don't need this trash on the net, so you shut down the culprit system's concentrator port as soon as you locate it, and it isn't heard from again until you have time to fix the problem and put it back on line. Similarly, you can shut down access to devices *en masse*, such as all workstations attached to a file server while rebooting the server.

Like SunNet Manager, SynOptics is built around the OSI model and specification. We see similar application areas:

- fault management

- configuration management

- performance management

- security management

- accounting

Comparing SNM with LNMS

While both SNM and LNMS are marketed as *network managers*, there are significant differences. SynOptics' LNMS is concentrator-oriented, is not user- or vendor-extensible, and is not a platform. Sun's SNM is extensible, is an open platform, and is not concentrator-oriented but designed to watch the overall network, either WAN or LAN. How do you choose between these two network managers? The answer is you don't. If you have a lot of concentrators on your net, you would benefit from having both of them. Plus, there are other good network managers that you could also purchase. In short, recommending a certain protocol analyzer, network manager, or any other network diagnostic tool isn't really possible. Just be aware that there are quite a few different tools that can help you monitor the activity on your net, and be prepared to take the time to research each one. The decision to purchase must be based on the distinct needs of your site.

Concord's Trakker Network Monitoring System

Concord's Trakker system is different from other network monitoring tools. It works by attaching probes to each network segment. These probes promiscuously monitor all traffic and summarize the packet information at no less than three network layers. A central system retrieves the information from the probes where it can be summarized, and any reasonable network statistics can be gathered from it immediately.

The biggest difference between this and other network devices is that with other devices you have to set traps and can only hope to catch what you need, but with Trakker, when you need the information, you have it.

Administrators will find network analyzers like Trakker extremely useful. It makes it possible for them to watch each network segment, in real time, without interfering with the network. Let's face it: Indigenous Unix tools like `etherfind`, `netstat`, and `ping` don't cut it, because they are limited in scope and operate on a single protocol layer. Other tools are available, but if they require network polling, that adds to network traffic — something that administrators are trying to minimize in the first place. And even if you have a comprehensive set of independent tools, you won't have all the information you need, because these tools were not designed to work together. For example, Sun Microsystems' SunNet Manager is an excellent tool, but it requires agents to interface the network elements, and such agents aren't always available when you need them.

However, Concord Communications' Trakker is well suited to UNIX networking. It monitors the network at all times without slowing it down with constant polling. It operates at all internetwork protocol layers, decoding most protocol families. Most important, it ties all its capabilities together under the capable orchestration of a single monitoring console.

Architecture

Trakker uses dedicated microcomputers (called segment monitors) to monitor each segment. Each of these machines attaches to a network segment or subnetwork through a standard MAU (multistation access unit). Segment monitors don't require a video monitor or keyboard except during setup. And segment monitors work with Trakker software, which runs on a central SPARC system under SunNet Manager. As system administrator, you monitor all network activity through this central Trakker console.

Segment monitors analyze network transmission, storing the results in Trakker's MIB. The Trakker console gathers information from the MIBs stored by each segment monitor. There are literally thousands of data objects in Trakker's MIB; these objects are further divided into sections based on protocol suites. Trakker monitors can also detect alarm conditions and send a notice to the console through an SNMP agent. Trakker coordinates all its information through intelligent analysis software, using its knowledge of each protocol to map communications from several protocol layers into dialogues between nodes on the multisegment network.

Real-Life Trakker

Installing any system this far-reaching is bound to take time and effort. Installing the segment monitors takes very little time, but preparing the console monitor is nontrivial. You will have to regenerate some kernel options, enabling semaphores and using a generous setting for maxusers.

Trakker runs almost error-free, and you will be surprised at how many minor problems you pick up on your network, no matter how well designed you think it is. You will find things like time daemons taking much too much CPU time, persistent error messages from an NFS client trying to access a file that is no longer there, and similar errors that would have gone undetected without Trakker. You will be able to track NFS traffic day by day, look at the real work habits of your users, and note how predictably they load each segment. Fix the errors Trakker shows you and redistribute the workload accordingly.

Trakker is convenient. You don't need to lug it around and plug it into the network segments you need to analyze. And you can use Trakker from the UNIX side of the network.

Documentation and Help

Trakker has voluminous documentation. You get separate guides to installing the segment monitor, monitoring TCP/IP and NFS, and tracing; there are also individual guides to LAT, DECnet, and the data link layer. Some guides (such as the Internet monitor guide) are so thorough, they provide a review of the basics of network protocols, encapsulation, and network layering for both the TCP/IP and OSI stacks.

All Network Layers

Trakker's most important feature is its ability to work at all network layers and with all protocols. It tracks down the TCP/IP family, the UDP family (including NFS), DECnet, and LAT. It also offers link-level monitoring of NetWare, AppleTalk, and PC-Net protocols. In addition, it formats protocol information before presenting it to the administrator, so you don't have to be intimately familiar with the details of each protocol.

Network Problems Vary

This chapter has given you ideas on how to diagnose and monitor your net, but there is more to the story. Just because you have the data in hand doesn't necessarily mean that you know what to do with it. And how can you tell when something's wrong with the network in the first place? Do network problems manifest themselves as network errors, computer errors, or both?

What usually happens is that you have some kind of problem, and then you must figure out what kind of diagnostics you need to solve the problem. There are no set rules to follow, because every problem is different, and the solutions vary widely. The best way to give you an idea of what it's like to solve network problems is to relate actual network problem scenarios, and that's precisely what we do in the last chapter of this book.

However, we have a few more networking topics to study before we do that. Perhaps one of the most difficult areas in inter-networking is the setup and administration of `sendmail`, our next chapter.

CHAPTER
16

Mail and Sendmail Administration

Our society has become so accustomed to electronic mail, it wouldn't be able to function without it. In fact, the volume of E-mail in large companies is so huge that many dedicate an entire mainframe just to handle mail. Fortunately, UNIX handles its own mail, so if a company has 1000 UNIX machines, it has 1000 machines that handle their own mail. Although each mail domain must have a mail master (usually a file server) as the final arbiter for mail delivery, partial use of a few file servers cost a lot less money than a mainframe.

The ability to handle mail on UNIX did not come easily; nor did it come overnight. UNIX mail started as a local affair, because in the old days it was common to have a single minicomputer handle everyone's computing. Thus, all mail was on one system, users could log in to any one of the system's terminals and get mail, and everyone who sent mail sent it to someone else on the same machine.

Some might say that the beginning of modern UNIX E-mail started when AT&T's UUCP extended mail delivery over the public telephone lines, but there have been many developments in electronic mail delivery, and we are not going to go into all of them here. However, as far as UNIX is concerned, perhaps we can say that the latest significant breakthrough in mail delivery occurred at Berkeley when mail was put on the Internet. Berkeley's `mail` understands the Internet because of the creation of `sendmail` by Eric Allman. This system is so complex it would probably require a book of its own to document fully, but we are only going to examine enough information to administer UNIX networks.

The Many Sides of UNIX Mail

UNIX mail can have as many as three parts: the front-end `mail` commands; a delivery agent, like `sendmail`; and a network agent to carry the mail.

Berkeley's `/usr/ucb/mail` and AT&T's `/bin/mail` are programs in their own right. They accept mail and (seem to) deliver mail, and, indeed, mail at its simplest is intended for mail collection and delivery on a local system. To send local mail to Bruce Hunter:

```
% mail bhunter
```

However, although local mail is still delivered directly to the recipient, users must also learn how to address mail for delivery away from the host system. UUCP uses another address form that uses the node name as well as the user's:

```
% mail jaeger!bhunter
```

UUCP is a switched network (it uses the telephone lines), and users use mail hops to send mail by way of other systems in order to keep down the cost of transmission. The address reflects this:

```
apex!acme!stalker!jaeger!bhunter
```

Note the hops from node `apex` to node `jaeger` through `acme` and `stalker` using the form `node!node!...!user`. Many addressing schemes for mail have been developed, but the one we are concerned with in this chapter is `sendmail`.

The User Interface

Like all things UNIX, the user's interface to mail can be readily customized through `~/.mail.rc`, aliases, and `~./forward`. The users' `$HOME/mailrc` is where the users' `mail` commands get customized, where their aliases are set up, and where features are defined. If a user wants the `vi` editor used from within `mail`, it is specified here. Subject lines, `cc` (courtesy copies), `biff` (mail notification), and other features are also turned on here:

```
17% cat .mailrc
set append dot autoprint
set folder=/usr/system/bhunter/acmemail
alias joanna jhunter@fsm1
alias eric ehunter@fsm1
alias chad chunter@fwu39
```

The `set` commands set mail attributes like:

- `append`   Appends new mail to end of user's mail file
- `dot`   Terminates the message with a period on a line (by itself) as the `EOF`
- `autoprint`   Prints each file to the screen as fast as the last is erased
- `alias`   Sets aliases

The `~/.forward` File

Nowadays, organizations move users about more than ever, with either temporary or permanent transfers. For example, if you get the attention of management as a troubleshooter, you may get temporarily transferred to another site to fix their problems. How do you get your mail to follow you?

The `~/.forward` file causes forwarding of user mail, and it only needs to contain the next name/address pair in standard UNIX *uname@host.org_name.org_ext* format, such as `knovak@acme.com`.

Folders

Not too long ago, there was an MVS mainframe mail system with two notable features: it was a resource hog of monumental proportions, and it had folders. Folders were its biggest selling point, and they were a good idea. They are a set of files in which mail that has already been read can be stored for future reference. UNIX folders start with a folders directory, which contains a mail folder file for each use, and UNIX `mail` is able to deal with a mail folder exactly as it would deal with mail stored in `/var/spool/mail/user_name`. To create folders, the user must set the folder option in `~/.mailrc`, create a folders directory (called `folders` or whatever else), and make empty folder files in that directory.

`biff` and `xbiff`

Mail doesn't do us any good unless we know it's there, so that's why the `biff` command was created. It beeps us whenever we get new mail. Supposedly, `biff` was named after its creator's dog, who liked to bark at the mailman. That story seems especially appropriate when you set up X Windows for the first time, because `biff` will beep as many times as you have windows. The X Window substitute, `xbiff`, was created so you only need to hear one beep, no matter how many windows you have.

Mail Message Components

Similar to surface mail, electronic mail comes and goes in two parts, the message and the "envelope." The message is what the user types in, and the envelope is the delivery information for the user agent that we see as header information (plus a little more). The envelope doesn't encapsulate mail as network protocol headers do, but rather it acts as a parallel file to show where the message file must go. Therefore, there are two files in the `mqueue` directory — the `df*` file is the message (data), and the `qf*` file is the queue information or envelope:

```
        # file dfAA07738    qfAA07738
   dfAA07738:           English text
   qfAA07738:           ascii text
```

Now let's look at the inside of a qf file:

```
 # cat qfAA07738
   P133519
   T717096347
   DdfAA07738
   MDeferred: Connection refused by Folsm3
   S<shilo@fms03.acme.com>
   H?P?return-path: ,shela@fms03.acme.com>
   Hreceived: from fms03 by ace(4.1/ace-SMTP...
     id AA07738; Mon, 21 Sep 92 10:25:47 PDT
   Hreceived: by fms03 (4.1/10.0i); Mon, 21 ...
   Hdate: Mon, 21 Sep 92 10:25:46 PDT
   Hfrom: shilo@fms03 (Shilo Jennings ~)
   Hmessage-id: <9209211725.AA23298@fms03>
   Happarently-to: acmeusers
   R<tom@folsm3.acme.com>
   R<thorn@folsm3.acme.com>
   R<ssweha@folsm3.acme.com>
   R<rpav@folsm3.acme.com>
   R<rmeyers@folsm3.acme.com>
     .
     .
     .
   R<altimari@folsm3.ame.com>
   R<baker@folsm3.acme.com>
```

Notice the focus (<>) on the recipient name-address triplets and the line prefixes. Later, they will become important in the headers section of the sendmail.cf file. Meanwhile, here are the single prefix meanings of the qf file:

D	The data file name
M	Message (printed by mailq command)

S	Sender address
H	Header definition
R	Recipients
E	Error

The data file looks like this:

```
# cat dfAAO7738
WARNING WARNING WARNING
AUSSIE File Server fms05 down 5-6PM Monday
downtime 60 minutes to add DISK SPACE
```

Together, both files make the mail message, with some or all of the header information prepending the message when it winds up in [var|usr]/spool/mail/user_name.

Mail Agents

Mail agents are sometimes referred to as user agents. The mail agent collects mail and makes the final delivery. Some of the better known mail agents are:

/usr/ucb/mail	The most familiar, BSD mail
/bin/mail	AT&T mail, the original; aka mail, mailx, bellmail (AIX)
uux	UUCP agent
mailx	Another name for mail
mailtool	SunOS for OpenLook or SunView
elm	A mail program from HP
mh	A mail program from Rand

Routing Agents

If a mail agent can deliver mail locally, it will, but today's networked computers always involve the Internet and/or UUCP, and that situation is far more complex. To get mail through the network requires a mail `routing` agent, and the one that concerns us in this chapter is `sendmail`.

A physical medium and protocols are also needed to get mail delivered:

- Ethernet-TCP/IP using (SMTP)
- UUCP (circuit-switched lines or hardwire)
- `/bin/mail` for local delivery

SMTP is the Simple Mail Transfer Protocol, used to deliver mail throughout the Internet.

Mailers

The last stop for outoing mail delivery is the mailer, a mail delivery program used by `sendmail` for the delivery of mail. Each mailer has a name that is internal to `sendmail` and located in the `mailer` section of the `sendmail.cf` file. The mailers `local` and `prog` are mandatory and are defined first. Other mailers are `tcpd` (TCP/IP for local domain), `tcp` (TCP/IP for Internet delivery), and `uucp` (UUCP).

Basic User Mail Files

Like most services in UNIX, mail has several files and directories. The repository for delivered user mail is the `/var/spool/mail` directory (`/usr/spool/mail` on older systems), which contains a mail file for each user (by the user's name) that has the header information followed by the message. Each message is appended to the file, and each starts with the string `From`. Try `grep`ing the word `From` with a space after it, and you will get the sender information. The queuing place for mail is `/var/spool/mqueue`.

The Basic `sendmail` System

All systems but one in a mail domain have simple `sendmail` configuration files. Each will try to deliver mail to a known host, but if
`sendmail` sees that it needs to use the network for delivery, and it
can't figure out how to deliver the mail, it sends it to the mail master, which has the complex `sendmail.cf` file needed to do the
address translation it takes to get mail to a relay host.

`sendmail` and `sendmail.cf` handle mail addressing.
Although users can get away with using many forms of addressing,
both complete and incomplete, mailers and mail routers need
specific address forms, and `sendmail` provides addresses that are
converted to specific internal and external address forms. It also
uses that addressing information to create the mail headers. The
`sendmail.cf` file must provide definitions of such things as delimiters, the domain name, router names, and individual host names,
and it must define a set of rules by which addresses will be processed (translated). With these rules, incomplete addreses like
`ajax!apex!sam` can be converted to full UUCP addresses that can
be handled by a system which does mostly local and Internet
delivery.

Relay Hosts

Relay hosts have direct connections to the Internet. Messages needing the Internet for delivery are routed there, and the relay host
then sends the mail on its way. The relay host works in the other
direction, receiving incoming mail from the Internet or UUNet.

Mail Working with DNS

Maintaining organization-wide `hosts` tables is the kind of nightmare you would wish on your worst enemy. Most sites use DNS,
because each local domain takes care of its own local host files, and
the DNS mechanism effectively merges all the local host files to
maintain a single, accurate host table. DNS uses enhanced mail
routing with MX records which specify a mail exchanger, and it is
so important that we cover it in more detail in Chapter 17.

An Introduction to `sendmail.cf`

The `sendmail` command, in conjunction with the file `/etc/sendmail.cf`, is critical in routing mail by analyzing mail addresses and rewriting them for final delivery. We are used to seeing the address form `user@host.domain.domain_type` as in `schultz@peanuts.determined.com`, but how about UUCP addresses like `determined!peanuts!schultz`, where the ordering and delimiters are different? Recall that `sendmail` via `sendmail.cf` readdresses the mail. One of the many areas of the `sendmail.cf` configuration file is the definitions section (known in the trade as *defines*). They usually come at the beginning, and we should look at a simple one so you can become familiar with them.

Mail Delimiters as an Example of `sendmail` Defines

Mail delimiters like `@`, `!`, `.`, and `::` make it difficult to go from one addressing scheme to another. The `sendmail.cf` files usually start with definitions, and one of the first is delimiters. The single-character mnemonic operator `D` in `sendmail.cf` is a *define*. What is defined is called a `macro`, which for delimiters is `o`. Therefore, in `sendmail.cf`, the definition of the `o` delimiter macro is :

```
Do.:%@!^/
```

Note the lack of white space; there is nothing to make it easy for humans to parse. Parsing is done by having one character for each mnemonic.

A First Look at Addressing Translations

Since mail is sent in two parts, the message and the envelope, the header information must deal with addressing schemes, and `sendmail` must do the address translations and the resulting transformation. Following are some possible addressing schemes and the address transformations required to work on UNIX with `sendmail` and other mail and routing agents:

FROM	*TRANSLATION*
`sam@mfg.apex.com`	`sam@mfg.apex.com`
`apex!acme!zenith!sam`	`sam@apex.uucp`
`apex::sam`	`sam@apex.dnet`
`apex (sam)`	`sam@apex.ibm`

Many address translations are so complex that they cannot be done in one change, but rather require many macros and definitions and several rule sets (made of many separate rules) showing how the transformations take place with the aid of numerous mnemonics and variables as well as a few constructs like conditionals.

Internal Names (Canonical Form) and Focus

To put mail delivery into effect, mail addresses must have a consistent form internal to `sendmail`. Additionally, a `focus` is added to underscore (in a virtual sense) part of the address. The focus operators (`<>`) cause parsing to focus on whatever part of the address is within. In the following examples, the address part is focused, while the `host@` part is not:

```
sam@<apex.uucp>

sam@<apex.dnet>

sam@<apex.ibm>
```

The `user@host.domain` form is called the canonical form, needed by Rule Set 0 for message delivery. We'll go into more detail on rule sets later in the chapter.

Some Ideas for Mail Routing within a Domain

We do not always know the domain names of the people to whom we want to send mail, but even if we do, we are even less likely to know the host name. If there are 10,000 nodes in an organization, how can we possibly know the *user@host.domain* name? If I send mail within an organization and know the name or acronym of a department, logic tells us that we should be able to get mail to a user in that organization. If the design tool group is know as CAD, we should be able to use

```
jsmith@cad
```

to get to John Smith. In fact, this is done today using DNS and well known aliases. The mail master has an alias of `cad` in the `/etc/hosts` file with the following information:

ADDRESS	NODE NAME	ALIAS
123.21.60.122	svr08	cad

Now all systems can find `cad`, even though no machine by that name really exists. This concept will be expanded further later in the chapter.

Mail Aliasing and Mail Groups

We have seen that mail aliasing also works at the user level in mail setup files like `~/.mailrc`.

```
alias joanna jhunter@apex.com
```

If mail comes in addressed to `joanna`, it will go to the proper address at `jhunter@aex.com`.

However, you can also set up an alias for an entire group:

```
alias mfg joanna, pnguyen, chad, cchang, eric, jperez
```

All you have to do to send a letter to everyone in the group is to send mail to `mfg`.

Forwarding

Forwarding is done by way of the users' `.forward` files and through aliases. The `~/.forward` file simply contains the *user_name@host.domain* to which the mail is to be forwarded.

Aliases

A domain-wide list of user aliases can be maintained and distributed via NIS (YP) with a central `aliases` file that is used by `mail`. Traditionally, this file is `/etc/aliases`, but NIS replaces it with a YP map, making mail delivery much simpler and more effective. Say my machine is called `jaeger`. If the mail master is `svr04`, aliases can tie the two together:

```
bhunter:bhunter@svr04
```

If you want further simplicity, don't have a separate `/var/spool/mail` directory on every machine. Have one huge mail directory on one server, and NFS-mount it to all the domain's systems with an alias to the domain's organizational name or TLA (three-letter acronym), and all of these names and name/address pairs will work:

```
bhunter

bhunter@jaeger

bhunter@svr4

bhunter@acme.com
```

Mail Setup for Server and Workstations

Mail was originally intended to exist on one system which would service all of that machine's users, but today's paradigm is tens to hundreds of workstations using several servers which form a single domain. Large organizations are made up of several domains, and within each one mail could exist, with each system having its own separate mail spool area (such as `/usr/spool/mail` or `/var/spool/mail`). However, there will be many problems with

- delivering mail to users whose system name is unknown

- delivering mail to users who move from workstation to workstation

- mailing to the domain without knowing the system name

- keeping the `/var` or `/usr` areas from filling with unread mail

- spooling error messages in a single place where they can be found and acted upon

To avoid these problems, it is easier in the long run to have a single mail server, a system that not only is the mail master but has all the mail on a single disk partition, disk pack, or concatenated virtual disk. Addressing mail from the outside is painless when that server's name is aliased to the domain or organization name. That server also has access to the YP `aliases` map, and therefore can find any user. Therefore, all that remains is to mount the master's mail directory to each workstation. If the directory names are simple, the mount should also be simple:

```
mount mlsvr:/var/spool/mail /var/spool/mail
```

You must admit that `/var/spool/mail` is a well known address.

sendmail as a Mail Agent

Mail is collected and delivered by a *mail agent*, traditionally, but not necessarily, the `mail` command. It is processed for delivery by a *routing agent*, most frequently `sendmail`, unless it is for local delivery, in which case it is passed on to the *transport* or *delivery agent,* typically the Internet or UUCP.

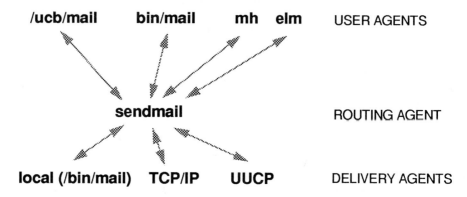

Figure 16.1: *Agents used for electronic mail*

Coming in the other direction, the *delivery agent* then passes mail to the *routing agent,* which passes it to a *mail agent.* Later in the chapter you will learn more about the `mailers` section of `sendmail.cf` and its reference to `local`, `prog`, and `smtp`.

Network Protocols

At the physical, link, and network layers, mail travels the same as any other traffic, but at the transport layer it must rely on SMTP and be able to find its own special port, TCP port 25.

```
telnet      23/tcp
smtp        25/tcp          mail
time        37/tcp          timeserver
```

`sendmail` listens (via socket) to that port for incoming mail, and it sends mail by way of the same port.

Mail delivery by way of the routing agent relies on the `sendmail` command to work as a daemon. In the system's run-command file (`rc` files), you will find lines like this:

```
if [ -f /usr/lib/sendmail -a -f /etc/sendmail.cf ]
   then
      /usr/lib/sendmail -bd -qlh
      echo -n ´ sendmail ´
```

This tests for the presence of the `sendmail` command and the
`sendmail.cf` configuration file. If they are found, the shell starts
`sendmail` with the appropriate flags to run as a daemon, and it
sets the queuing time. `sendmail` then uses its configuration file to
define how it delivers mail.

How the `sendmail.cf` File Works

The `sendmail` command works with the configuration file
`sendmail.cf` to configure the routing agent. In the broadest view,
the `sendmail.cf` file defines the mail environment (sets definitions for macros and set options), rewrites addresses to be accepted
by other mailers (by way of rules and rule sets), and does address-
to-instruction mapping (such as finding the appropriate mailer).

All vendors ship their systems with at least one version of
`sendmail.cf`, but most use two, one for the mail master and the
other for all subsidiary systems. Both are do-all, fits-all versions
that have too much code for most sites. Additional sources for
more streamlined versions of `sendmail.cf` (`tcpproto`,
`uucpproto.cf`, and `tcpuucpproto.cf`) can be gotten by
anonymous `ftp` from `ftp.uu.net`, and many a network has
relied on these files in a pinch.

At first you can get confused when you see two `.cf` files in
the standard distribution, but their uses soon become clear. One,
`sendmail.cf`, is intended to be used for all systems, whereas the
other, `main.cf`, is used by the mail master system. The
`sendmail.cf` file, like so many UNIX configuration files, is
divided into multiple sections, and the first is for general macros.
Each macro is represented by a single letter, such as D for *define*.
The definitions are for things like domain aliases, host name, rely
mailer and host, and DNS. But there are other macros besides the
defines, such as

C	Classes
V	Version number
D	Special macros
O	Options

Most of the macros are already defined in conventional `.cf` files, so usually all the administrator has to do is provide a few definitions for things like the domain name. Other macros are automatically provided by `sendmail`'s internal macros (such as `hostname`).

Configuring `sendmail` with `sendmail.cf`

The `sendmail` configuration file for individual nodes is always the smaller, simpler of the two configuration files; it only needs to get the mail routed to the mail master. Most `sendmail.cf` files are heavily commented; that's the way the file is documented.

A "frozen" (compiled) configuration file called `sendmail.fc` can be used for speed in reading the configuration files, but unlike the `.cf` file, it is not an ASCII file:

```
31% su
Password:
# file send*
sendmail.cf: ASCII text
sendmail.cf.save: ASCII text
sendmail.fc: data
sendmail.hf: English text
sendmail.st: data
```

While it does machine-read faster, it cannot be changed without recompilation. If there is no `.fc` file, the machine will always read the `.cf` file, but if you have an `.fc` file, you must remember to compile it into a new `.fc` file every time you change the `.cf` file (or be prepared to face the embarassing consequences).

To understand `sendmail.cf`, you have to understand that
`.cf` lines are jammed together for easy machine parsing. There is
no white space used unless it is part of a string. Therefore, white
space is significant to the macros being set and are not a part of the
parsing of macro tokens. Here is an example of a conditional:

```
Dq$g$?x ($x)$.
```

This is the total name format, and it is standard in host `.cf` files.
In this example, `q` is defined in terms of `g`, the sender address. It
says that if `s` (the sender name) is set, use it.

Format for Lines

Each line to be acted on (in the first part of the file) starts with an
uppercase letter for an action like define, class, option, and so on.
Here is the full set:

D	Definition
C	Class
0	Options
H	Headers
T	Trusted users
M	Mailer
P	Precedence
F	File for class definition
R	Address rewrite rule
S	Define rule set

Following this single-letter action (with no space) is the macro name, also a single letter. The ones defined regularly by `sendmail` are in lowercase. Those created by the administrator are local and in uppercase by convention.

Essential Macros

Here are the essential macros:

`w`	`hostname` (internal to `sendmail`)
`o`	Separators
`j`	"Official" domain name
`e`	SNMP entry message
`n`	Daemon name for error messages
`q`	Default sender name format
`l`	`From` line format

Initially, you may find yourself confused because you can't find a macro in a `sendmail.cf`. However, when a macro is undefined, no amount of searching will find it. These macros are internal.

Macros Internal to `sendmail`

Here is a partial listing of internal `sendmail` macros. Again, they are internal, and thus already known, so they are used but not defined in the `.cf` file.

`$`	`hostname`
`$s`	User's name from GECOS field
`$r`	Delivery agent protocol

$i   Queue ID (like **AA999999**)

$d   Date in UNIX **ctime** format

Rules and Rule Sets

Most of the .cf file is devoted to translating addresses. The defines set the values for the macros used by the rules, and the rules are used by the rule sets to translate addresses. Therefore, most of the configuration file sections preceding are a warm-up for these rules and rule sets. Here is where the addresses are reordered into a consistent internal format and readied for delivery.

A rule set is defined by the mnemonic S. There can be an arbitrary number of rule sets, but Rule Sets 0 through 4 are standard and are the most critical for administrators:

S0   Message delivery rule set applied to recipient address

S1   Sender rule set

S2   Recipient rule set

S3   Preamble rule set (applied to all addresses)

S4   Final output rule set

Also added to the addresses are:

D   Sender-domain addition

S   Mailer-specific sender rewriting

R   Mailer-specific recipient rewriting

Here is a diagram of how the rule sets are read:

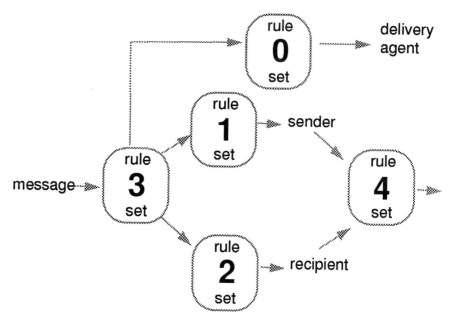

Figure 16.2: Message flow through the rule sets

`From:` addresses are handled in a more linear fashion:

```
-> 3 --> D --> 1 --> S --> 4 --> To:/CC:
```

Rule Set 3 gets the `To:` or `CC:` address first (Rule Set 3 is always first), and then it passes the address to get the sender-domain addition (like `acme`). Then it passes to Rule Set 1 and gets mailer-specific sender address rewriting.

Now let's go even deeper into the rule sets, one at a time. Rule Set 3 typically

- removes empty focus < >
- changes the address from the form *foo,bar;snarg* to *foo:bar:snarg*
- applies focus on the domain part (such as `bhunter<@acme>` or moves the focus right to the domain port

• orders old-style and UUCP addresses to the conventional "Internet" triple

In short, Rule Set 3 takes any form of addressing, strange or regular, long or short, and puts it into one format that the rest of `sendmail`'s rule sets can handle.

For the record, here's the code:

```
s4
R$*<$+>*        $2                   basic RFC822 parsing
R@$+,$+:$+      @$1:$2:$3            change all "," to ":"
R?@$+:$+        $@$>6<@$1>:$2        src route canonical
R$+:$*;@$+      $@$1:$2;@$3          list syntax
RS+@$+          $:$1<@$2>            focus on domain
R$+<$+@$+>      $1$2<@$3>            move gaze right
R$-!S+          $@$>6$1@$2>          already canonical
RS-!$+          $@$>6$2<@$1.uucp>    uucphost!user
R$-.$+!$+       $@$>6$3<@$1.$2>      host.domain!user
R$+%$+          $@$>3$1@$2           user%host
```

It looks almost unreadable now, but it won't seem that way after we look at the address rewrite rules and figure out what most of it means.

Address Rewrite Rules

The address rewrite rule section is the first place where white space is used for parsing where it is not a part of the string needed by the macro. The form is *right-hand-side TAB left-hand-side TAB comment*. The left-hand side (lhs) are pattern match symbols for the tokens, while the right-hand side (rhs) are the symbols used to do address (pattern) rewriting.

The token-matching symbols are:

$*	0 or more
$+	1 or more
$-	Exactly 1
$+x	Match any in class x
$~x	Not in class x
$x	All in macro x

NOTE: The set that Sun uses is extended.

Let's examine a pattern match. **$-@$+** matches not only `bhunter@stalker` and `bhunter@stalker.acme.com`, but also `bhunter@stalker.ace.acme.com`. On the other hand, **$-@$-** matches only `bhunter@stalker`.

Here are the rhs symbols:

$1	A match of the first metasymbol
$2	A match of the second metasymbol
$3	A match of the third metasymbol

It is important to note that exact tokens match exact tokens. So, for **$-@$+** on `bhunter@stalker.acme.com`, **$1** is `bhunter`, and **$2** is `stalker.acme.com`.

Address Transformations

The following are address transformation metasymbols:

`$N`	Substitute the indefinite token N
`$#mailer`	Resolve to mailer (used in Rule Set 0 only)
`$[strings$]`	Substitute canonical string
`$[hosts$]`	Map to primary host name (takes name from YP hosts.byname)
`${x names$}`	Map name through YP (Sun)
`$>N`	Call Rule Set N

The following are prefixes:

`$@`	Terminates rule set, returns remainder of the right-hand side
`$:`	Terminates rewrite rule but continues with the rule set

Prefixes cause immediate termination of the (S0) rule set and tell **sendmail** that the resolution of the name is finished. Note the syntax $#*mailer*@*host*$:*user* for the *mailer/host/user* triple needed by the mailer. The `$@` terminates the rule set, and the `$:` terminates rules to keep an address from looping; otherwise, a rule or rule set would keep acting on the address as long as the left-hand side was applicable. Take as an example a line out of a generic **main.cf** file from the Rule Set 3.

```
r$+<@$+>$@>     6$1<@$2>     already canonical
```

This rule states, "Take an address in canonical order like

`bhunter<#ace.acme.com>`, pass it through Rule Set 6, and return it in the same order in which you found it. The fixed tokens `<@ >` are to be left alone." Now if the prefix `$@` weren't there to tell `sendmail` to stop after the first pass, it would take most addresses and loop forever. For example, applying focus, the address `bhunter@jaeger` must transform to `bhunter<jaeger>`, so the rewrite rule is `R$+<$+>`. In the transformation

```
$1@$2<.$B>
```

where `$B` is defined as `acme.com`, the address alone changes from `bhunter@jaeger` to `bhunter@jaeger.<acme.com>`, and the rule is written to use the organization's full Internet address:

```
R$<@.$+>$1@$2<.$B>
```

Now that we've gone through the *rewrite* and *transformation* rules, Rule Set 4 shouldn't seem so mysterious:

```
S4
R$*<$+>$*            $2                 basic RFC822 parsing
R@$+,$+:$+           @$1:$2:$3          change "," to ":"
R@$+:$+              $@$>6<@$1>:$2       src route canonical
R$+:$*;@S+           $@$1:$2;@$3        list syntax
RS+@$+               $:$1<@$2>          focus on domain
R$+<$+@$+>           $:1$2<@$3>         move gaze right
RS+<@$+>             $@$>6$1<@$2>       already canonical
R$-!$+               $@$>6$2<@$1.uucp>  uucphost!user
R$-.$+$+             $@$>66$3<@$1.$2>   host.domain!user
R$+%$+               $@$>3$1@$2         user%host
```

Let's take apart the first few lines. The `S4` is Rule Set 4, and the first rule is `R$*<$+>$*     $2`. It states that the line of any number of strings (`$!`) followed by one or more tokens within the focus (`$2`) and again followed by any number of tokens (`$3`) are to be resolved into only that part within the focus, `$2`.

Here is a master's version:

```
S0
# On entry, the address has been canonicalized and
# focused by rule set 3.
R@                  $#local $:$n           handle <> form
# For numeric spec, you can't pass spec on to
# receiver, since receivers are not smart enough
# to know that [x.y.z.a] is their own name.
R<@[$+]>:$*       $:$>9 <@[$1]>:$2      Clean up, then...
R<@[$+]>:$*       $#smtp $@[$1] $:$2    numeric inet spec
R<@[$+]>,$*       $#smtp $@[$1] $:$2    numeric inet spec
R$<@[$+]>         $#smtp $@[$2] $:$1
```

Not all `.cf` files have to be this complex. For example, if you don't do UUCP, bitnet, or DECnet, you don't need those parts of Rule Set 4.

The mail address gets munched by several rule sets, but the last one it has to pass is Rule Set 4. Since it's the end of the line for the address, all final post writing takes place here. The rule set puts uucp addresses back into *host!user* form, and it removes the (<____>) focus and performs other clean-up operations. Here is some typical code:

```
S4
R$+<@$+.uucp>     $2!$1         u@h.uucp => h!u
R$+              $: $>9 $1      Clean up addr
R$*<$+>$*        $1$2$3         defocus
```

Notice how the first rule changes the order of uucp addresses.

```
R$+<@$+.uucp>     $2!$1
```

Also note how the second rule calls Rule Set 9:

```
RS+              $: $>9 $
```

The third rule simply writes out the address (as it exists at that point) and removes the focus. Rule Set 9 cleans up a name for passing to a mailer but leaves it focused.

```
S9
R@                  $@$n              handle <> err addr
R$*<$*LOCAL>$*      $1<$2$m>$3        change local info
R<@$k+>R*:$+:$+     <@$1$2,$3:$4      <rte-addr> canonical
```

NOTE: Rule Set 9 is not a standard rule set.

On the `From:` side, it's nearly the same, except Rule Set 1 is replaced by Rule Set 2, and mailer-specific recipient rewriting takes place.

```
        -> 3 ;;> D --> 2 --> R --> 4 --> From:
```

A rule set may be empty, and Rule Set 2 is a classic example.

```
    # Recipient field Pre-rewriting
    S2
    # None needed.
```

All messages must pass Rule Set 3, which turns all addresses into canonical form:

```
    local-part@mail_domain. org.maj_domain
```

as in

```
    bhunter@ace.acme.com
```

If there is no `@` part, it is taken from the sender name. If I were to send a letter to `shilo`, the `@` part is taken and appended as in `shilo@ace.acme.com`.

One organization's Rule Set 3 is S3. To the user it appears that canonical addressing is unnecessary, but as you can see, it is appended by sendmail if it is not put on by the user.

```
# rules for vms dni softswitch addressing
R$-O@sswvax            mrgate::ssw::acme::$1@sswvax
R$-@sswvax.acme.com    mrgate::ssw::acme::$1@sswvax
R$-@ssw                acme.$1@fmln.acme.com
R$-@ssw.acme.com       acme.$1@fmln.acme.com


# rule for old VMS style addressing
R$-::$-           $2@$1


# handle "from:<>: special case
R<>              $@@          turn into magic token


# basic textual canonicalization
R$*<$+>$*         $2          basic RFC822 parsing


# make sure <@a,@b,@c:user@d> syntax is easy to
# parse -- undone later
R@S+,S+:S+       @$1:$2:$3          change all "," to ":"
R@S+:S+          $@$>6<@$1>:$2      src route canonical


R$+:$*;@$+       $@$1:$2;@$3        list syntax
R$+@S+           $:$1<@$2>          focus on domain
R$+<$+@$+>       $1$2<@$3>          move gaze right
R$+<@$+>         $@$>6$1<@$2>       already canonical


# convert old-style names to domain-based names
# All old-style names parse from left to right,
# without precedence.
R$-!$+           $@$>6$2<@$1.uucp>  uucphost!user
R$-.$+!$+        $@$>6$3<@$1.$2>    host.domain!user
R$+%S+           $@$>3$1@$2         user%host
```

Remember the rule flow diagram? Sender addresses pass Rule 1 while recipient addresses must pass through Rule Set 2. Both output to Rule Set 4.

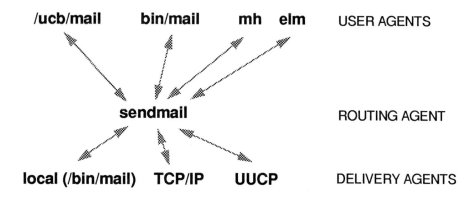

Figure 16.3: Agents used for electronic mail

Rule Set 0 is the message *delivery* rule set. It handles the envelope's destination address; therefore, it changes the envelope (qf file) information, not the address in the message itself. Rule Set 4 expects *name<@host.domain>*. It removes the localhost from the address.

Rule Set 0 applies to names that actually specify recipients and resolve to the triple *mailer/host/user*. (reference $h and $u). This rule resolves the address to the required mail triple, *uname@domain.organization*. Here is where we see internal conventions not seen in the user's address input or in the output modified by Rule Set 4. The first example is the introduction (and removal) of the string LOCAL. The full version of sendmail for a mail-master system has a lot of code, much of which is multiline address conversion. .cf files vary with each organization and distribution. Here is one sample:

```
S0
# On entry, the address has been canonicalized
# and focused by rule set 3.
# Handle special cases....
R@                    $#local $:$n        handle <> form
```

```
# resolve the local hostname to "LOCAL".
R$*<*S=w.LOCAL>$*    $1,$2LOCAL>$4        thishost.LOCAL
R$*<$*$=w.uucp>$*    $1<$2LOCAL>$4        thishost.uucp
R$*<$*$=w>$*         $1<$2LOCAL>$4        thishost


# Mail addressed explicitly to the domain gateway (us)
# terminate rule set (no-loop), call rule set 30,
# strip focused @LOCAL
R$*<@LOCAL>          $@$>30$1    strip our name, retry
$<@LOCSL>:$+         $@$>30$1    retry after route strip


# For numeric spec, you can't pass spec on to receiver,
# since old rcvr's are not smart enough to know
# that [x.y.z.a] is their own name.
R<@[$+]>:$*          $:$>9 <@[$1]>:$2    Clean up, then...
R<@[$+]>:$*          $#ether $@[$1] $:$2 num inet spec
R<@[$+]>,$*          $#ether $2[$1] $:$2 num inet spec
R$*<@[$+]>           $#ether $2[$2] $:$1 num inet spec


# deliver to known ethernet hosts explicitly
# specified in our domain
R$*<@$%y.LOCAL>$*    $#ether $@$2 $:$1,@$2>$3
# etherhost.uucp is treated as etherhost.$m for now.
# This allows them to be addressed from uucp as
# foo!sun!etherhost!user.
R$*<@$%y.uucp>$*     $#ether $@$2 $:$1<@$2>3


# Explicitly specified names in our domain --
# that we've never heard of
R$*<@$*.LOCAL>$*
    \ $#error $:Never heard of host #2 in domain $m


# Clean up addresses for external use -- kills
# LOCAL, route-addr ,=>:
R$*                 $:$>9 $1               Then continue...


# resolve UUCP-stype names
R<@$-.uucp>:$+      $#uucp  $@$1 $:$2    @host.uucp:...
R$+<@$-.uucp>       $#uucp  $@$2 $:$1
```

```
# Pass other valid names up the ladder to our forwarder
#R$*<@$*.$=T>$*      $#$M    $@$R $:$1,@$2.$3>$4
# Replace following with above to only forward
# "known" top-level domains
R$<@$*.$+>$          $#$M    $@$R $:$1<@?$2.$3>$4

# if you are on the DDN, then comment-out both
# of the lines above and use the following instead:
#R$*<@$*.$+>$        $#ddn   $@ $2.#3 $:$1<@$2.$3>$4

# All addresses in the rule ABOVE are absolute
# (fully qualified domains).
# Addresses BELOW can be partially qualified.

# deliver to known ethernet hosts
RS $*<@$%y>$*        $#ether $@$2 $:$1,@$2>$3

#other non-local names nowhere to go; return to sender
R$<@$+.$->$*         $#error $:Unknown domain $3
R$*<@$+>$*           $#error $:Never heard of $2 in domain $m
R$*@$*               $#error $:I don't understand $1@$2

# Local names with  are really not local!
R$+%$+               $@$>30$1@$2     turn % =>  @, retry

# everything else is a local name
RS+                  $#local $:$1
```

The `.cf` File's First Part

Now that you have a better understanding of how the rule and
rule sets work, let's look more thoroughly at the part of the `.cf`
file that precedes the rules.

Defines

It is important to understand that the first part of the `.cf` file sets
up `sendmail` for everything that comes after it. Here is where

most things are defined, options defined, trusted users named, and so on, before the rules and rule sets are created from the definitions and options. Here is a line-by-line explanation of the lines that precede the rules section of acme's master .cf file. We have already broken down rules 0 through 4, but note the local modifications for softswitch and SMTP.

```
# Part one -- the define

# The .cf version for the SMTP bannermacro Z
DZace-SMTP-version-5-14-92
# The local -- domain acme.commacro D
DDacme.com
#  The mail server (master's) full name acemacro R
DRace
#  Our official domain name!macro J
#  note $w is an internal macro for the hostname
Dj$w
#  The /usr/spool/mail moutn hostmacro U
DUsu04
#  Some soft-switch macros to define
#  "acme" and "ssw" (soft switch)
DIacme
DWssw
DTfmln
#  Name for error messages macro n
DNPostmaster
#  UNIX header format macro
#  note the builtins $g (sender addr) and $d date
DlFrom $g $d
#  Delimiter charactersmacro o
#  focus translated sender address
Dq<$g>
#  SMTP login messagemacro e
#  domain_name(j) "Sendmail" vers-no(v)/
        \ ready at date(z)
DE$j Sendmail $v/$Z ready at $b
```

Options

Options are not options in the `sendmail` command line sense (O), but options for configuration within the `.cf` file. In the options sections, you do things like set the default delivery mode, set the temporary file mode (reference `chmod`), set the default network name, define a queue directory, set queue `timeout` time, and so on. Most of the options are preset, for better or for worse, but some you will want to set yourself. For example, at the very beginning of the `.cf` file for the main or master you must decide if you want the gateway machine to identify itself as the domain. If so, you form the macro

        Dj$M

If you want the gateway machine to appear to be inside the domain, use

        Dj$w.$m

as *hostname.domain name,* such as `fmwu00.ace.acme.com`.

   If you are using `sendmail.ms` (or have a fully-qualified hostname), use

```
#DJ$w
#OPTIONS
# substitution for space (blank) characters --
# dot for blanks
OB.
# default delivery mode (deliver in background)
ODbackground
# temporary file mode -- note the umask-type mode
#OF0600
# log level
OL9
# default network name (D = acme.com)
#ON$D
# default messages to old style header format
Oo
# queue directory
OQ/usr/spool/mqueue
# read timeout = 20 minutes
```

```
Or20m
# statistics log file
OS/usr/lib/sendmail.st
# queue up everything before starting transmission
Os
# set queue timeout to 4 hours
OT4h
# time zone names (V6 only)
#OtEST,EDT
# default UID1 = daemon
Oul
# default GID 1= daemon
Og1
# load average at which we just queue messages
Ox11
# load average at which we refuse connections
OX12
```

Message Precedences

Message precedence controls how quickly a message will be delivered. The higher the precedence number, the faster it is delivered. Negative precedences are delivered about as fast as bulk mail.

```
Pfirst-class+0
Fspecial-delivery+100
Pbulk=-60
Pjunk=-100
```

Trusted Users

Trusted users are the only users that `sendmail` will listen to.

```
Troot daemon uucp dni
```

Headers

Headers are critical to mail delivery and the "envelope" information. To understand the headers section of the `.cf` file, take a look at the header part of any mail message. Short mail messages are over half header information, and that is how important headers are to `sendmail`. As a result, `sendmail.cf` spends a lot of its space defining headers. Here is a header format conditional's format using the x macro, the user's name as taken from the GECOS field of the password file:

        $?x $x $.

An example would be the format of a total name for the default sender name format, which must include the sender's name as it appears in the `passwd` comment (GECOS) field:

        D1g?x ($x)$.

This defines q (Dq) as the sender address ($g). The `sendmail` internal macro ($x) is the user name taken from the GECOS field. It sets q to g if g is already set. Here is a header line that shows the application of $g, $x, and sender address (sender name):

        From: bhunter@ace.acme.com (Bruce H Hunter)

Tha last $. is the end of the conditional.

Here is an example of a header:

```
# EXAMPLE
# H?P?return-path: <javani@ace.acme.com>
# Hreceived: from fmwull by ace
# (4.1/ace-SMTP-gateway-version-8-r-92)
# id AA01298; Mon, 5 Oct 92 14:16:41 PDT

H?P?Return-Path: <$g>
#  H?P?return-path: <javani@ace.acme.com
H?M?Received: $?sfrom $s $.by $j ($v/$Z)
id $i; $b

#  Hreceived: by fmwull
#  (AIX 3.1/UCB 5.61/ace-SMTP-version-5-14-92)
#  id AA14396; Mon, 5 Oct 92 14:16:39 -700
```

Following is the `headers` section of the `.cf` file example:

```
H?D?Resent-Date: $a
H?D?Date: $a
H?F?Resent-From: $q
H?F?From: $q
H?x?Full-Name: $x
HSubject:
H?M?Resent-Message-Id: <$t.$i@$j>
H?M?Message-Id: <$t.$i@$j>
```

Mailers

The mailer definitions are last in the `sendmail.cf` for the master. `local` and `prog` are standard in all `sendmail` files, but `smtp` is a classic example of mailers added since the original `sendmail` was created (display truncated):

```
Mlocal, P=/bin/bellmail, F=lsDFMmn, S=1, R=1,
Mprog,  P=/bin/sh,        F=lsDFM,   S=1, R=1,
Msmtp,  P=[IPC], F=mDXMueXLN,  S=1, A=IPC $h,
```

Rule Set Commentary

Our `sendmail` file system simplifies the five basic rule sets, 0-4. Set 3 is traditionally the most complex. Here is a typical Rule Set, broken down with commentary.

```
S3

# handle "from:<>" special case
# note $@ is terminate rule set
RS*<>$*        R@@         turn into magic token

# basic textual canonicalization
# keep only the focused part
```

```
R$*<$+>$*        $2          basic RFC822 parsing

# make sure <@a, @b, @c:user@d> syntax is easy to
# parse -- undone later
$@S+,S+:S+       $@1:$2:$3       change all "," to ":"
R@$+:S+          $@$>6<@$1>:$2   src route canonical

RS+:$*:@$+       $@$1:$2;@$3     list syntax

R$+@$+           $:$1<@$2>         focus on domain part
# note $: is terminate rewrite rule
# (to prevent looping)

RS+<$+@$+>       $1$2<@$3>       move gaze <focus> right
R$+<@$+>         $@>6$1<@$2>     already canonical
```

Naming conventions are ironed out here, and the rule reads

> *one_token!tokens   host!user -> call ruleset 6 -> user@host.uucp*

```
   # convert old style names to domain-based names
   # all old-style names parse from left to right,
   # without precedence
```

This one reads:

```
token!tokens (call rule set 6) -> user@host.uucp
R$-!$+        $@$>6$2<@$1.uucp>     uucphost!user
token.tokens!tokens (call rule set 6) ->
     \ user@host.domain>
R$-.$!$+      $@$>6$3<@$1.$2>         host.domain!user
```

> *tokens%tokens (rule set 3) user%host -> user@host*

Note the call-back to Rule Set 3 ($>3):

```
   R$+%$+              $@$>3$1@$2     user%host
```

Rule Set 6 has been called above, but what is Rule Set 6?

```
# Rewriting rules
# special local conversions
S6
R$*<@$*$=m>$*   $1,@$2LOCAL>$4   cnvrt local domain
```

tokens<@tokenstoken_in_class_m>tokens

Debugging Rule Sets

A large part of the executable `sendmail` code is devoted to debugging, by invoking with the executable (`/usr/lib/sendmail`) with the debugging flags and by handing `sendmail` the name of the file to be debugged. The command is interactive, so it will ask you for the name of the rule set to be tested and for an address to be worked on. The command will then show you the address line by line as it works on each token. Look at the following example, which takes the address `bhunter@stalker.acme.com` and works it with Rule Set 3:

```
# /usr/lib/sendmail -bt -C/etc/sendmail.cf
Address Test Mode:
Enter <rule set> <address>
> 3 bhunter@stalker.acme.com
rewrite:rule set 3    input:"bhunter" "@" "stalker"
                             "." "acme" "." "com"
rewrite:rule set 3 returns:"bhunter" "@" "stalker"
                             "." "acme" "." "com"
> 1,3 bhunter
rewrite:rule set 1    input:"bhunter"
rewrite:rule set 1 returns:"bhunter" "@" "ace"
                             "." "acme" "." "com"
rewrite:rule set 3    input:"bhunter" "@" "ace"
                             "." "acme" "." "com"
rewrite:rule set 3 returns:"bhunter" "@" "ace"
                             "." "acme" "." "com"
```

```
> 1,3,4 knovak@ssw
rewrite:rule set 1    input:"knovak" "@" "ssw"
rewrite:rule set 1 returns:"knovak" "@" "ssw"
rewrite:rule set 3    input:"knovak" "@" "ssw"
rewrite:rule set 3 returns:"knovak" "@" "ssw"
rewrite:rule set 4    input:"knovak" "@" "ssw"
rewrite:rule set 4 returns:"acme: "." "knovak" "@"
                              "fmln" "." "acme" "."
                              "com"
```

Note the conversion in Rule Set 4 for `acme's softswitch`.

Here is Rule Set 4 from an *acme* AIX system:

```
S4
 #
 # rule added to make soft-switch addressing
 # easier changes
 # "anything@ssw" to
 # "acme.anything@fmln.acme.com"
 #
 R$-@$S$*              $I.$1@$T.$D

#    Some soft-switch macros
DIacme
DSssw
DTfmln
```

```
token 1                2  3
lhs    1               @  $S
novak                  @  ssw
Token  2   3   4   5   6   7
  $I       $1  @   $T  .   $D
acme  .  knovak @ fmln . acme.com
```

Now let's use this knowledge to look at Rules 1 and 2 with `sendmail` in debug mode:

```
> 1,2 bhunter
rewrite: rule set  1    input:  "bhunter"
rewrite: rule set  1 returns:  "bhunter" "@" "ace"
                               "." "acme" "." "com"
rewrite: rule set  2    input:  "bhunter" "@" "ace"
                               "." "acme" "." "com"
rewrite: rule set  2 returns:  "bhunter" "@" "ace"
                               "." "acme" "." "com"
```

And let's not forget Rule Set 0 to get to a mail router:

```
> chad@linus.mitre.org
rewrite: rule set 0    input:  "chad" "@" "linus"
                               "." "mitre" "." "org"
rewrite: rule set 0 returns:  "^V" "smtp" "^W" "ace"
                               "^X" "@" linus" "."
                               "mitre" "." org"
>
```

And finally, let's review the rule set:

```
S0
R$*          $#smtp$@$R$:$1              punt to Relay
```

This reading takes the entire string and prepends it with
`R#smtp$@$R$`. The result of the *rhs* expansion is:

```
    "^V" "smtp" "^W" "ace" "^X"
```

Address Transformations and the Different Rule Sets

Notice how the addresses have changed with each rule set. Focus
is added, moved, and deleted. Triples (when used) change. Internal constants (like LOCAL) are added and then removed, all a function of which rule set is in use. Canonical form is used and dis-
carded. Whereas Rule Set 3 used the canonical form
local_part@host_domain_spec, Rule Set 0 wants the triple
mailer,host,user.

Mail Debugging with the mqueue Directory

One more advantage to a large central mail server is that tracking down delivery problems is made easier by putting all the error messages in one place in the mqueue directory. If the master has a problem delivering a message, it will register its complaint in the log file in mqueue. If a user has problems getting or sending mail, check /var/spool/mqueue for error messages. Look for the times required to complete the delivery as an indicator of potential problems. Mail delivery is stopped or hampered when:

- the recipient system is not up or not on the network

- addressing is erroneous

- the wrong user name is used (a solid argument for first initial/last name user-naming conventions)

- the *user-name/address/aliases* combination is not correct in the mail aliases file

Here are some typical error messages from the file mqueue/syslog:

```
24% grep -v xntp *
syslog:Oct  2 04:05:42 syslog restart
syslog:Oct  2 14:15:27 localhost: 15918 sendmail:
    AA15918: message-ID =<921002211
5.AA15918@fmcs04>
syslog:Oct  2 14:15:27 localhost: 15918 sendmail:
    AA15918: from=burton, size=81
23, class=0
syslog:Oct  2 14:15:28 localhost: 15920 sendmail:
    AA15918: to=ptin,
delay=00
00:01, stat=Sent
syslog.0:Oct  1 04:05:42 syslog restart
syslog.0:Oct  1 20:03:30 localhost:
    elcsd:file system almost full
CAN'T log err
ors to /syserr.fmcs04
```

```
syslog0.Oct  1 20:04:21 localhost:
    elcsd:file system almost full,
CAN'T log err
ors to /syserr.fmcs04;
```

Testing Mail with the `usr/ucb/mail` Command

There are ways to debug mail without `sendmail` in debug mode by using the `mail` command, and a quick way is with the `mail` `-v` flag:

```
# mail -v chad@linus.mitre.org
Subject: mail.test
forward to dev-null
.
Cc:
root... setsender: A user number or a group number
                   is not valid.
chad@linus.mitre.org... Connecting to ace.smtp
chad@linus.mitre.org... Connecting to ace (smtp)...
220 ace Sendmail 4.1/ace-SMTP-gateway-version-8-...
7:18 PDT
>>> HELO jaeger
250 ace Hello jaeger, pleased to meet you
>>> MAIL From:<root@ace.aacme.com>
250 <root@ace.acme.com>... Sender ok
>>> RCPT To:<chad@linus.mitre.org>
250 ,chad@linus.mitre.org>... Recipient ok
>>> DATA
354 Enter mail, end with "." on a line by itself
>>> .
250 Mail accepted
>>> QUIT
221 ace delivering mail
chad@linus.mitre.org...Sent
#
```

Note the mail delivery mechanism coming out of the woodwork as we see the domain (`ace`) connecting to `smtp`.

`sendmail` **Isn't Enough**

`sendmail` can't get mailed delivered without node names being resolved into Internet addresses. This is the job of DNS, the subject of the next chapter.

CHAPTER
17

DNS and BIND

The Domain Name System

The difficulties of managing a name space go up incrementally to the square of the number of hosts when done without DNS. Look at the ease of managing the name space of a standalone organization of 100 nodes. All you have to do is keep one accurate `hosts` file and propagate it to each system. And if you incorporate NIS, it will propagate itself.

Now imagine an organization large enough to have several suborganizations, each 100 nodes in size. When other groups or organizations (let's call them domains) change their host tables, you will have no knowledge of these changes. Likewise, when you change yours every few days with additions, deletions, and modifications, they will have no knowledge of the changes. It doesn't take too long before a lot of nodes become unreachable. Naturally, those will be precisely the ones you need.

How to get around this problem? Assume that you can get some poor trusting soul to act as a central authority and maintain a single central master YP-class hosts file. Every few days (or every few changes, whichever is relevant), you carefully cut your portion of the `hosts` file, with all the changes, and send it to the central authority. That individual would have to take your changes, merge them with the changes of others, and put them in the master `hosts` file, being careful to delete all records that might be duplicates. For example, if host `stalker` moves its Internet number because it has gone to another subnet, the central authority would have to remove the old `stalker` before the new one was added. Of course, every deletion would also have to be updated also. It's obvious that no would would last long in a job like this, because it would drive anyone crazy.

Fortunately, there is a better solution — DNS. It is implemented (in UNIX) by BIND, the Berkeley Internet Name Domain Service. We know the domain name system conventions of Internet addresses from working with `sendmail` and `sendmail.cf`, so let's create a mythical company on the Internet called Acme, Inc., with a *zone* or *domain* for manufacturing called `mfg`. The canonical address for a user named George is

```
george@mfg.acme.com
```

This shows that George's address is in the Internet itself, and therefore its address is in `in-addr.arpa`. If the node `mfg` is at address `143.234.60.24`, its full address is

```
134.234.60.24.in-addr.arpa.
```

but we don't ever see it that way in the `hosts` file because the `in-addr.arpa` part is understood. In this example, the domain is the `com` (commercial) zone of the Internet. Within that huge name domain the address is Acme's, and within `acme.com` the host address is `mfg`. The purpose of DNS is to find hosts in specific domains (within the name space of the Internet). IP addresses determine domains. It is important to understand that each IP address can be mapped directly to a fully qualified domain name; otherwise, there is no particular relationship. A domain can have several IP addresses as well as a multiplicity of subnet addresses, all of which can be legitimately described as one name, like `acme.com`:

```
acme.com.in-addr.arpa.
```

Outside of DNS, it is customary to see addresses written from the smallest subdomain to the larger organization, as in

```
mfg.acme.com
```

Interestingly enough, we will see that they are written backwards for use in DNS.

Bind Configurations

The BIND service resolves names to addresses. It caches them for rapid resolution. This service is done through DNS servers. Bind is a part of DNS, and bind systems can be set up for several different kinds of configuration:

- as a resolver only
- for caching only
- as a primary name server
- as a secondary name server

Name Servers

Name servers are both programs and the systems that run them which have the *authority* for a zone. A zone is their part of the name space and the terms *zone,* and *domain* are nearly synonymous.

Name servers fill a request for name data and come in two types, depending on where they get their data.

Primary master	Gets data from the host it runs on
Secondary master	Gets data from another name server

Note the similarities to YP — a YP *master* has its own data, and a YP *slave* gets updated from the master. Secondary masters query the primary master from time to time with a *zone transfer* and update their information. Secondary masters can transfer this data from the master or from another secondary master.

Primary master servers must, at the very least, maintain these files:

```
named.hosts

named.rev

named.boot

named.ca
```

These files are traditionally kept in the directory /etc in /etc/named. They can be put anywhere, as long as the location is known in the configuration file. Here is a typical listing of a namedu directory.

```
47% pwd
/etc
48% ls name*
named.boot           named.db            named.local
named.ca             named.db.save       named.pid

named:
acme.hosts           named.ca.bak        rev185.143.hosts
acme.hosts.00024     named.ca.null       rev215.128.hosts
isc.hosts            named.local         rev233.133.hosts
named.boot           rev137.46.hosts     rev233.133.hosts
named.ca             rev183.143.hosts
```

The prefixes and suffixes are ca for cache, rev for reverse (name resolution), and db for database.

Effect on the `/etc/hosts` File

Before DNS, `hosts` files had as many entries as there were nodes. A `hosts` file with over 10,000 names and addresses has obvious problems. With DNS, our YP master's `hosts` file only has a few hundred entries. Here is part of an `/etc/hosts` file from the Acme YP master:

```
127.0.0.1    localhost lcl me loopback
133.233.70.1      syn1a
#      Synoptics concentrator sub-1 fm3-124
133.233.70.2      syn1b
#      Synoptics concentrator sub-1 comp room
133.233.70.3      syn1c
#      Synoptics concentrator sub-1 m2-13
133.233.70.10     svr03-1
133.233.70.11     svr04-1
133.233.70.12     svr05-1
133.233.70.13     teru-1
133.233.70.13     svr01-1
133.233.70.14     svr01-1
133.233.70.15     jaeger
133.233.70.16     wkst50
133.233.70.20     wkst00
133.233.85.21     wkst03
     .

     .
133.233.90.43     fmpc24 #+
133.233.90.44     fmpc25 #+
133.233.90.45     podor 133.233.90.100
          \ sub90-gw1 ssd.gw
133.233.90.165    seaview
133.233.90.166    graph23 #SD graphics sparc
133.233.181.6     svr03
133.233.181.7     mfg mailhost dnihost svr04 svr02
133.233.181.8     svr05
133.233.181.9     ps03
143.185.80.2      gaff
```

Nodes within an organization get information about hosts that are not in the local YP hosts map from their own name server's files like `/etc/named/acme.hosts`.

Notice how, in the following example, there are over 51,000 lines in the `hosts` file:

```
19% pwd
/usr/named
20% wc -1 acme.hosts
51700 acme.hosts
22% head acme.hosts
$ORIGIN com.
acme IN SOA pallas.acme.com.
     \ postmaster.pallas.acme.com. (
                    92111909 14400 300 604800 86400 )
              IN        NS        aurora.acme.com.
              IN        NS        pallas.acme.com.
              IN        NS        ssd.acme.com.
              IN        A         128.215.62.139
```

Observe the surface similarity to `/etc/hosts`. We see that authority is given to `pallas`. `aurora`, `pallas`, and `ssd` are name servers.

Here, in `acme.hosts`, is the node `jaeger`:

```
jaeger            IN        A         133/233/70.15
                  IN        MX        0 jaeger.acme.com.
                  IN        MX        5 hermes.acme.com.
                  IN        MX        10 aurora.acme.com.
                  IN        MS        20.ssd.acme.com.
```

Here again, the line

```
jaeger            IN        A         133/233/70.15
```

is more like a line in `/etc/hosts` than you might expect. It states that `jaeger` is an Internet address at address 133.233.70.15. It just takes more space and a couple of extra keywords to do it.

Resource Records

All the configuration files use resource records. In our examples, most of the files in the Acme directory `named.*` work with resource records. Their format is similar and use the same recording-type notation. Here are the keywords:

SOA	Start of authority defines parameters of zone's data
A	Address converts host name to address
PTR	Pointer converts address to host name
MX	Mail exchange where to deliver mail
CNAME	Canonical defines alias host name
hinfo	Host information host software and OS description
WKS	Well known service advertises network services
IN	(Internet DNS resource record)
NS	name server

The format of a DNS resource record is *[name] [tt1] IN type data,* where *type* is what kind of resource record it is, and *data* is information specific to the record.

Resolvers

Backing up a bit, DNS is implemented by the BIND software. It is typical server-type software, and the client side is called the *resolver*. Therefore, resolvers are client (code) that access the name servers for domain information. A resolver queries the name server, interprets its response, and returns the information to the calling program.

To set up a resolver-only system, configure `/etc/resolv/conf`:

```
domain acme.com
primary 133.233.85.166    galadriel
primary 128.215.62.139
primary 128.215.49.30
primary 143.185.65.2
```

Here is a prime example of multiple addresses resolving to just one name, for the name attached to all of these addresses is `galadriel`.

Caching

In the process of resolving names, a server makes a lot of queries and gets a lot of answers, and this takes time and network bandwidth. It learns the addresses of other servers and then gets the data it sought. The servers can cache this data to speed up any further inquiries. Caching-only servers run name-server software but do not keep name-server database files. They extract and cache their data from full-service name servers. Here is part of the cache file, `named.ca`:

```
;   BIND data file for initial cache data
        \ for root domain servers.
.                    99999999  IN NS ns.nasa.gov.
.                    99999999  IN NS ns.nic.ddn.mil.
.
.
.
                     99999999  IN NS SRI-NIC.ARPA.
SRI-IC.ARPA.         99999999  IN A 10.0.0.51
USC-ISIC.ARPA.       99999999  IN A 10.0.0.52
BRL-AOS.ARPA.        99999999  IN A 128.20.1.2
BRL-AOS.ARPA.        99999999  IN A 192.5.22.82
ns.nasa.gov.         99999999  IN A 128.102.16.10
ns.nic.ddn.mil.      99999999  IN A 192.112.36.4
```

The 99999999 is ttl, time to live, so large a number that the data will never be removed from the cache. Usually, ttl is left blank.

Full Resolution

How do names get fully resolved? Resolution starts at the root of the DNS system and eventually works out to the node. Name resolution is done by a name server for both the name space for which it has authority and the space for which it does not. A name server can always query a *root* name server for information out of its zone of authority. A *root* name server provides a list of names of servers on the level below it, and those servers do the same at the next level. With this scheme, names can be resolved from the topmost level down until DNS gets to the host itself.

Name/Address Order

We are used to seeing the canonical forms of names used by mail and sendmail and Internet numbers or addresses in the host file form as in 133.233.70.15, so now let's reexamine them using a little white space for clarity:

```
133.      233.      70.      15
```

which, when using the symbolic names, is

```
com       acme      mfg      stalker
```

Notice that with this scheme, if the numbers are in the order you expect, the name is not, so you need the reverse order to go from leaf to root:

```
stalker   mfg       acme     com
```

which, when going back to the Internet numbers, is

<pre>
15   70   233   133
</pre>

So, in reality, both the symbolic name and the Internet number can be expressed in either order if the software is ready for it. Note that you will find this *reverse* address order in the file `/usr/named/rev233.133.hosts`. The reverse file for the Acme 133.233 subnet is

```
$ORIGIN 70.233.133.in-addr.arpa.
125          IN         PTR       fmps01acme.com
127          IN         PTR       siva.acme.com
131          IN         PTR       valentino.acme.com
1            IN         PTR       fmsyn1a.acme.com.
2            IN         PTR       fmsyn1b.acme.com.
3            IN         PTR       fmsyn1c.acme.com.
04           IN         PTR       fmswg02.acme.com.
.
.
54           IN         PTR       stalker.acme.com.
55           IN         PTR       wkst61.acme.com.
```

When reading this file, the keywords are `IN` and `PTR`. As we've already seen, `IN` is the Internet DNS resource record, and `PTR` is the pointer that converts an address to a host name.

nslookup

One of BIND's biggest contributions to the administrator's tool box is the `nslookup` command. We can use `nslookup`, for example, to get information about a name server

```
# nslookup pallas.acme.com 128.215.62.139
  Server:   acme.com
  Address:  128.215.62.139

  Name:     pallas.acme.com
  Address:  128.215.62.139
```

The command can also be used interactively. Note the – flag and the > prompt.

```
gayland# nslookup - 128.215.62.139
 Default Server:  acme.com
 Address:  128.215.62.139
 > set type=ns
 > ssd
 Server:  acme.com
 Address:  128.215.62.139
 ssd.acme.com      nameserver = ssd.acme.com
 ssd.acme.com      nameserver = ns.uu.net
 ssd.acme.com      nameserver = aurora.acme.com
 ssd.acme.com      inet address = 137.46.201.30
 ns.uu.net         inet address = 137.39.1.3
 aurora.acme.com   inet address = 143.185.65.2
```

Setting Up for DNS

One of the first steps in setup is to make YP go outside the local
domain (YP.mfg) to get names that are not in the YP master's
/etc/hosts file. The changes to the system start with the YP
Makefile. Set the B variable to -b to have YP use the resolver.
Note that all NIS servers must be individually configured to use the
resolver. Here is the DNS part of the make file:

```
B  =  -b
#B =
```

Daemons

To be a server, the server runs the named daemon

```
# ps -ax | grep named
  118 ?   IW   11:30 in.named -b /usr/named/named.boot
22517 p8 S   0:00 grep named
```

The daemon is started in rc.local:

```
39% grep named rc*
    rc.local:if [ -f /usr/etc/in.named -a -f
        /usr/named/named.boot ]; then
    rc.local:    in.named -b /usr/named/named.boot :
        echo -n ´ named´
```

Name Server Files for Setup

The file `/etc/resolv.conf` is used to configure the resolver. Note: To be technically accurate, the *resolver* is not a program or a node but a set of library routines. Typical configuration files use the following keywords:

> *nameserver*   *address*

The keyword `nameserver` identifies (by Internet address) the server that the resolver will ask for zone information.

Another entry uses the keyword `domain`, which defines the default domain name.

> *domain*   *name*

Below, you will not see the *nameserver* line, but you will see keywords `domain` and `primary`:

```
% cat resolv.conf
    domain acme.com
    primary 133.233.85.166
    primary 128.215.62.139
    primary 128.215.49.30
    primary 143.185.65.2
```

The primary address `133.233.85.166` is for the server `gayland`, and, in fact, all these addresses will track back to the server `gayland`. Again, one organization can have multiple addresses for the same name:

```
gayland# nslookup 133.233.85.166
 Server: gayland.acme.com
 Address:    133.233.85.166
 Name:       [133.233.85.166]   Address 133.233.85.166

gayland# nslookup 128.215.62.139
 Server: gayland.acme.com
 Address:    133.233.85.166
 Name:       [128.215.62.139]
 Address:    128.215.62.139

gayland# nslookup 143.185.65.2
 Server: gayland.acme.com
 Address:    133.233.85.166
 Name:       [143.185.65.2]
 Address:    143.185.65.2
```

This file is read each time a process accesses the resolver. If this file is not there, the server will fall back on a default configuration. The local host is the default name server and the default domain name = `hostname`.

named Configuration Files

When working with named configuration files, here are the key words to look for:

directory   The directory for all file references

primary   The primary server for this zone

secondary   The secondary server for this zone

cache   The cache file

forwarders   Forward queries to these servers

slave   Forces the server to use only the forwarders

Here is one version of the file:

```
; type domain                              source host of host
directory /usr/named
; domain acme.com
secondary  acme.com     128.215.62.139    acme.hosts
secondary  215.128.IN-ADDR.ARPA 128 215.62.139
        \ rev215.128.hosts
secondary  185.143.IN-ADDR.ARPA 128.215.62.139
        \ rev185.143.hosts
secondary  183.143.IN-ADDR.ARPA 128.215.62.139
        \ rev183.143.hosts
secondary  233.133.IN-ADDR.ARPA 128.215.62.139
        \ rev233.133.hosts
secondary  ssd.acme.com 128.215.62.139
        \ 137.46.201.30 ssd.hosts
secondary  isc.acme.com 128.215.62.139
        \ 137.46.201.30 isc.hosts
primary    0.0.127.in-addr.arpa   named.local
cache                             named.ca
; forwarders 143.185.65.2 128.215.62.139
```

named.hosts

named.hosts is the zone file for name-to-IP address resolution. This is typical:

```
jaeger          IN      A       133.233.70.15
                IN      MX      0 jaeger.acme.com.
                IN      MX      5 hermes.acme.com.
                IN      MX      10 aurora.acme.com.
                IN      MX      20 ssd.acme.com.
ctdcs2          IN      A       128.215.97.1
```

named.rev

named.rev is the zone file for *reverse* domain for IP address-to-host resolution. Here is a typical portion.

```
$ORIGIN 70.233.133.in-addr.arpa.
125          IN        PTR          fmps01.acme.com.
127          IN        PTR          siva.acme.com.
131          IN        PTR          valentino.acme.com.
```

Notice the difference in the two files. The hosts version keys on the host name, the reverse version on the address with the address backwards from the way most of us are accustomed to seeing it.

named.local

Like the mandatory loopback entry in /etc/hosts, named.local exists to cvonvert the 127.0.0.1 address to loopback. It is the zone file for 0.0.127.IN.ADDR.ARPA.

```
;
; BIND data file for local loopback interface.
;
0 IN     SQA   gayland.acme.com.  tcpip.cadev6.acme.com. (
                   1          ; Serial
                   3600       ; Refresh
                   300        ; Retry
                   3600000 ; Expire
                   3600 )   ; Minimum

      IN     NS    gayland.acme.com.
   1  IN     PTR   localhost.
   localhost.  IN   A          127.0.0.1
```

Frequently, it has a companion, named.rev.

X Marks the Spot

The purpose of this chapter was to give you a better idea of where mail manages to get its names resolved to addresses for delivery. Next, we will look at how to maintain one of the most well known of all network services, The X Window System.

CHAPTER

18

Administering the X Window System

Administering the network involves more than administering network software. You must also deal with applications that run on the network. In short, if it's a network application, and it's on your domain, you own it, and it's up to you to keep it going. Thus, no book on UNIX networking would be complete without one example of a network software application, and the X Window System is ideal because it is so popular and because it was developed for working with the network. In fact, X Windows, as it is informally called on occasion, is so common on UNIX distributed systems that eventually it will be considered standard.

It's possible to administer the X Window System without understanding its internals, but it's much easier to troubleshoot if you understand some of them. Therefore, we're going to take the time to carefully examine X Windows, but not from a user's perspective. We're going to look at X Windows from an administrator's perspective, an entirely different slant. NOTE: Administrators are not X Window gurus. They need to know enough to install and keep a moderately vanilla version alive.

GUIs and X Windows

The X Window System is often called X Windows or X. X's early beginnings started at both Stanford, with a windowing system called W, and MIT with Project Athena, in which a consortium of OEMs and the university developed a network where all computers could be reached with a common interface. The result of this research was graphical user interfaces, also known as GUIs (pronounced "gooeys").

GUIs give users visual interfaces with both the operating system and applications, thus allowing them to be more productive and to learn the system quickly. Other GUI ideas emanated from MIT's Sketchpad (1962), SRI International's NLS tiled windows, University of Utah's Flex, and PARC from XEROX. The first common commercial application of a GUI was seen in 1983 on Apple's Lisa machines.

A graphical user interface gives a common look and feel from system to system, and even from operating system to operating system. Consider OSF's Motif, which is largely associated with IBM in spite of OSF origins, since IBM pushed it so heavily and used it in its AIX systems. However, other early usage by OEMs like SCO guaranteed the propagation of Motif across several operating systems, so users can be working on Motif on OS/2 and then go over to a DOS machine running Motif. The point is that GUIs make it easier for users, because they can go across operating systems and still have a familiar interface.

GUIs are becoming complex, and it takes several layers to make a complete system. Let's take a look at the big picture:

```
LAYER   DESCRIPTION                        EXAMPLES
================================================================
1       desktop manager                    Xdesktop
2       user model (window manager)        Motif, Open Look, twm
3       windowing model                    X10, X11
4       imaging model (not on UNIX)        GDI, Quickdraw
5       OS                                 UNIX, DOS, OS/2
6       Hardware                           Sun, DEC, HP, IBM
```

The first four layers make up a GUI. SCO's Open Desktop, for example, has a built-in *desktop manager* (which might be thought of as a window for your window's icons), and it can be used to take care of reaching common commands and functions. Users simply point to an icon of the function they need (such as an editor or the file system manager), then click, and they have it on the tube. The desktop manager is on Layer 1.

Layers 2 through 4 are known as the *applications programming interface* or API. SCO's choice of a Layer 2 window manager is Motif, and their Layer 3 X version is X11. UNIX has no imaging model (Layer 4). Be aware that not all UNIX systems have a desktop manager, either, and thus they consist of only two layers: the window manager and the X version. SunOS has Open Look as its window manager, and it uses X11 for its windowing model.

Just because your systems come with a desktop manager doesn't automatically mean that all of your users will want to use it. Some of your users will prefer a fully embellished GUI with a deskstop manager, because it is a user-friendly interface that reduces most of their work to *point-and-click* operations with the mouse. However, many of your more technical users may prefer to do without a desktop manager, instead running on something like **twm** on top of X11, because they'd rather manually do tasks like create windows, go into **vi**, and manipulate files. User preferences vary widely.

Because Open Desktop is prepackaged, the choices of desktop manager, window manager, and windowing model have already been made for you, and there is no question that prepackaged software like this is easier to administer. However, this kind of

simplicity isn't possible on most of the larger technical sites with
file servers. Some user tools will only run on a certain version and
release of X, so administrators may have to run them all to
accommodate all of the tools your users need. You will probably
also have to run several different window managers as well to
satisfy user preference and need.

Now let's look at the API from an entirely different perspective,
the programmer's point of view:

```
LAYER    API              PROGRAM
==========================================
1        -                desktop manager
2        Xm               mwm, twm
3        Xlib, Xt         X server
4        imaging model    -
5        OS
6        hardware
```

Layer 1, the desktop manager, is a way to get to lower layers, and
thus is not easily user-programmable. However, at Layer 2 the
Motif library (Xm) is the applications programming interface to the
window managers, and on Layer 3 the X libraries and the X tool kit
are the API for the X server, X11. Thus, one typical API consists of
the X Window System libraries, Xt and Xlib, in combination with
the Motif library, Xm. Clearly, X Windows is perceived from
different points of view.

The buzz words *look and feel* are widely associated with the
varying versions of the X Window System, and they merit a more
precise explanation. Think of *look* as the consistent appearance of
widgets, gadgets, icons, window borders, and cursors, whereas *feel*
relates to the consistent behavior of the methods used to expose,
iconify, move, focus, and activate those widgets, gadgets, icons,
and windows. The consistent *look and feel* is what makes the X
user interfaces truly user-portable.

X Basics

The key to understanding *any* system in UNIX is to understand its underlying technology and design, and the X Window System is no exception. Let's look at a model of the X architecture:

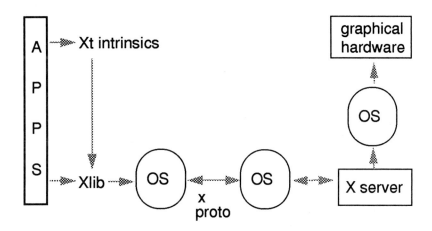

Figure 18.1: Model of the X architecture

The graphical hardware (the display device, the mouse, and the keyboard) reaches the X server through the operating system. The X server attaches to the network via TCP/IP and the X protocols. At the other end is the client side of the model, where applications are reached by way of the X library primitives, X intrinsics, and the X tool kits.

It's time to start building a glossary and defining some terms:

X server	The software and hardware that owns the keyboard, terminal, and mouse.
graphics hardware	The keyboard, display device (CRT), and mouse.
Xlib	The subroutine libraries that provide the underlying primitives for X.

event	An input device action like a key, a button click, a screen, or a program event that can have a similar effect.
action	The desired effect of an event, such as moving a window.
Xt	The X Toolkit, the higher-level X routines of the X library.
intrinsics	The toolkit to build toolkits, the glue or matrix that supports the creation of widgets and translating actions into callbacks.
widget	A user interface object such as an on-screen button or a scroll bar which lives in its own window and causes an action when the user activates it.
callbacks	Map actions to application functions, procedures called under prespecified conditions.
resource	The data associated with a widget or other X object settable by applications or clients.

So far, all we've done is present you with data. Let's start putting the information together and making some sense out of all this.

The X Client/Server Relationship

A server is the entity that owns the (physical) resources. The file server owns the disks, the print server owns the printers, and the X server owns the keyboard, mouse, and display device (such as the tty or the monitor). An X client, on the other hand, is a process that takes input from the X server and gets the desired work done. The magic of all this is that the user's X server and its input-output devices can get work done by any X client anywhere on the network. This makes particular sense when looking at an X terminal or a DOS PC working as an X terminal, running applications on other hosts within its local domain.

The X Stuff on the Screen

Let's dissect an X screen full of X objects. All the larger, discernible objects are *windows* — an `xterm` is a *window*, a menu is a *window*, and all of the graphic utilities like `xload` and `xeyes` are *windows*. Taking the familiar `xterm` window apart, at the very least you will find things like *scroll bars* or *sliders*, push buttons for iconifying the window or for resizing, and a title bar. In the mushy vernacular of X, these are *graphical objects*. A graphical object that "resides in its own window" and causes an action when interacted with is a *widget*. There are also *gadgets* created at a higher level than widgets to save space and improve performance. The latter take less code and are simpler to implement, but they cannot be created without the former. Widgets are X-toolkit user-interface building blocks, and each has a single job. Widget sets are collected to create a user-model-level entity that the user recognizes, such as Motif, MIT's Athena system, or AT&T and Sun's OLIT.

One way to move an `xterm` window with `twm` is to move the cursor with the mouse to the title bar of the window, press the middle button of the mouse, and with the button still down *drag* the window to a new location. Applying X terminology, the title bar is the *location*, the sustained holding down of the mouse's middle button is the *event*, and the move of the window is the *action*. The *mapping* of the *event*, the push of the mouse button to an *action* (the window movement), is a *translation*. This definition is important, since all keys and buttons must be mapped with translation tables.

Equally important is understanding that this takes place on the X server, and the X clients are totally independent of all this, for X was designed to free clients from the burden of translations. A side benefit is that you don't have to suffer the additional network traffic.

X Resources

An X resource is an attribute of a graphical object like the width (in pixels) of a border or the color of a window's background. It is the data in a widget changeable at the command level, and therefore settable by applications and clients and highly customizable by the user. To some extent they are the things you see on the screen, including the details of windows, your cursors, fonts, pixmaps, and colormaps. Resources are abstracted at the programming level and have associated integer indentifiers. A user may easily alter resources by manipulating the resource files by modifying the resource specifications in files like `.Xdefaults` or `.Xresources`. The format of a resource specification is:

```
object[.*]subobject[.*]subobject[.*]
      ... attribute: value
```

Now let's look at a few more definitions:

object   Client program.

subobject   A piece of the widget-level hierarchy, like a window, slider, button, or menu.

attribute   A feature of the last subobject, including font, label, geometry, bitmap, and background.

value   The setting of the attributes, such as `blue`, `currier-14`, and `80x66`.

We will go into resources in greater detail further on in the chapter.

Widget Hierarchy

Applications are constructed from hierarchies of widgets, the same sort of widget hierarchy seen in the subobjects of a resource specification. A simple window like `xcalendar` has its own widget hierarchy, and the hierarchy starts with `xcalendar` itself. The hierarchy descends into the `xcalander`/Form and branches to `controls`/Form to describe the buttons functions. The controls form branches down to a `quitButton`/Form, a helpButton/Form, and a date/Label. At the other side under calendar/Form, the branches go down to daynumbers/Form and daynames/Form. The latter branches to daynumbers/Command and SUN/Command, while daynumbers/Form branches to 1/Command through 31/Command.

Classes and Instances

The resource files are made up of definitions that use the widget hierarchy, objects, and their subobjects, attributes, and values, all bound together to named resources. Another part of the resource naming are *classes* and *instances*. A class is a group or collection of graphical objects or applications that share similar properties, and every component of the resource specification has a class. The first letter of a class is traditionally uppercase, as in Foreground. Instances are a single occurrence of an item in a class, and are therefore existing objects. They start with a lowercase letter.

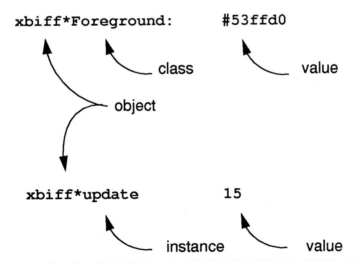

Figure 18.2: Classes and instances

Bindings

To do a tight binding of a resource, you have to know the entire widget hierarchy, but few people do. A tight binding is used to fully specify a resource and match only those objects that are an exact match, and tight binding specifications separate subobjects with a dot. Full knowledge of the hierarchy can be avoided by using loose binding (symbolized by the asterisk, *), which partially specifies a resource, close enough for most applications.

With this foundation of X basics, administering X should make a little more sense. Most of the battle of understanding a new technical area is won by taking the "magic" out of it.

Administering the X Window System

Users view X Windows in many ways. To the casual user, it is a visually exciting interface that offers speed, ease, and convenience, but it is also one more thing to learn in order to be functional. To system and network administrators, X represents another major subsystem that must be supported and provided with substantial resources.

X is only one layer of the GUI, and systems administrators must deal with it. Naturally, any software new to the systems has an impact on the people who install and maintain the systems and software, and X administration duties are many and varied. For example, they must request and install physical resources for X, install the X releases, provide for multiple versions, create and install user start-up file scripts, and install and maintain X file systems on file servers. They must set up and maintain X on workstations and set up X terminals and X terminal servers, if they are used. They also must understand X process management, maintain X's resource files, and be able to troubleshoot X and understand its resource requirements.

One of the first things you learn about X as an administrator is the difference between the X Window System and X Window managers. What the user perceives as X Windows (and may perceive as an X *specification*), the system administrator perceives as one of many available *window managers*, including Motif's or Open

Look's. From the system administrator's perspective, regardless of which window manager is used, the actual windowing *system*, X, is the same. There are even virtual window managers such as `olvm` (Open Look virtual window manager) and `mvwm` (Motif virtual window manager).

There are many window managers, and `uvm`, `twm`, and `mwm` (Motif) are just a few. Window manager choices are partly determined by user preference and prejudice, and partly by other factors, but since window managers are user interfaces to the system and the network, be prepared to support numerous X Window managers on your site. You may also need to support more than one version and/or release of X, but we'll get into that later.

Resource Requirements

Other sites may have different requirements, but for commercial sites that do a lot of work, X heavily affects workstations in terms of resource use, and you will find that X is CPU-, network-, and memory-intensive. Eight megabytes are required for black and white terminals. At our site, color systems were happily running `sunview` with eight megabytes, but they all dropped dead trying to run the same applications on X10. When we gave each of them 12 megabytes, they ran great until we moved to X11, and then they all fell down and died again, requiring 16 megabytes to revive and run comfortably. You may be able to get by with less memory on your site, depending partly on your machines but mostly on the kind of applications you run. Try your applications with each successive X version and release, and be prepared to increase real memory if necessary.

Our experience is that all X versions and releases need at least 4 MIPS, and they should have 64 megabytes of swap space. In fact, X Version 11 Release 3 and 4 was dismally slow for us even at 4 MIPS, but it looks great at 18 MIPS. We've also found that X looks better on a high-resolution screen (pixels per inch), equal to or greater than 1024x840, so be prepared to invest in high-resolution terminals or monitors. We have run X applications like FrameMaker at 840x600, but small fonts suffer.

X also affects your file servers. At least ½ to 1 gigabyte of additional file server disk space is required for multiple versions of X and multiple tool versions and applications running with X. Some computers on the network that run X have to serve X terminals, and additional CPU capacity is needed for these X terminal servers, since they must respond to TFTP and NFS from each server as well as tend to the servers' boot-up needs. X terminal servers require 30 plus megabytes for storing the software, but you can also have an X terminal server take its files from a file server.

It's easier to install and administer X if you know how it works, and at first its terms may be confusing. Initially, X may seem to redefine the terms *server* and *client*. In fact, the meanings may seem almost reversed from the conventional file server and workstation relationship. However, the meanings make more sense if you think of the X server as the owner of the resource.

Typically, you work at a workstation, PC, or X terminal, and the work goes out to a server; however, from the X perspective, your keyboard, screen, and the immediate X process associated with them are known as the *X server*, and the *clients* are the processes that the *X server* is running. Although users can have any number of X *client* processes anywhere on the net, they can have only one *X server*, which takes input from the keyboard and the mouse, gets output from the *clients*, and displays it on the users' screens.

Most workstation and PC users use their system as their *X server* and run *clients* there as well, but the base part of X is a text- and graphics-oriented system designed to do its work across the network between the *X server* and its *clients*. Thus, X is also designed to run on one system and display on another. As a result, users can run *client* processes anywhere on the net that they have access, and they can have the results in graphics and glorious X colors right at their desks. Users also love the way they can customize their X Windows.

The user model of X, the window managers, are easily customized, and X customization is highly practical for administrators, too. Picture having one window open on your own machine for weekly utilization reports, another open on a user's workstation doing a fix, and three more open on the servers.

The system administrators are responsible for building and populating the directories that will house X's programs and for creating the startup files at both the system and user levels to get the users going. The more versions of X that you have, the more times you will do this. Theoretically, executables should be located in /usr/bin/X11 libraries in /usr/lib/x11, but in practice there are no hard and fast rules for file locations or even the names of the start-up scripts. On the other hand, you might as well try to adhere to any precedents that you find. Most system administrators aim for /usr/bin/X11 or /usr/local/bin/X11 and /usr/lib/X11 for the X locations on the X servers (workstations and PCs), but the locations on file servers will vary greatly.

Installing X from MIT Source Tapes

Installing and updating X can be easy, difficult and time-consuming, or anything in between. If it is part of the OEM's distribution, it is already installed or is just another software package to install. Installing the latest version of Motif on an AIX system, for example, requires that you create temporary space for the software to be read in from tape. You install Motif with the aid of smit, and the entire installation takes less than 15 minutes with almost no effort since smit does all the work. All you need to do is answer its questions properly. At the other extreme is the installation of the X consortium tapes.

MIT source tapes are not needed by everyone; indeed, many commercial sites get along quite well without them. However, porting houses and GUI programmers would have a tough time without MIT source tapes. If you are willing to try your hand at installing X from MIT source tapes, just be aware that you have your work cut out for you. There are four tapes — one required, one recommended, and two optional. There are at least a dozen

pages of installation instructions, so be sure to read all the
READMEs. If you have never done this before, start with the release
notes, RELNOTES, too.

Short of the MIT installation, the hardest installation is taking X
from another system and bringing it to your own. It would be
easier to take it off the distribution, but X is often customized for
particular applications at certain sites, and the distribution versions
won't have everything your users need. Sometimes you may find
yourself having to take if off a machine that belongs to another
group, and they have different ways of doing things, so you may
have a hard time finding the X software. The system's startup
script is the place to start your search, because it points to most of
the file locations directly, and others indirectly through the scripts
it calls.

Move to each X directory and create an archive file with `tar` or
`cpio` with the `o` option. Don't forget the X-related files in `/etc`.
If you have to install more than one system, which is usually the
case, create an installation script to go along with the archive files,
and put it all on one tape. Put the installation script on the tape
first, and then the files and directories. At the other end, all you
have to do is read in the installation script. When it executes, it
will read in the files and directories.

MIT Tape Installation Specifics

On most commercial sites, X is part of the OEM's distribution. It is
present when you install the system, like SCO's Open Desktop, or
on a preinstalled system, as in the case of most Suns. All that the
administrator needs to do in these cases is to reinstall it on the file
servers for access by the workstations in order to conserve disk
space and to have a consistent environment. The MIT source code
is not necessary. On the other hand, larger commercial installations may find MIT source handy for a sanity check.

Short of telling you how to get the tapes from the X consortium, following is a sketch of how to install X11 from the Athena
tapes. The base of MIT X is installed from a set of four tapes, and
the contents of the MIT X11 R4 source tapes are:

README	Initial install instructions
RELNOTES.PS	R4.LI release notes in PostScript
RELNOTES.txt	R4.LI release notes in plain text
RELNOTES.lpt	R4.LI release notes in *lpt* format
tape-1/	core.LI software for X Window System (required)
tape-2/	contrib.LI clients and core doc (recommended)
tape-3/	contrib.LI libraries and other toolkits (optional)
tape-4/	contrib.LI Andrew, games, etc. (optional)

Many sites take the MIT source from a central distribution system. To extract the sources into another directory, such as /usr/local/src/X11R4/, here's what you do:

```
% cat *.??|uncompress|(cd /usr/local/src/R4/;
       tar xvf -)
```

Building the Release

The MIT X11 distribution has two parts:

- core software supported by X Consortium (./mit/)
- user-contributed software (./contrib/)

The *core* distribution is set up for easy configuration; the user-contributed distribution requires being built by hand. Makefiles in the core software are generated automatically by imake. The program combines machine-independent descriptions (called imakefiles) of targets to be built with machine-dependent sets of parameters. Initial versions of all of the Makefiles are included for those sites that cannot use imake.

Installation Summary

1. Read the Release Notes.

2. Create a release directory named `/usr/local/src/X` or `/src/R4/` or something similar. 100 to 300 megabytes will be required.

3. Read the tapes in. (They are in `tar` 1600 BPI format.)

4. Read the file `mit/config/README` for instructions on how to configure the build for your particular site.

5. Carefully check the `imake`-configuration parameters in `mit/config/imakemdep.h` and `mit/config/Imake.tmpl`.

6. Look at the configuration file (`.cf`) for your system; set the make variable `BOOTSTRAPCFLAGS`. If you can't find it, use:

   ```
   % make World >& make.world &
   ```

   If you do find the variable, you should append that definition to the command line, using the `make` variable `BOOTSTRAPCFLAGS`. This is used by `imake` to set particular `cpp` symbols for all compiles. (Now if you are porting to a different platform, see `mit/util/imake/imakemdep.h`.) Special `BOOTSTRAPCFLAGS` are required on the following systems for which `.cf` files are supplied: MacII, AT&T 6386, IBM workstations, and the Tektronix 4310 series. Example:

   ```
   % make BOOTSTRAPCFLAGS=-DmacII World >& make.world &
   ```

   This will rebuild all of the `Makefiles` and execute a `make -k all` to compile everything in the core distribution.

7. Make backup copies of your old X header files, binaries, fonts, and libraries.

8. Go to the top of the build tree and type

   ```
   # make install >& make.install
   ```

   For manual pages, type `# make install.man`. If your system is not a window system, you may have to add device drivers or reconfigure your kernel and create additional pseudoterminals.

Considerations

The `imake` sources and configuration files have been consolidated into the directory `./config/`. The machine-dependent files are named `*.cf` and use `cpp` symbols instead of `make` variables so that defaults can be provided. The `imake` and `makedepend` predefined constants have been moved into `./config/imakemdep.h` so that there is only one file to edit when porting to a new system. Here is what you need to do to build:

1. Set the `OSMajorVersion` and `OSMinorVersion` variables in the appropriate `./config/*.cf` files.

2. Check the parameters in `./config/site.def`.

3. Look in `./server/ddx/*/README` for any specific instructions.

4. Type `make World >& make.world &` (do not name the log file `make.log` or it will get deleted).

5. Run the install.

6. Check the log file for any errors. The release should build clean (except for optimizer warnings on some systems).

7. Save your old `/usr/bin/X11/`, `/usr/include/X11/`, `/usr/lib/X11/`, and `/usr/lib/libX*`.

8. Do a `make install` if you want manual pages installed. Type: `make install.man`.

9. Check to see that `xterm` is `setuid` to `root` and `xload` is either `setuid` to `root` or `setgid` to whichever group owns `/dev/kmem`.

10. Remove any `xterm -L` lines from `/etc/ttys`.

11. Check the `xdm` configuration files in `/usr/lib/X11/xdm/`. In particular, make sure that the `.Xservers` file contains the appropriate name for your type of server (such as `Xqvss`, `Xqdss`, `Xsun`, `Xibm`, `Xapollo`, `Xhp`, `XmacII`, `Xcfbpmax`,

Xmfbpmax, or Xtek) or that you have created a link named
/usr/bin/X11/X.

12. Make sure that /usr/bin/X11 is in your path.

MIT Release File Locations

By default, the release will install its files into the following places.
These locations set the standard for where X software is to be
located.

/usr/bin/X11/	Executable programs
/usr/lib/X11/	Fonts, color databases, and application default resources
/usr/lib/	Programming libraries
/usr/include/X11/	Programming header files

Porting to a New Platform

If you are trying to port this release to a new platform, you will
need to do the following:

1. Read the release notes.

2. Follow the directions in ./config/ about setting up a .cf
    file and adding an #ifdef block to Imake.tmpl. The best
    way is to find a system similar to yours and start from there.

3. Check the definitions in ./include/Xos.h.

4. Check the networking code in the following files in the
    ./lib/X/ directory: Xlibos.h, Xlibint.h, XlibInt.c,
    XConnDis.c, Xstreams.h, Xstreams.c.

5. Check the definitions in ./lib/Xt/Xtos.h.

6. If you plan to build the server, check the definitions in
    ./server/include/os.h, the networking code in
    ./server/os/*, and add appropriate blocks of definitions to
    ./server/Imakefile.

7. If you are not building a server, make sure the `BuildServer` parameter in your `.cf` file is set to `NO`.

8. Type `make World >& make.world &`.

Kernel Configuration

On a first-time install, you may have to add peudoterminals to the kernel's configuration file. It may even be necessary to add device drivers:

```
config  vmunix  swap generic

pseudo-device   pty     # pseudo-tty's,
                        # also needed for SunView
pseudo-device   ether   # basic Ethernet support
```

With the `ptys` added, an `ls -l` of `/dev` will show the pseudo-driver entry points.

```
crw-rw-rw-  1 root       21,    0 May 21 18:01 /dev/ptyp0
crw-rw-rw-  1 root       21,    1 Jan 15 15:19 /dev/ptyp1
crw-rw-rw-  1 root       21,    2 May 28 11:26 /dev/ptyp2
  .
  .
crw-rw-rw-  1 root       21,   20 Nov 16  1988 /dev/ptyq4
crw-rw-rw-  1 root       21,   21 Nov 16  1988 /dev/ptyq5
crw-rw-rw-  1 root       21,   22 Nov 16  1988 /dev/ptyq6
```

Useful MIT Tape Documents

Even with the documentation, you have your work cut out for you. Following is a minimal set of documentation:

Release Notes - `./RELNOTES.ms`

X general information man page - `./X.man`

`Xlib` Changes - `doc/Xlib/R4Xlib.tbl.ms`

Server Changes - `doc/Server/r4.tbl.ms`

xdm man page - `clients/xdm/xdm.man`

Copyright infomation - `./COPYRIGHTS`

Standards information - `./Standards.man`

Running X Clients

Remember, by definition X *clients* are the programs running under X that *generate* data but cannot *display* them. What you type in on the command line to make an X client run depends on where your job is running. The system was designed to run jobs from one node on the network to another, although they can run locally as well. For example, if you want to graphically show the CPU load on your local workstation, you type **xload &**. This is a typical use of X. However, if you want to see what the load is on the server, but from your own workstation, the job must be started on another system and the display shown on your system. In other words, your X job runs remotely with local windows:

```
% rsh snoopy 'xload -display stalker:0:01' &
```

Note that in both cases, the process is run in the background to free the window. Also note that **xload** is fired on the server **snoopy** by **rsh**, but the **-display** flag is set to put the output on the local workstation **stalker**. This same task can be accomplished in many other ways under X, but this way it's easy to demonstrate what's happening.

X Terminals and Requirements

Whenever you type in an ASCII character on an ASCII or ANSI terminal, it uses what precious little intelligence it has to translate and print the character on screen. Graphics monitors on workstations are far more sophisticated, requiring a frame buffer to aid in the translation. However, because X provides actual *terminal emulation* with the **xterm** program, emulating a DEC VT102 for character work and a Tectronix 4014 for graphics, the systems administrator must set up the user's TERM and TERMCAP variables accordingly whenever creating a new account or bringing an old one over to X. For C shell, the user's TERM constant will usually be set to `xterm`:

```
setenv term xterm
```

but for Bourne shell, use:

```
term=xterm; export xterm
```

Naturally, there must also be an `xterm` entry in `termcap` or `terminfo`, but since `termcap` is such a huge file, use `grep` to make sure the information is there:

```
% grep xterm /etc/termcap
vs|xterm|vs100:\
```

Now the environment knows the terminals we can start on a script to start X.

Startup Sequence

Systems administrators must understand the basic startup sequences of X, because they have to support and create startup scripts at both system and user level:

1. The user types in the script name, and then the startup script in the user's regular path is executed.

2. That script will do some initialization, and the startup script executes `xinit` and runs `xinitrc`.

3. `$HOME/.Xdefaults` is read.

4. `$HOME/.xinitrc` is read.

5. The window manager is executed.

6. The window manager's `rc` file is read.

In the process, `xrdb` gets the information about the resources. Much of the resource initialization comes from the system's `.Xdefaults` or `.Xresources` file. If the system's `.Xdefaults` and `.xinitrc` are fired but the files are not there, the system will execute the user's own version of these files.

Thus, following is a rough sketch of the typical homegrown command sequence interacting with existing X commands. Note the arbitrary command names and paths:

```
1) /usr/local/bin/X11 ----------------|
                                       |
2) /usr/local/X11/bin/xinit[X11]--| <-|
                                  |
3) ~/.xdefaults (from (2)) <------|
                                  |
4) ~/Xinitrc (from (2))-| <-------|
                        |
5) _wm  -----| <--------|
             |
6) ._wmrc <--|
```

Ref. xrbd, xset and xmodmap

To reiterate, the script will exist in two versions, the system's and the user's. The system's is always executed, and eventually the user's will be also if it is found. Here is the startup script pseudocode:

```
if already running X Windows
   then
      complain
      quit
if not console
   then
      complain
      quit
test arguments
# set environment

set open-window_home, news_home
set lib_path
set local_dir, man_path
set x11_only   # and other sun
               # open look goodies
# extend user path for X

path = $path + xpath
# set version and revision
remove old logfile
```

```
# execute xinit with .xinitrc
if file local/bin/xinitrc exists
  then
     local/bin/xinitrc
     else
        ~/.xinitrc
# xinitrc
```

Here's how it looks when you add some Bourne shell flesh:

```
#!/bin/csh -f
# user's startup script
if ( $?WINDOWS )
 then
    echo "The "'$WINDOWS'" environment \
           variable is set to $WINDOWS."
    echo "$WINDOWS is already running"
    exit 1
 endif
curtty=`tty`
if ( ${curtty} != "/dev/console" )
  then
    echo "You can't start X from the console"
    exit 1
 endif
# Set the location of local X11 information
setenv X11LOCAL /usr/local/X11t
setenv XSERVERRC $X11LOCAL/bin/xserverrc
setenv XMANPATH \
        $OPENWINHOME/share/man:$X11LOCAL/man
set xpath = ($OPENWINHOME/bin $X11LOCAL/bin)
setenv XPATH `echo $xpath | sed 's/ /:/g'`
# identify the current window version
setenv WINDOWS X11
setenv XVER 11
setenv XREL 3
# Extend the user's path
set path = ($xpath $path)
if ( ! $?MANPATH )
```

```
   then
     setenv MANPATH /usr/man:/usr/local/man
   endif
setenv MANPATH ${XMANPATH}:${MANPATH}
# Remove old X log file
rm -f /tmp/xinitrc.$USER
# Start X11 using commands from
# $X11LOCAL/bin/xinitrc.X11
if ( -f $X11LOCAL/bin/xinitrc.X11 )
   then
     exec xinit $X11LOCAL/bin/xinitrc.X11> \
         & /tmp/xinitrc.$USER
     else if ( -f ~/.xinitrc.x11 ) then
       exec xinit ~/.xinitrc.x11>& /tmp/xinitrc.$USER
       else
         exec xinit >& /tmp/xinitrc.$USER
   endif
```

Note how the script calls `xinitrc`, the next link in the startup chain. It is neither long nor complicated. Here is its pseudocode:

keymap with the keymap file   #xmodmap

load the resource database   #xrdb

if HOME/.xinitrc exists
 then
   execute $HOME/.xinitrc

create the console window

Now the `xinitrc` script itself:

```
#!/bin/csh -f
setenv WINDOW_PARENT /dev/win0
# Redefine the X11 keymap according to the
# X11 version being run...
if ( -f $X11LOCAL/lib/keymap.X${XVER}R${XREL})
  then
    xmodmap $X11LOCAL/lib/keymap.X${XVER}R${XREL}
  endif
# Setup X resources...
if ( -f ~/.Xdefaults.x11 )
  then
   xrdb -load ~/.Xdefaults.x11
   else
    if (-f /usr/local/X11/lib/sys.Xdefaults)then
    xrdb -load /usr/local/X11/lib/sys.Xdefaults
  endif
# execute the user's .xinitrc file
if ( -f ~/.xinitrc.x11 )
  then
    (~/.xinitrc.x11 &) >> /tmp/xinitrc.local.$USER
  endif
exec $X11LOCAL/bin/xterm -C -name console\
    >> /tmp/xinitrc.$USER
```

Recall that mapping is the connection between an event, a location, and an action. An example is to click *middle* on the title bar and move. The *event* is click the middle mouse button, the *location* is the tile bar of the window, and the *action* is to move the window. Critical in the `xinitrc` script is the keymapping done by `xrdb` loading `.Xdefaults` (or `.Xresources`) into the resource database and `xmodmap`, which creates and modifies the key map. During this process, notice that several subsidiary commands are called, including `xmodmap` for key mapping, `xrdb` to manipulate the X resource database, and `xset` (called repeatedly to set characteristics).

Keymapping and Translation Tables

All keys used for X must be mapped. Some keys are mapped for user- or system-defined X functions, like "F" keys (the function keys at the top of the keyboard), others are mandatory for X, like the "meta" key (X's unique give-it-another-function key), and finally, all mouse buttons and related keys must be mapped.

Definition of *mapping*:

The connection between an *event*, a *location*, and an *action*. *Example*: Click middle on title bar and move.

Definition of *translation*:

Mapping of an event to an action is a translation. Translations are kept in the translation table.

Reference the `xmodmap` command and the translation tables.

What Is `keymap`?

Mapping instructions and information occurs throughout the X initiation files. However, there are separate and distinct keymap files dedicated to X. Look at the X11 lib directory:

```
% ls /usr/local/X11/lib            # site-specific lib
app-defaults
keymap.X11R3                        # keymap for X11 rev 3
keymap.X11R4                        # keymap for X11 rev 4
rbg.dir
rbg.text
sys.Xdefaults
system.mumrc                        # Motif rc
```

Now the contents:

```
% cat keymap.X11R3
keysym R10 = Left
keysym R12 = Right
```

```
keysym R8 = Up
keysym R14 = Down
add mod1 = Meta_L
add mod1 = Meta_R
add mod1 = Alt_L
add lock = Caps_Lock
```

Note the syntax:

keycode	number = keyname
keysym	keyname = keyname

Keymappings can be seen with **xmodmap**, and separate keymaps are required for different architectures and models.

```
% xmodmap -pk
There are 2 KeySyms per KeyCode; KeyCodes range from 8 to 132.

    KeyCode  Keysym (Keysym)    ...
    Value    Value   (Name)     ...

       8     0xffc8 (F11)
       9
      10     0xffc9 (F12)
      11
      12     0xffbe (F1)
      13     0xffbf (F2)
      14     0xffc7 (F10)
      15     0xffc0 (F3)
      16     0xffc8 (F11)
      17     0xffc1 (F4)
      18     0xffc9 (F12)
      19     0xffc2 (F5)
       .
       .
     125     0xff6a (Help)
     126     0xffe5 (Caps_Lock)
     127     0xffe7 (Meta_L)
```

```
128       0x0020 (space)
129       0xffe8 (Meta_R)
130
131
132       0xffab (KP_Add)
```

Resource Naming `.Xdefaults` **and** `.Xresources`

Resources are controlled in the system's and the user's files, `.Xresources` or `.Xdefaults`. We need to review a few definitions in order to understand these resource files, so with deliberate repetition we will look at objects, subobjects, and binding again, only this time in greater detail.

Definitions:

object	Client program.
subobject	Widget level hierarchy, such as windows or menus.
attribute	A feature of the last subobject.
value	The setting of the attribute, such as color or size.

Let's review the syntax used in `Xresources` or `.Xdefaults`:

object.subobject[.subobject].attribute: value

EXAMPLE: `xlock*Background: black`

As we see in the example, the object is bound to the attribute. How they are bound is important, because there are two kinds of binding and two ways to show those bindings:

Tight   *   Loose

Within bindings there are also classes and instances, so we have another set of definitions:

class: Every component of the resource spec has a class.
                     It always starts in uppercase.

instance: A single occurrence of an item in a class.
                     It is always lowercase.

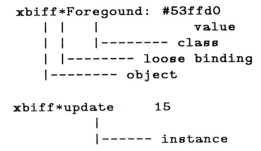

```
xbiff*Foregound:  #53ffd0
     |  |    |              value
     |  |    |-------- class
     |  |-------- loose binding
     |-------- object

xbiff*update      15
         |
         |------ instance
```

Now putting all of this together, here is a example of a typical `.Xdefaults` or `.Xresources` file:

```
OpenWindows.MultiClickTimeout:        4
OpenWindows.Beep:                     always
OpenWindows.SetInput:                 followmouse
OpenWindows.ScrollbarPlacement:       left
OpenWindows.PopupJumpCursor:          True
OpenWindows.IconLocation:             right
OpenWindows.SelectDisplaysMenu:       False
OpenWindows.DragRightDistance:        10
OpenWindows.MinimalDecor:             xbiffXmanxclock
bitmap*Background:                    wheat
bitmap*Border:                        maroon
bitmap*Foreground:                    maroon
bitmap*Highlight:                     SlateBlue
bitmap*Mouse:                         SlateBlue
xclock*Hands:                         #ffc92c
```

```
xclock*InternalBorder:          0
xclock*Mode:                    Analog
xclock*Update:                  1
xclock*BorderWidth:             2
    .
    .
    .
xperfmon*Border:                Magenta
xperfmon*Foreground:            MediumGoldenrod
xperfmon*Update:                2
xterm*ActiveIcon:               on
xterm*AllowIconInput:           on
xterm*Background:               #4e3e43
xterm*BodyFont:                 12x20
xterm*Border:                   #4e3e43
xterm*BorderWidth:              1
xterm*Foreground:               #ffc92c
xterm*Geometry:                 80x56+0+0
xterm*JumpScroll:               on
xterm*Mouse:                    Yellow
xterm*ReverseWrap:              on
xterm*SaveLines:                1024
xterm*Scrollbar:                off
xterm*TitleFont:                12x20
xterm*Font:                     9x15
```

Where Are the User Tools?

The X user tools complicate matters considerably. Users must be able to access X tools without having to resort to using separate path names, because no one wants to remember or use paths like `/usr/local/X11/bin`. They just want to type `xeyes` or whatever and be done with it. Therefore, logical tool location and path setting are a priority for administrators. If you are reverse-engineering an existing system, remember that the locations of X's executables, data files, and configuration files are arbitrary, so look first in `/usr/bin/X11`, and after that, you may have to go on a tool hunt to find them, depending on how many machines and architectures you have. They will seldom be in the same path on a file server as on a workstation. Start with `/usr/bin/X11` and `/usr/lib/X11`.

But what if you are on a commercial site, running machines with several different architectures on a single domain, and your users use extensive CAD and CASE tools, some of which run on only one version and/or release of X, and some another? We have had X10, X11R3, X11R4, and X11R5 running on the same domain, because some of our key design tools wouldn't make it over to the next X version and/or release. A relatively complex environment had to be set up to include an endless number of variables for all these design tools and X tools; and to keep track of them all, they had to be segregated by architecture, X version, and X release level. For example, we put them on the servers by separate directories catering to separate architectures, such as `/exports/sun4/X11` and `/exports/risc6000/X11`. The version directories were added below that.

Aside from whatever application tools you have at your site, you also have to handle miscellaneous stuff like DOS emulation, `sunview` emulation, or whatever. Thus, extending the users' paths and setting other path variables in the users' environment can get complicated quickly.

The User's Line of Execution for X

The key to X Windows startup and function are in three major executables:

```
xinit -> ?wm -> xterm
```

`xinit` provides the windowing base for X, the window manager `?wm` provides the visual part (the user interface), and the user's actual working tools comes from `xterm` and fun tools like `xclock`, `xeyes`, and `xbiff`.

Users can bring up X manually by typing in some commands like

```
% xinit          # start X
% twm &          # start a window manager
                 (in background)
% xterm &        # start a window
                 (in background)
```

which will give the user basic windows with no defaults and no customization, so of course a lot of functions won't work because the "meta" key may not be mapped. Besides, most users want to type in one command for X and have everything come up.

Thus, while it is possible for a user to bring up X from the X distribution without help from the system administrator, it is customary for the administrator to create a series of startup scripts for X, which makes its initiation transparent and painless for the user.

Here is a simple sample startup script for users:

```
#!/bin/sh
node=`hostname`
DISPLAY=${node}:0
xrdb -Dhostname=$node $HOME/.Xresources
# set screensaver
xset s 600
twm &
# then start a few windows and x-things
xterm -n stalker -fn 9x15 -sb -geometry =80x24+0-2 &
xclock &
xbiff &
xeyes &
xterm -n drifter -fn 9X15 -sb -geometry =80X36-0-0 &
```

Note the `xrdb` line, which sets the contents of the RESOURCE_MANAGER; that is, it loads the resource database. The `-Dhostname=$node $HOME/.Xresources` defines the host's name and gives the location for the file for the C preprocessor. In short, here is where the user's resource file is loaded to define what her resources are to be.

Starting the Window Manager

Administrators need to create (or borrow) an `rc` script for each of the window managers used in the domain. In fact, there must be two versions, the system's, which is the default, and the user's. The window manager initiation file is stylized and has a distinct form, as the following pseudocode of the script shows:

```
SECTIONS (PARTS)

variable section:
  settings
  fonts, volumes, colors

key bindings section:
  defines keys, buttons,
  pointer buttons ...
 button-name= keys : context : function

function subsection:
  describes functions used
  (later) in menu section

menus section:
  defines contents of menus

VARIABLES SYNTAX:

 variable value such as

    BorderWidth    2  !assignment

    Zoom              !boolean

  list variable (multiple value)

  Autoraise
```

```
{
  "stalker"
  "drifter"
}

button/key bindings:
  button-name = key(s) : context : function such as
  Button2 = m   : window|icon : f.iconify

function (subsection):
  Function "function-name"
  {
     !"command [args]"
  }

menu
  menu "menu_name"
  {
     "item_name"      action

  }
```

A bare-bones color version of the finished script will run six pages.

A Real Example of an OEM X Installation

We have discussed a broad general view of the way many UNIX systems exist today, with no specific location for X files and no specific choice of a window manager. In contrast, let's look at an SCO Open Desktop system that has been set up by the OEM for use in the as-is condition. It is a full graphical user interface with a desktop manager sitting over the top of the applications programming interface, and it was conceived to offer a full operating system with little or no need to buy additional software. It will be useful for us to see what an X system can look like in an isolated environment.

SCO followed the pattern established by the X consortium (reinforced by the O'Reilly X series), for the bulk of the X implementation is in /usr/lib. A listing of /usr/lib shows an X11 directory:

```
% ls -al /usr/lib/X11
total 102
drwxr-xr-x   10 bin    bin      304 Sep 13 1990 .
drwxr-xr-x   45 bin    bin     1632 Jul 18 18:08 ..
-r--r--r--    1 bin    bin     1453 Sep 05 1990 .Xsight.cfg
drwxr-xr-x    2 bin    bin      176 Sep 13 1990 app-defaults
drwxr-xr-x    5 bin    bin       80 Sep 13 1990 fonts
drwxr-xr-x    2 bin    bin       80 Sep 13 1990 images
drwxr-xr-x    2 bin    bin      144 Sep 13 1990 keymaps
-r--r--r--    1 bin    bin    16384 Sep 05 1990 rgb.dat
-r--r--r--    1 bin    bin     4352 Sep 05 1990 rgb.map
-r--r--r--    1 bin    bin     6656 Sep 05 1990 rgb.txt
-r--r--r--    1 bin    bin      590 Sep 05 1990 sample.Xdefs
-r--r--r--    1 bin    bin      191 Sep 05 1990 sys.startxrc
-r--r--r--    1 bin    bin     1931 Sep 05 1990 system.mwmrc
drwxr-xr-x    2 bin    bin      160 Sep 13 1990 xdm
drwxr-xr-x    7 bin    bin      144 Sep 13 1990 xdt
-rw-r--r--    1 bin    bin     4662 Sep 05 1990 xman.help
drwxr-xr-x    2 bin    bin       64 Sep 13 1990 xrdb
drwxr-xr-x    2 bin    bin      160 Sep 13 1990 xsconfig
```

This is clearly a classic X installation, for SCO stayed with MIT's Project Athena model.

The next trick is to find the startup script. This will give us the path extension to locate the executables, since /usr/lib is only half the battle. The SCO command to start X11 is called startx, and common sense tells us it must be located in either /bin or /usr/bin. Since Version 7 UNIX sets the pattern for what is in /bin and substantially predates X, /usr/bin is a fair guess as to the location of startx. Sure enough, a quick listing shows us it is there.

The startup script for X11 is /usr/bin/startx. Let's look at a few of the more important parts. The first part of the script will set the location of the fonts, but more important to our current quest, it will set the location of the X executables and the library:

```
XFONTS=/usr/lib/X11/fonts/misc\
  ;/usr/lib/X11/fonts/75dpi\
  ;/usr/lib/X11/fonts/100dpi
XPATH=/usr/bin/X11
SYS_RC_DIR=/usr/lib/X11
SYS_RC_FILE=sys.startxrc
USER_RC_FILE=.startxrc
```

A critical part of any X environment is the setting of the DISPLAY constant. If it is not set to :0.0, there will be no end of trouble.

```
        DISPLAY=:0.0
```

Now start X and the initial clients specified in either $HOME/.startxrc or $SYS_RC_DIR/$SYS_RC_FILE.

```
if  [ -f ${HOME}/${USER_RC_FILE} ]
 then if [ $REMOTE_SERVER ]
  then /bin/sh ${HOME}/${USER_RC_FILE}
  else XINIT /bin/sh ${HOME}/${USER_RC_FILE} $*
 fi

 elif [ -f ${SYS_RC_DIR}/${SYS_RC_FILE} ]
  then if [ $REMOTE_SERVER ]
  then /bin/sh ${SYS_RC_DIR}/${SYS_RC_FILE}
  else XINIT /bin/sh ${SYS_RC_DIR}/${SYS_RC_FILE} $*
 fi

 else if [ $REMOTE_SERVER ]
  then :
  else XINIT $*
 fi
fi
```

To verify the contents of /usr/bin/X11, do this (display truncated):

```
% ls -CF /usr/bin/X11
X*            mwm*          xclock*         xfd*
Xsight*       mxdtinfo*     xconfigure*     xhost*
atobm*        mxdw*         xcutsel*        xinit*
bdftosnf*     myni*         xdm*            xkill*
bitmap*       odtterm*      xdpyinfo*       xload*
bmtoa*        resize*       xdt*            xlogo*
ico*          showsnf*      xdtnewuser*     xlsfonts*
image*        tellxdt*      xdtusersetup*   xlswins*
lccdm*        xanswer*      xdtwait*        xmag*
mfyi*         xbiff*        xedit*          xman*
mgti*         xcalc*        xev*            xmodmap*
mkfontdir*    xclipboard*   xeyes*          xpr*
```

Here we find the one and only window manager, mwm (Motif). Also note the x* executables like xclock, xeyes, and xkill, showing clearly that we are in the home of the X executables.

Now let's go back to /usr/lib/X11 and examine some of the default files used in SCO X11's initialization. A bare-bones .Xdefs is started in /usr/lib/X11/sample.Xdefs.

```
xterm*background:Navy
xterm*foreground:yellow
xterm*jumpScroll:on
xterm*ScrollBar:on
xterm*cursorColor:yellow
xterm*c132:on
xterm*scrollKey:on
xterm*menuFont:vtbold
dos*Foreground:White
dos*Background:magenta
xclock*foreground:magenta
xclock*background:MediumBlue
xclock*hands:yellow
xclock*highlight:yellow
```

```
xclock*update:5
xload*foreground:black
xload*background:green
xcalc*foreground:black
xcalc*background:lightblue
xcalc*NKeyFore:black
xcalc*NKeyBack:White
xcalc*OKeyBore:DarkGreen
xcalc*OKeyBack:blue
xcalc*FKeyFore:White
xcalc*FKeyBack:red
xcalc*DispFore:black
xcalc*DispBack:orange
```

If nothing else, there will certainly be a colorful display.

Looking further, you can see a `keymap` directory. Further examination will show keymaps for several countries. The UK `keymap` looks like this:

```
!
! Keymap for UK 102 key keyboard
!
keycode        0x08  = Escape NoSymbol
keycode        0x09  = 1              exclam
keycode        0x0a  = 2              at
keycode        0x0c  = 4              dollar
keycode        0x0d  = 5              percent
keycode        0x0e  = 6              asciicircum
keycode        0x0f  = 7              ampersand
keycode        0x10  = 8              asterisk
keycode        0x11  = 9              parenleft
keycode        0x12  = 0              parenright
        .

        .
keycode        0x6a  = F15            NoSymbol
keycode        0x6b  = F23            NoSymbol
keycode        0x6c  = Print          NoSymbol
keycode        0x6d  = Mode_switch    NoSymbol
!keycode       0x6e  = F35            NoSymbol
```

```
!keycode      Ox6f  = Cancel       NoSymbol
!keycode      Ox70  = NoSymbol     NoSymbol
!keycode      Ox71  = F18          NoSymbol
!keycode      Ox72  = F22          NoSymbol
!keycode      Ox73  = Menu         NoSymbol
```

Note the classic form

```
keycode                number=keyname
```

or

```
keysym                 keyname=keyname
```

as in

```
keycode    Ox41    =     Caps_Lock
```

There is an `app_defaults` directory in `/usr/lib/X11`, and in it are configuration files for Motif. The generic `mwm` file looks like:

```
# general appearance resources that apply to Mwm
# (all parts)
#
*font:                    fixed
*backgroundTile:          background
*activeForeground:        Black
*activeBackground:        Cyan
*activeTopShadowColor:    LightCyan
*activeBottomShadowColor: Black
*makeActiveColors:        false
*foreground:              Black
*background:              Gray
*topShadowColor:          White
*bottomShadowColor:       Black
```

```
*makeColors:                     false
*buttonBindings:                 DefaultButtonBindings
*keyBindings:                    DefaultKeyBindings
*rootMenu:                       RootMenu
*windowMenu:                     DefaultWindowMenu
*useIconBox:                     true
*showFeedback:                   restart
# general appearance resources that apply
# to specific parts of Mwm
*menu*background:                Gray
*menu*topShadowColor:            White
*menu*bottomShadowColor:         Black
*menu*makeColors:                false
# Mwm - specific appearance and behavior resources
*positionOnScreen:               false
# prevents xterm downsizing on ega
*xGranularity:                   8
# VGA/EGA Optimization
*transientDecoration:            title
# no resize frame for popup windows
*execShell:                      /bin/sh
# f.exec shell
```

We also see the system's `mwmrc`. If a user were to create a
`~/.mwmrc`, this would be the source.

```
# menu pane descriptions
# Previously the system menu.
Menu DefaultWindowMenu MwmWindowMenu
{
    Restore     _R    Alt<key>5      f.normalize
    Move        _M    Alt<key>7      f.move
    Size        _S    Alt<key>8      f.resize
    Minimize    _n    Alt<key>9      f.minimize
    Maximize    _x    Alt<key>O      f.maximize
    Lower       _L    Alt<key>minus  f.lower
    no-label                         f.separator
    Close       _C    Alt<key>4      f.kill
```

```
}

Menu WorkspaceMenu
{
    "Workspace Menu"              f.title
    "Clients"            _C      f.menu ClientsMenu
    "New Window"         _N      f.exec "odtterm -sb &"
    "Shuffle Up"         _U      f.circle_up
    "Shuffle Down"       _D      f.circle_down
    "Refresh"            _R      f.refresh
    no-label                     f.separator
    "Restart"                    f.restart
    no-label                     f.separator
    "Quit"                       f.quit_mwm
}

Menu ClientsMenu
{
    "xclock" f.exec "xclock &"
    "xload"       f.exec "xload &"
    "xcalc"       f.exec "xcalc &"
    "xbiff"       f.exec "xbiff &"
    "xmag"        f.exec "xmag &"
    "bitmap"      f.exec "bitmap $HOME/tmp_bitmap &"
    "xeyes"       f.exec "xeyes &"
    "ico"         f.exec "ico &"
}
# key binding descriptions

Keys DefaultKeyBindings
{
 Shift<Key>Escape  icon|window f.post_wmenu
 Meta<Key>space            icon|window f.post_wmenu
 Meta<Key>Escape    root|icon|window f.next_key
 Meta Shift<Key>Escape    root|icon|window f.prev_key
 Meta<Key>Tab             root|icon|window f.next_key
 Meta Shift<Key>Tab       root|icon|window f.prev_key
 Meta Ctrl Shift<Key>exclam
     \ root|icon|window f.set_behaviour
}
```

```
# button binding descriptions

Buttons DefaultButtonBindings
{
        <Btn1Down>        root            f.menu        WorkspaceMenu
        <Btn3Down>        root            f.menu        WorkspaceMenu
        <Btn1Down>        frame           f.raise
        <Btn2Down>        frame|icon      f.post_wmenu
        <Btn3Down>        frame|icon      f.post_wmenu
        Meta<Btn1Down>    icon|window     f.raise_lower
        Meta<Btn3Down>    icon|window     f.move
}
```

SCO's implementation is an example of what a good, solid X system can look like, but it uses only one version of X at one revision level and only one window manager at one revision level. This pristine environment is not possible on file servers with X environments set up for several architectures, several X versions, and several window managers.

Installing X and X Applications on Open Desktop

You don't install X on SCO's Open Desktop, because it is already installed, so getting X going is only a matter of having the monitor's graphics be compatible. Running ASCII is no problem, for it will even run on VGA++ at 1024x840, but when you bring up X, the display gets double to quadruple vision if the OEM hasn't made provisions for it. Now you must suffer with 600 pixels per inch, even though you paid for 1024. If you do have the wrong pixel count, the cure is to reset it to something that will work, like 840x600, with `makedev vga`. Then X is running. Interestingly enough, although X is a network software application, it will run without the network being up. FrameMaker, on the other hand, is an X-only application that won't run unless it thinks the network is up.

FrameMaker is a windowed, graphic desktop publishing system that has become firmly entrenched in the UNIX world, and its network software is typically served from a file server and run by any workstation that can access that server as long as it has a *license*. However, the network is such an integral part of commercial UNIX systems today that applications software is created to run on the network, and if you try to install FrameMaker on a free-standing micro, you will get a socket error. How can you get a socket error if TCP/IP isn't even up? The socket isn't there, and if the software can't reach the socket, it will fail.

Therefore, even if you don't have a network card, you must "bring up the network" anyway by getting TCP/IP going. With SCO Open Desktop, bring the system to single-user mode. System V types should do an `init 1` from multi-user mode and run `mkdev` with a `tcp` option:

```
# mkdev tcp
```

If you have an Ethernet card supported by a driver, tell the command what kind. If you have no card, fake it and enter `q` to quit. You will have enabled TCP/IP at least to the point of having `rc` bring up the daemons and the necessary sockets.

It's interesting to note that on Berkeley UNIX systems, you can walk through your `rc` files and figure out the boot sequence, but the SVR3 system is too complex and has too many directories for that.

If you are going to go on the net, put off bringing up Frame until you are safely on the net. Whether on the net or off, do a ping to your loopback local host to see if you are up. Also stay alert going from `init S` to `init 2` and watch the console messages. If it complains at `portmapper`, you didn't make it. If you get the usual network `daemon started` messages, you are in.

Setting Up a Workstation for X

Most often, the workstations will take their X files from a file server. Therefore, the place to start is `/etc/fstab`. Many sites will have separate server directories for each architecture, and sub-directories for each X version and release. Pick the architecture and version needed for the workstation being configured, and create the `fstab` entry.

```
fsvr01:/usr/sun4/X11R4 /export/X11 nfs ro 0 0
```

Here the directory for Sun SPARC (`sun4`) architecture for X11 Release 4 is mounted to the workstation's `/export/X11` mount point. The mount is `hard` (by default), and it is mounted read-only. Don't forget to make a directory for it before mounting, of course.

That is basically it for the system side, but the user's home directory will need some work. (The user's home directory should exist on the file server, not the workstation). Add all the appropriate X-related dot files to each user's `$HOME`.

User Dot Files

Fundamental to initiation and executed even before the first start-up script are the user's initiation files (`.profile`, `.login`, and `.cshrc`), which must have the user's path set to where the initial X startup script is. You can extend the user's path there or simply put that script where the user's path is already pointed, like `/usr/local/bin`, which not only exists on most systems but is certainly in the `path` variable. There are certain advantages to putting the initiation scripts where they can be accessed without resetting or initially extending the user's path.

Setting Up a File Server for X

Place the file trees that your workstations and X-terminal servers will need on the file servers, separating by directories into logical groups. X-terminal servers may well not have enough space for the X-terminal server software, so they may need the file servers to hold it.

X Terminals

Computer sites used to have a large central system supporting scores to hundreds of users on terminals connected to the central system by terminal controllers, multiplexers, or a number of other schemes. Next came clustered systems, the first approach to distributed systems. The most common computing environment today for engineers and scientists is one workstation for each user. These workstations take data from file servers, and neither need be central because data can always be exchanged over the net.

Once the server/workstation paradigm was a new innovation, but today most of us have become quite familiar with it. However, we shouldn't get too comfortable, because the computer industry never stands still, and a new pattern prompted by multiprocessor servers has been evolving in the industry that it is starting to emerge.

In two years, we saw workstation power rise from less than 4 MIPS up to as high as an incredible 100 MIPS, and no end is in sight. Our appetites for system performance are voracious, because sophisticated graphics, such as windows, place increasing demands on our systems, so much so that we need more room for our applications to run. Faster CPUs, I/O coprocessors, multiple buses, and channels are no longer enough. The only way to appease our hunger for power is multiprocessors. Anticipating this need, many vendors have already gone multiprocessor. AT&T has an MP version of SVR4, SCO has an MP version, and Sun, Encore, DG, Silicon Graphics, Apollo (HP), and many others all have MP machines.

With 50 to 70 MIPS on high-end workstations common now, and a solid potential of multiprocessor workstations with 100+ MIPS in the immediate future, several changes in our computing environments may occur. First of all, large multiprocessor workstations will be costly, way too much to spend for use by the average user alone. Granted, there are times when a single application will floorboard a large computer, but most of the time it will be more cost-efficient to partially return to the concept of time-share computing for access to the high-end systems. It's ironic, but it's also extremely logical. In time, of course, smaller inexpensive MP systems will appear as well. This is good because oversized applications like computational chemistry, finite element analysis, chip simulations, and so on will always be run on systems that are in fact too small for them.

Second, think about how many workstations you have on your site that are rapidly becoming obsolete. What should be done with the 4-MIPS systems that were the flashiest game in town a few years ago? They will be good for only limited applications when used individually, but on the net they can be used to access those powerful MP workstations. In other words, they can be used as X terminals to access larger, more powerful machines.

Let's pursue the thought further. It costs a lot of money for service contracts to support aging workstations, and it will be expensive to replace them. However, X terminals cost a lot less to purchase and are not as expensive to maintain. If aging workstations are going to be used as X terminals anyway, when it comes time to replace them, wouldn't it be more cost-effective to replace them with dedicated X terminals?

If we could look into the immediate future with a crystal ball, we might see an image of future computer sites with a fair number of high-powered MP systems supporting a large number of users on X terminals. Users who can keep a mid-range workstation constantly busy will have their own workstations, but most of the users who can't will access central MP computers, and the rest will use whatever older, low-end workstations are available. Consider that many "low-end" workstations of the future will have the MIPS of today's mid- to high-end workstations.

What Is an X Terminal?

First we must look at what makes an ANSI or ASCII terminal. Character-oriented devices, they send bit sequences as bytes in the range of 0 to 127 for each keystroke, and there are no other input devices other than the keyboard. In the ASCII range they send only 0 to 127, and the *function* keys send a series of two to three of these integers. The *break* key is the only maverick, sending nothing but simply interrupting carrier. The tube, the display device, responds to these characters, whether they come from the computer or directly from the keyboard, and it prints a recognizable representation to the screen. They are updated by the transmission of `keysym`. Some additional intelligence is used to position the characters, such as *scroll* and *home*.

Now let's compare character terminals with X terminals. X terminals are graphics devices that take bit-mapped images from a computer and print them to the screen. They do not know what they are printing, nor do they need to. The X terminal has at least two input devices — the "keyboard" and the mouse — and each keystroke or mouse button produces a unique string of bytes. They need not be uniform from one vendor's system to another's (although it's nice for us when they are) because the X Window System provides for keymapping, key and button signals translated to meaningful instructions. They do not have to work independently, either. They can work in concert, such as pushing the mouse button and holding down the shift key.

The major difference between character terminals and X terminals is intelligence. An intelligent terminal can redraw the screen as you work on it (if you erase a line, it closes up the line on the screen), and it can map or remap its non-ASCII (function) keys. However, the X terminal is much more intelligent, for it it is a computer in its own right. Although working on an X terminal seems similar to working on a diskless workstation without an apparent operating system, X terminals do have an "operating system" called an *image* that is loaded by the X terminal server when the X terminal is booted. They are really quite sophisticated.

X terminals are not only less costly than workstations, but they will usually perform faster than a workstation's monitor, and their graphics are usually better. Of course, there are a few drawbacks, too. They will definitely add a load to the network, for sending bit maps and `keysym` is more taxing than sending the simple stream of characters that an ASCII terminal requires. It's no big deal to make any UNIX computer an X terminal server, but that's just one more kind of server to add to your administration list along with file servers, mail servers, YP servers, printer servers, and so on. But look on the bright side: X terminals are less of a network load than diskless workstations are, and they don't swap across the network. The problem of their contribution to an increased network load can be overcome with subnetting.

How Do X Terminals Work?

The X terminal is married to an X terminal server. It has a permanent Ethernet address and is assigned an Internet number, thus making it a legitimate node. It boots from a PROM, and when when it boots it sends a RARP (reverse address resolution protocol) to its server. It knows its Ethernet address, but it doesn't know its name or Internet number yet, so it will request that information from its server, which will look up the Internet number in the /etc/ethers file. After a few more exchanges, the X terminal will learn its name.

In addition to booting information, the X terminal server must provide font and environment information, and installation and configurations information can also be exchanged. The more expensive X terminals store most of the boot information on PROMs, and the least expensive ones get most or all of that information from the server.

When the X terminal has completed its boot, it becomes a classic X server (the display and input device), and each of its potentially many remote processes are X clients.

The administration required for both X terminals and X server is:

- Installing X terminals

- Creating and maintaining server files (like /etc/ethers)

- Enabling server demons like TFTP

- Creating or installing server setup files

- Setting up the boot host

- Downloading new code for upgrades

- Doing remote configuration and rebooting

- Enabling the xdm daemon if XDM is used

XDM

We're going to finish X Windows by taking a short look at XDM. Users must first log in and then initiate X Windows, and some X users, particularly those using X terminals, want X as soon as they log on. XDM provides this instant X. To have XDM, the user must first have an ~/.Xsessions file, which requests a display manager, authenticates the host, displays the login window, and starts an X session. To make XDM work, the administrator must add the **xdm** daemon to /etc/rclocal and make an XDM addition to /etc/services as well:

```
xdm 177/udp
```

Enough Theory

We've looked at the network in almost every possible way. We started with a bird's eye view of the net by discussing network topology, and then we zoomed down to network level to examine network media. We delved into the inner workings of networking by learning about network protocols, which are invisible to users but not to administrators. We've explored different network designs, we've seen how vital addressing is to network administration, and we've examined most of the major network hardware available today, such as routers, servers, clients, and workstations. We learned how to keep the net as secure as possible with access control and network security, and we even learned how to diagnose network problems in theory. We've studied *sendmail* and DNS, and we've examined one of the most popular network applications on UNIX today. But studying theory is not enough. In the next chapter we examine actual networking scenarios, so you can see networking in practice.

CHAPTER
19

Network Scenarios

No one is an instant network guru. We all learn best from experience, and the mistakes we all make as we work through various problems are what point us towards true understanding. This chapter documents a few actual network problems that actually occurred at a commercial site. What's important about these scenarios is that they give you an idea of what it's really like to be confronted with a network problem. First of all, you are on the spot, because you don't know what's the matter, and no book will be able to give you an answer. Instead, you must use the knowledge you have to try whatever you can think of; what often happens is that you gradually eliminate what the problem isn't until you arrive at a solution. In any event, study the problem-solving methods used to fix each problem, both the mistakes and the eventual successes. Because it is impossible to show you every possible scenario that could occur, there are only a few scenarios here, and only a few problem solving-methods are presented. Therefore, you must develop your own methods as you work through the network problems at your own site. However, these scenarios will give you a good idea of what's in store. They are told in a narrative style by an administrator.

Full `root` **File System**

One day, when doing a routine check of system and network diagnostics, a `df` on the pride-of-the-fleet file server showed the `root` partition at 105 percent. A full `root` file system on any computer is a concern, but it's hard not to panic when it happens on a major file server in an engineering domain. Major processes had been running and accessing this server for hours, perhaps days. If the cause of the problem could not be found soon, the server would have to be rebooted, and that would hamper the work of the entire organization. In short, it would be a disaster.

Immediately going into battle mode, I went directly to that server's window on my system and in sequence moved to `/tmp`, `/var/adm`, and `/var/spool/mail`, cleaning out everything of any size. However, continuous `df`s showed no decrease in partition size, and time was running out. As soon as the system needed to write to `/tmp`, it wouldn't be able to, and it would hang.

New administrators never think of looking in `/dev` for mutant files, but I've often found real files in there that didn't belong. Sometimes they get written there by accident. Unfortunately, a

```
find /tmp -type f -exec ls -l {} \;
```

came up with nothing.

Because time was of the essence, I asked a fellow administrator to help me find the problem, and then I moved to `/var/spool`, because on this system `/var` is on the `root` partition. Using `find` again, I looked for files larger than 50,000 characters:

```
find /var/spool -type f -size 50000c -exec ls -l {}\;
```

I found two files short of a megabyte `mqueue`, and even though they weren't big enough to fill the disk, I removed them anyway. These two files should have rung a mental alarm in my head, but they didn't yet.

The removal of several large files should have given back some room on the disk, but the disk was still full. This problem was reminiscent of similar problems I had had on mainframe UNIX systems when VM, the host operating system, tried to write a 10-

megabyte error file to a 5-megabyte console-log disk on the virtual UNIX system. UNIX held the superblock captive on a write that could not complete. Since adding up all the used space on the disk wouldn't come close to filling the disk, but nevertheless the system reported the disk full, perhaps a similar kind of problem was haunting this file server.

A `ps` of the few processes running on the server that were attached to a terminal or the console showed two processes that were accumulating time:

```
% ps -qax
PID     TTY    S     TIME    COMMAND
 .
20256   pty0   S     2:20    -From standard (sendmail)
20258   pty0   S     1:57    -From standard (sendmail)
 .
```

There was a good chance that these processes could be stuck on a write. The `s` process state is supposed to signify that the process is sleeping for less than 20 seconds, but `2:20` and `1:57` were naps worthy of Rip Van Winkle.

Up to this point I had been using my window to the server, but it was time to look at the actual console in the computer room. The console was spewing out `disk write` errors. It couldn't write because the disk was full, so my problem still appeared to be an unfinishable write.

While I was in the computer room, the other system administrator came in and told me that he had found a strange process running on the server listed as -From `stalker`, one of our system group's machines that was also the YP master.

A `ps` of a mail process generates a -From *system_name* process name when invoked, but it only takes a second or two. Since `mqueue` is the mail queue, and two processes there had accumulated time, unusual for `mail`, the two large files in `/var/spool/mqueue` that I had removed must be the other half of the puzzle. I killed the process, and immediately the death grip on the `root` partition was released.

We had destroyed most of the evidence, but we reconstructed the event as best we could. Apparently, a mail message sent from `stalker` ran away, writing a monster file to `/var/spool/mqueue`. As more disk space was freed, the process would continue to write even more. The only two cures were to kill the process or reboot the system, which would have caused a major loss of service to 70 systems using the file server that day.

Stale File Handle

A system administrator was setting up some shared special directories on the server's `/usr/local` directory. (Recall that `/local` has as much to do with being *local* as `usr` has to do with *users*.) There were a number of tool directories immediately below `/usr/local`, and he wanted to mount a new one on his SPARC-stations. The directory `/usr/local/gem` was going to be mounted by mounting all of `/usr/local` from the server.

He added `/usr/local` to the server's `/etc/exports` file, but he ran into a slight problem : `/usr/local/tool` was already in the file. Then, when he ran `exportfs`, it returned an error. You can't mount a file system when you have already mounted part of it at a lower level. When he did an `exports -u` on the older directory to fix things, his problems really started. Nearly 50 workstations mounting the old directory were in trouble and throwing out `stale file handle` error messages right and left. Although he tried to correct the `exports` file, it was too late — the workstations wouldn't respond. Most of the laser printers were dependent on the now unmounted directory. Now there were no laser printers, and the queue was growing fast.

By now, every user in the three departments that the systems served were stopping by his office one by one, popping their heads over the partition, and saying things like "Did you know I can't get to the printer?" and "I just lost a lot of software ..." and "Did you know `/usr/local` is empty?" It was not a comfortable situation. One obvious solution was to reboot all the workstations, but the cost in lost time to the users would be staggering. Some had been running jobs since the day before, and they hadn't finished running.

We all have bad days, but fortunately this system administrator kept his cool. He tore through the manual looking for a way out, when suddenly he remembered that the system kept a file of its mounts, `/etc/mtab`. It looks like `fstab`, but if files are added or removed manually, the changes are reflected in `mtab`, not in `fstab`.

The administrators on this site wrote a utility that executes shell commands or scripts on all the systems in any file specified as an argument, similar to a superuser `rsh`. Our hero's plan was to write a script to remove the `/local/tool` entry from each system's `mtab` file with `sed`, copy the results to `/tmp`, and then copy the `/tmp` file back to `/etc/mtab`. Then the script would manually mount `/usr/local`. He fired his script and waited tensely as it ran on more than 50 systems. Fortunately, the suspense didn't last long, because all service was soon restored. He smiled, because he knew that it was a clever recovery, showing a knowledgeable understanding of the system's internals.

The System that Wouldn't Join The Network

A CAD tool vendor's team was at our site to show their wares, and they brought their own system with them. The salesman and engineer set up for the demo in one of the labs downstairs, but they couldn't finish because they didn't have a disk big enough to run their application. They explained that they were planning to use one of the lab's disks so that they would have enough storage to demo the software with our data.

Unfortunately for them, relying on the lab to have a large disk was a major oversight, because the lab's computer budget was smaller than the chance of world peace. So the lab people and the demo team came upstairs to our group for a disk, but they came to the wrong place because we rely on service contracts and therefore have no spare disks. The unit they were using to display their software was a Sun SPARCstation, but the only expansion unit we had with a disk had 370 megabytes, and it was already configured with a full operating system, something I was not about ready to lose just to be a good neighbor.

Then they came up with a bright idea: I could save the day if I let them attach to our fileserver. We were on the same extended LAN, so it was possible. To keep good relations going with the lab, I reluctantly agreed.

I decided to call their system `bromine`, a name used once by another transient system we had. The host part of the network address would be 254, also reserved for transient systems. `bromine` and its Internet address were added to the YP database's source file and I ran a `make` on YP. The file system to be accessed, `/usr/lab`, was added to the server's `exports` file. The directory already existed and took up an entire 1-gigabyte disk.

My work done, I went down to the lab to see how they were doing. Separated by a floor, we were also separated by network topology, for the lab was directly attached to the company's extended LAN, while we enjoyed our own, bridge-isolated segment. I advised them on altering their `hosts` table to include the demo system's new name and Internet number as well as the name and Internet number of the server. I stood by and watched them boot their system, but it died with a `portmapper / RCP` . . . error. I sympathized, because I never had much luck getting from the lab's network segment to ours in any reasonable time, probably because the lab was on the building network, notoriously dirty and slow, and we were not. They all looked to me for help, and the only cure I could think of was to bring the machine upstairs and plug it into a connector attached to one of the concentrators used by our network segment.

I went back upstairs to work, and they went to fetch their machine. The computer, expansion cabinets, and all were dragged upstairs and plugged into a LattisNet/IBM connector, attached to a concentrator, and in turn attached to one of our file servers, but instead of coming up right, the poor system showed the same behavior as in the lab: `portmapper / RPC` . . . . They came to me sheepishly and told me what had happened. By now, it was apparent that I had better take a more active role in the install.

A `ping` from my own system to the demo system timed out. The net didn't even know the system was there. A `ping` from the demo system to anywhere also timed out. I asked the team's tech to run `hostname`, and it came up with the same name it had when it left the vendor's shop. Its Internet address was equally old.

We ran Sun's configuration program on the system and gave it some good information. A check on all the `rc` files starting with `boot.rc` showed the new name and address. This time the rebooted system finally came to life, but it was too late. Several hours had elapsed from the time these salespeople had arrived to the present. They were half dead, our tech was exhausted, and I have been in better moods, all because no one had thought to check out the configuration in the beginning. Had the `hostname` and Internet number been changed in the first few minutes of the setup, there would have been no story to tell, and their firm would have had a better chance of making its sale.

Mail Stopped

One of my favorite users, Eric, stopped by my office and pleaded with me to get his mail going. His mail stopped one day while I was gone, he said, and he hadn't received any mail ever since. The systems in this scenario are a Sun/DEC mix running full networking and BSD `sendmail`.

I told him I'd get right to it, so he ran off to a meeting. Because the mail master under `sendmail` is both mail router and final arbitrator for mail delivery, the first place I looked was the mail master's `aliases` file. A quick `grep` of `/etc/aliases` showed that Eric was at the right address. So I logged in on his system and went immediately to `/var/spool/mail`, where I found an empty `mail` file a few days old. It looked as if `mail` delivery had been attempted but didn't make it, because `sendmail` was working to the system but wasn't necessarily working on this system. Why? Eric's system was one of the first systems I had installed for this group, and it had a long history of good service, `mail` included.

Mail is stored in `/var/spool/mqueue` when it's going to be transferred over the network, and when I looked in this directory on Eric's machine, it was empty. I wasn't surprised. On an individual   workstation   it   is   unusual   to   find   files   in

`/var/spool/mqueue`. Only on the mail master will you always find mail or an active log file, `syslog`, in that directory.

I went to the mail master and directly to the `mqueue/syslog` file, which shows a log of everything sent within the mail domain, whether delivered or not. Using `vi` to move to the end of the file, I searched backwards on Eric's log name, from the newest entry to the oldest entry. The last mail sent was from me, and it was a couple of days old. A glance at `syslog` on the mail master said that the mail had been delivered. The delay time was only a few milliseconds, and its status was clearly `sent`. As far as the mail master was concerned, Eric's system was a reliable, fully usable mail system. Thus, the trouble had to be internal to Eric's machine.

Back at the errant system, a look at `/etc/sendmail.cf` showed that its creation date was only five days old, precisely the number of days that I had been gone. Had someone reinstalled `mail`'s configuration file? I reloaded `sendmail.cf` from a distribution area, killed the `sendmail` daemon, and restarted it. Voila! Test mail sent from my own system reached Eric's system and deposited itself in `/var/spool/mail` in a second or so. The problem was solved.

Once you solve a problem, take the time to find out what happened. Then, when the same problem comes up, you know exactly what to do. I had to find out why a system worked flawlessly for months and then suddenly lost a single service. Frankly, I was stumped.

I didn't see Eric until lunch, and I told him that he should read his mail, because it was accumulating. Then I asked him if he knew that the `sendmail` configuration file had been altered the previous Wednesday. He said it must have happened when another administrator installed SunOS 4.0.2 on his system. The other administrator had installed a new system, but had failed to configure `sendmail`. This was something I usually did myself because it was somewhat esoteric.

Had I known that a new system had been loaded, I could have shortcut the detective process from an hour to a few minutes. The fault was lack of communication. Users don't understand that running on a new system is something that administrators know. Administrators must be exhaustive about asking questions, because the answers can save hours of time.

The Repercussions of the Removal of an NFS Directory

This scenario started innocently enough at a system's staff meeting to organize existing file server disk space. One of the targets for reclamation was a huge tool directory. More than a directory, it was a full-gigabyte disk pack, which contained all the tools used by our engineering group as well as other shared items like FrameMaker, Sun's `clusters` files, all the X Windows software, and other software.

This disk had been used by a development group, but it it was going to be replaced by a new tool area that was shared by all groups in the domain. We were all sure that no one was still mounting to this old tools disk, so one of the systems staff unceremoniously removed its contents without renaming it, saving that for later. Unfortunately, this would turn out to be a mistake.

The morning after the change, my system started acting strangely in X Windows. I moved to `sunview` to start my problem resolution, when I was approached by a panicked user — `ftp` would not work on his system. When I went to investigate, I found `ftp` in `/usr/ucb`, but it was a symbolic link.

Before I could get much further with my investigation of the missing command, another user hit me with yet another problem. X Windows was not working on her system. The day was starting with a rash of software problems, and it was possible that they were all related.

The second user's system was throwing `stale file handle` errors to the console window, and that provided me with some direction. A `df` of the system's mounted file systems showed that it was linked to that old, and now empty, tool directory mentioned at the beginning of this scenario. No wonder this user's system couldn't find X. The `stale file handle` error came when the system sensed that the old tool directory had been unmounted and remounted again.

The system's `fstab` file was quickly modified to point to the tool directory on the alternate file server. The old directory was unmounted and the new one mounted. X came back, and so did everything else.

Moving to the first user's system with no `ftp`, the problem was the same. This system was used to taking its `clusters` files from the old, now empty, directory. The `clusters` directory is Sun's way of serving nonvital system software to diskless and dataless workstations. Files on the workstation appear to be where they should be, traditionally found by way of symbolic (soft) links. However, when we retired the old disk, all the commands in `clusters` went away, including the network software.

By using `rsh` and `grep` in a script run across all systems, I was able to find two more systems on the wrong disk, for their `fstab` entries told it all. Modifying each `fstab` file and remounting their tools disk, the problem was solved.

The moral of this scenario is, we should have checked the systems the night before.

A YP Epidemic — The Sickness and the Cure

If there was ever such a thing as a YP plague, our systems had it. It came on so slowly, it was hardly noticeable at first. Our one and only YP slave server threw an occasional `block error`, but we could live with that. YP's `make` grumbled about nonexistent maps when run on the master server, but it had always complained, so because we were so busy, we put that problem on the back burner.

Then one day the `ypserv` daemon died on the slave, which will be known from now on as *Slave I*. When doing a `make` on YP, the master's console would get a message telling it that a YP slave was `registered but not responding`. We didn't know what the message meant right away, but in our experience, you definitely have a problem if you ever see this message. I restarted the daemon, but it died again in a few hours. Before restarting it a second time, I created a log file for YP errors just in case the problem would leave footprints. Each successive death came more quickly, but the only error message each time was `block error`.

Without an effective slave server for YP, we needed another slave server quickly. A large, rack-mounted Sun file server, similar to Slave I, was chosen for Slave II. I modified the system's `rc.local` by uncommenting `ypserv` and ran `ypinit` with the `-s` flag to get the maps from the master, and the console filled with errors about missing maps. What I had considered as innocuous warnings about maps had come back to haunt me, for the new slave could not be made.

I felt like the only doctor at the battle of Gettysburg. The master was sick, YP was dead on Slave I, and Slave II refused to be born. What should I do? Since the work in our organization would stop if the YP master went down, I decided to concentrate on the master.

Pondering the map connection, I remembered that a month earlier, YP's `Makefile` had been cut back to the bare necessities in order to make it run quickly and successfully. After the `Makefile` was modified, the YP domain's map directory still contained empty unused maps that were no longer referenced by the `Makefile`. All of the unused ones were removed and the remaining maps checked for consistency with the `Makefile`. This must be done, because when running `ypinit`, every map that `ypinit` *thinks* you need is set up, and it is your job to remove those that you know you don't want. Only with consistency between `/var/yp/Makefile` and the YP domain's directory below it will running `make` on YP be successful. Then you `yppush` the maps to the slave.

While recalling all this, I decided to move over to Slave II, run `ypinit` again, and this time note all error messages. Sure enough, there was a very odd error message about `awk`, and `/usr/bin/awk` was checked and found to be missing. How `awk` was ever lost in the first place was a mystery, but it had completely disappeared. I took a copy from Slave I and made it executable. Then I ran `ypinit` again, and it worked. The clean map directory on the master and `awk`'s presence made the difference. `ypserve` was started, and YP was checked by running `ypwhich` from a workstation. Now the YP master and Slave II responded. I was on a roll.

I moved over to Slave I with high hopes. When a subsystem like YP is in such bad condition, it is easier to rebuild it. I removed the YP domain map directory's contents, and then ran `ypinit` as if it were the first time. The execution was good, and the maps matched those on the master. Now the `ypserv` daemon was restarted, and it stayed alive.

A series of tests was run, executing `ypwhich` from different systems, and all three YP servers were responding. For the first time in months, the YP master was taken off line and rebooted successfully. Slave I was rechecked, and its `ypserv` daemon was functioning beautifully.

Note that in this scenario, I had not one problem but a series of unrelated bugs, errors, and omissions to find and fix before I could get the systems in top running form.

YP Server Not Responding, and Worse

Error massages are not always what they say they are; nor do scenarios move smoothly from one piece of problem determination to another. Frequently, problems drag on for a long time before you finally come up with a reasonable answer. It takes persistence.

One Monday morning a Sun workstation couldn't boot. It would get to the network initiation part of `rc.local` and then hang, complaining that a YP server was not available. How could I believe that error message? Running `ypwhich` from several systems showed no less that three out of four YP servers responding, and all four servers were alive and well, on line, and reachable from the net.

As I was trying to figure out this problem, another workstation of the same architecture got hung up trying to get YP services for a user login. Then a short time later, still another workstation tried to boot and got hung up at `rc.local`. What on earth was going on?

On today's distributed systems, it is all too easy for administrators to get used to talking to their servers from the windows on their workstations. This time, I got up and walked to the computer room so I could look directly at the file server's consoles. A pair of nearly identical Sun workstations were complaining about problems with their (one) Ethernet interface, `ie0`, and an Auspex file server was also complaining about the network interface (on the same net segment) with a slightly different message. All three machines were telling me that the network wasn't there, but a `ping` to each of them or to random workstations was good. However, `spray` shed a little more light: The net was there, but it was dropping 88 percent of the packets, while receiving only 11 to 15 good packets per second.

Back in the office battlefield, a couple of DEC servers started giving NFS errors. Whatever the problem was, it was rapidly getting worse, but that could be good news, because if something broke, we would be able to find out what was wrong.

I went back to the computer room and found one of the servers whining about loss of carrier in spite of the fact that it was in touch with the segment. It was cable-checking time.

The cable at the computer end was secure. All Suns shed their Ethernet cables easily, so we rigged a protective loop in the cable at the backplane in order to avoid having an accidental nudge on the cable pull it loose. The other end to the transceiver connection to an older SynOptics concentrator *looked* good, but with nothing else to blame, we decided to change concentrator ports.

Checking back in the office again, we found the DECs back on NFS and the two Sun workstations booted. Apparently the concentrator was the source of the problem, or was it? The solution didn't feel right, especially after `spray` showed that network traffic was still dropping 85 percent, with only 13 packets per second received.

A week later, the network was still maxed out. We started to monitor the network 24 hours per day, and we plugged in the protocol analyzer. Continuous traffic monitoring showed that the single subnet line shared by the servers was averaging 30 percent plus, and spikes were hitting 100 percent with unnerving frequency.

There were no quick solutions waiting in the wings to rescue us on cue this time. Our network was maxed out, and we badly needed to subnet once again. Fortunately, we had already made plans to resubnet, with four to six subnets at each server, depending on the card capacity of the architecture, and we were only a few weeks away from implementing that plan. We had already changed the concentrators for the users' end of the net, and when we resubnetted, part of this subnet plan was replacing the ancient local concentrator with a newer, instrumented model. Clearly, we were moving none too soon; in fact, we had cut this move much too close.

Even though the challenges and cost of subnetting might make you inclined to put it off as long as possible, by all means subnet *before* you reach the practical capacity of the segments. Conventional Ethernet's capacity is around 30 percent of its theoretical maximum, for it is a CSMA/CD protocol, and 30 percent is its collision threshold. Beyond that you have runts, collisions, and retransmissions. All of this is bad enough for UDP, but an absolute disaster for TCP-dependent upper-level protocols like NFS; when the lines become this overloaded, YP doesn't work, and that jeopardizes the work of the entire group.

Summing Up

This chapter marks the end of your long journey through UNIX networking. We started with general networking concepts that happen to also apply to UNIX networks, but gradually we moved into chapters that cover numerous networking topics specific to UNIX alone. To end the book, we gave you a small sample of some actual UNIX networking problems, because a working knowledge of all the prior chapters is needed in order to actually diagnose network problems and fix them. However, this book is only an introduction to UNIX networking, for the field is developing rapidly at this writing, and computer sites are barely keeping up with all the changes. Indeed, there will be many exciting developments in the years to come.

INDEX